BLACK STUDENTS
IN
HIGHER EDUCATION

BLACK STUDENTS IN HIGHER EDUCATION

CONDITIONS AND EXPERIENCES IN THE 1970s

Edited by Gail E. Thomas

Contributions to the Study of Education, Number 1

Greenwood Press
Westport, Connecticut • London, England

Library of Congress Cataloging in Publication Data

Main entry under title:

Black students in higher education.

    (Contributions to the study of education;
no. 1 ISSN 0196-707X)
    Bibliography: p.
    Includes index.
    1.   Afro-Americans—Education (Higher)—Addresses,
essays, lectures. I.   Thomas, Gail E. II.   Series.
LC2781.B466   378′.198′08996073   80-1702
ISBN 0-313-22477-3 (lib. bdg.)

Library of Congress Catalog Card Number: 80-1702
ISBN: 0-313-22477-3
ISSN: 0196-707X

First published in 1981

Greenwood Press
A division of Congressional Information Service, Inc.
88 Post Road West, Westport, Connecticut 06881

Printed in the United States of America

10 9 8 7 6 5 4 3 2 1

To the
Dupree, Kennedy, and Matthews
children with love, and to
Chuck Baldwin, and Will and
Gloria Scott for their
support and friendship
throughout the years.

All royalties derived from the sale of this book will go to the American Sociological Association's Minority Fellowship Program and the United Negro College Fund.

Contents

Tables and Illustration

TABLES

Chapter 17

Chapter 21

Chapter 26

Chapter 27

ILLUSTRATION

Chapter 9

Foreword

By
Charles V. Willie
Harvard Graduate School of Education

Gail Thomas has presented a comprehensive analysis of black students in higher education. The book is a well organized look at the past, and a realistic projection into the future. I say realistic because Thomas and her authors talk of the future in terms of the resistances to black educational progress. They appropriately conclude that the attitudes and actions of the majority and the minority will jointly impact upon the question of continuing educational progress for blacks. And they suggest that a conflict model of social change is an appropriate frame of reference.

The facts presented in several chapters indicate the significant educational progress by blacks. But Thomas knows that the price of this progress has been high for members of the minority. In describing earlier attempts to educate black people at the college level, W. E. B. DuBois said that "the opposition to Negro education in the South was at first bitter and showed itself in ashes, insult, and blood" (DuBois, Souls of Black Folk, 1903). Now a new pattern is emerging: Black people are educated in colleges and universities in the West, the North, and in the South, and in predominantly white and predominantly black institutions. It remains to be seen whether this new development in higher education for blacks also will be met with "ashes, insult, and blood." Some interracial confrontations in higher education have been bloody; but most, have not.

Standardized tests are examined, and their function as excluding devices is considered. A strong case for the future of black colleges is made; and ways in which predominantly white colleges can improve their retention rate of minorities are suggested. In viewing higher education as a continuum, this book examines the significant role of two-year colleges as well as that of graduate and professional schools in furthering the education of blacks. The two-year and junior college are not put down as second-best institutions because they accommodate a higher proportion of minorities; and graduate and professional schools are not portrayed as beyond the educational grasp of minorities merely because some tend to score low on standardized admissions tests. The book is enriched because the discussion of these and other important issues is from the perspective of majority and minority scholars. Such a diverse perspective is something of value and may help all Americans to understand better our national system of higher education. More importantly, it is possible that whites may develop a better understanding of black and brown populations and of themselves by reading this book.

Preface

This volume grew out of a symposium on the access and representation of racial minorities in higher education organized by the editor and presented at the 1979 annual meeting of the American Association for the Advancement of Science (AAAS). The participants at that symposium were: Helen Astin, James Blackwell, Frank Brown, Doris Wilkinson and Charles Willie. These individuals discussed the role of standardized testing, the access of blacks and other racial minorities to graduate and professional schools, the status of black women in higher education, and methods to increase minority access to higher education.

Since the 1979 conference, the original topic was extended beyond access, to look at the past and present experiences of blacks in higher education; their distribution and completion rates in various types of colleges and universities; their participation in the basic sciences and other academic majors; programs and strategies designed to increase the access and retention of minorities in the basic sciences and in higher education; and broad economic and educational policies affecting the future of blacks in higher education. These topics are presently addressed by a conscientious group of majority and minority specialists with diverse experiences and perspectives. Together, their contributions offer a broader definition of equality of higher educational opportunity for blacks and other minorities that extends beyond access. It is hoped that these contributions will provide some direction in the 1980s for policy and research on minorities in higher education.

This volume would not have been possible without the patience and dedication of a number of individuals. Therefore, sincere thanks and appreciation are extended to the following individuals and organizations: to the authors for their commitment and valuable contributions; to James McPartland and the Center for Social Organization of Schools staff for their total support and the provision of all the resources which greatly aided in the production of this volume; to John Hollifield and Carolyn Moore for their patience and excellent editorial assistance which contributed to the quality of this book; to my student assistant Noel Kirnon who will soon become a part of the critical mass of black professionals; and to the impressive team of secretaries for their ability to cope and persist throughout this massive project: Barbara Hucksoll, Hazel Kennedy, Jean Williams, Connie Acuin, Maryann Battaglia and Nancy Javins.

I am also deeply indebted to my own colleagues who sacrificed their time and busy schedules to read and offer valuable comments which strengthened this work: Jomills Braddock, Joyce Epstein, Antoine Garibaldi, Linda Gottfredson, Lorenzo Morris and Richard Scott. Finally, I am grateful to my Creator, family and friends who provided me with the strength and incentive to pursue and complete this project as well as other endeavors.

BLACK STUDENTS IN HIGHER EDUCATION

Introduction

Black students have been more visible in higher education in the decade of the 1970s than in previous decades. In 1970, 21 percent of the blacks between the ages of 18-24 were enrolled in some type of college compared to only 13 percent in 1960 (National Advisory Committee on Black Higher Education, 1979). In addition, black enrollment in U.S. colleges and universities has increased far more rapidly than white college enrollment within the past six years. The five most important historical events that have affected the increased presence of blacks in higher education are: The Civil Rights Movement, the Brown decision, the Equality of Education Opportunity (EEO) Report, the 1965 Higher Education Act, and the recent Adams decision. The Brown decision and the EEO report, which focused primarily on racial inequality in elementary and secondary schools, had an indirect impact on black access to higher education.

The EEO report (Coleman et.al., 1966) was a response to Section 402 of the Civil Rights Act of 1964 which mandated that the Office of Education undertake a study concerning the lack of availability of equality of educational opportunity in U.S. public schools for persons by reason of ethnicity, color, and religion. The report documented inequality in school inputs and outputs between blacks and whites as measured by school facilities, the racial composition of the schools and black-white performance on standardized achievement tests. The results of the report were to become a tool for legal and social action to bring about equality of educational opportunity for blacks and other minorities. Various compensatory educational efforts and other strategies of intervention were undertaken in elementary and secondary schools as a result of the Coleman Report. However, no major programs were implemented at the higher

educational level as a result of the EEO report. One year
prior to the report, the Higher Education Act of 1965 was
passed. This important Act provided for the Basic Educational Opportunity Grant (BEOG) and a variety of other
financial aid packages which subsequently contributed to an
increase in minority enrollment in U.S. colleges and universities.

Following the Higher Education Act, a series of affirmative action efforts and special admissions programs were
established in the late 60s and early 70s. These programs
also aided in increasing the enrollment of minorities in
higher education. In 1973, the Adams decision was passed
which mandated states to desegregate their dual systems of
higher education. It increased the representation of blacks
in higher education and provided blacks with the opportunity
to pursue their higher education in institutions other than
the traditionally black colleges.

All four of the events described as impacting black
access to higher education have been viewed by many Americans
as having paved the way toward equality of educational
opportunity for minorities. Recent census and news media
reports have emphasized the increased college (i.e., undergraduate) access of blacks in the 70s. However, Alexander
Astin (1977) and others have pointed out that higher educational access for minorities must be defined and evaluated
beyond these students' ability to enroll in any college.
Other important factors that must be considered are the type
and quality of colleges that minorities attend, the type of
academic majors that they invest in, and their success in
completing college, graduate and professional degrees. The
academic and social experiences of minorities in various
types of colleges and universities are also important in
assessing how blacks fare in higher education.

The purpose of this book is to evaluate the experiences
and progress of blacks in higher education within the decade
of the 70s based upon a very broad definition of higher
educational access and equality of educational opportunity.
The present definition extends beyond simple descriptive
analyses of college enrollments of blacks. The collection of
papers in this volume considers the degree attainment
statuses of blacks in undergraduate, graduate and professional
schools, their distributions in various academic majors, and
their academic and social experiences within various types
of institutions.

The volume also places the experiences of blacks in higher education within an historical context by describing the initial participation of blacks in U.S. colleges and universities. This historical context is extremely important because the present status of blacks in higher education cannot be understood without some knowledge of the past events that have shaped their present educational experiences. For example, one can hardly understand the high percentage of blacks currently majoring in education without some appreciation of the traditional teaching emphasis of black institutions in the black community.

The current conditions of blacks in higher education must also be understood within the context of U.S. race relations and the intimate relationship that exists between America's educational system and the larger social structure. Bowles and Gintis (1973) and Carnoy (1974) noted the critical role that the educational system plays in differentially socializing individuals of different races and social class statuses and in varying their educational and subsequent status opportunities according to the prevailing societal norms. Thus when Jim Crow was the predominant norm in society, it was also the norm operating in the educational system. However, as U.S. society is currently attempting to become a more integrated society, higher education must also adjust to reflect this developing norm.

The various transitions and adjustments that U.S. colleges and universities have made and are continuing to make have largely come about as a result of minority group protest and pressure and majority-minority conflict. Pierre van den Berghe (1967) has criticized social scientists for their exclusive application of consensus-based functional theory to U.S. race relations. This volume acknowledges the importance of conflict and the dynamics of U.S. race relations for understanding the past and present status of blacks in higher education. The Civil Rights Movement of the 60s and the controversy surrounding the Adams and Bakke decisions in the 70s clearly exemplify the critical role of conflict associated with social change for blacks in higher education and in the larger society.

In addition to recognizing the role of history and conflict in understanding the current conditions of blacks in higher education, we must acknowledge the operation of values surrounding the subject matter of blacks and minorities in higher education. Social scientists often claim that their data speaks for itself. However, this author is not able to identify any empirical or descriptive piece of social

scientific work which has not been interpreted within some
general value framework or specific perspective of the
writer(s). Thresher (1966) has made this point more directly
with reference to higher education by noting that access to
higher education is primarily a social process deeply embed-
ded in society's entire cultural pattern and value system.

The majority of the contributors in this volume are
minority and bring with them some common interest and perspectives. Some social scientists would view this as creating
bias, however, it may be that the minority perspective is an
asset. This perspective has been largely omitted from the
existing literature on blacks in higher education. Therefore,
the collections in this volume should aid in broadening the
existing perspectives and approaches to the problems of
blacks in higher education. The contributors represent a
broad cross-section of the higher education and professional
community. They include higher educational administrators,
admissions officers, counselors, teachers, research scientists, medical physicians, and lawyers. In addition, many of
the contributors are formally and informally engaged in
increasing the access and retention of minorities in higher
education.

Organization of the Book

This book addresses three issues: (1) black access to
higher education; (2) the academic, social and psychological
experiences of blacks in various types of higher educational
institutions; (3) the retention and completion status of
blacks in higher education. Section I of the volume reviews
the history of black participation in higher education and
provides a profile of blacks currently participating in
higher education. Section II addresses the importance of
academic admissions criteria and financial aid on black
student access and persistence at various levels of higher
education. Section III presents descriptive and analytical
data on the current enrollment, major fields, desegregation,
and the degree attainment status of blacks throughout higher
education. This section also describes the academic achievement, aspirations, and social experiences of black students
in predominantly black and white four-year colleges and in
community colleges.

Section IV focuses on the critical issue of black access
to professional schools and identifies critical factors
necessary for the survival of blacks in higher education.
Section V proposes a variety of strategies and programs
designed to improve the access and retention of blacks in

engineering and the basic sciences and at all levels of higher education. Finally, Section VI deals with educational, governmental and economic policies that affect the future status of blacks in higher education. The concluding chapter in the volume highlights the major points, observations and implications of the previous chapters. Recommendations are proposed for policy and research consideration concerning the future of blacks in higher education.

Dissemination and Outcome

The narrative, descriptive, and analytical data in this volume are intended for a broad audience of individuals in federal and state government, in the higher educational community, and in the local school, residential, and political community. It is hoped that this volume will provide some basis for formulating more effective policy to enhance the progress of blacks in higher education.

References

Astin, A.W.
    1977   "Equal access to postsecondary education: myth or reality?" UCLA Educator 19:8-17.

Bowles, S. and H. Gintis
    1973   "I.Q. in the U.S. class structure." Social Policy 3 (Nov. - Feb.):65-96.

Carnoy, M.
    1974   Education as Cultural Imperialism. New York: David McKay.

Coleman, J.S., E.Q. Campbell, C.J. Hobson, J.M. McPartland, A.M. Mood, F.D. Weinfeld and R.L. York
    1966   Equality of Educational Opportunity. Washington, D.C.: U.S. Government Printing Office.

Mosteller, F. and D.P. Moynihan
    1972   On Equality of Educational Opportunity. New York: Vintage Books.

Thresher, B.A.
    1966   College Admissions and the Public Interest. New York: College Entrance Examination Board.

Van den Berghe
    1967   Race and Racism. New York: John Wiley.

Section I
History and Profile of Blacks in
Higher Education: Overview

Knowledge of the historical events that have shaped the current status of blacks in higher education is critical to understanding present conditions. It is also important to have some knowledge of the characteristics and backgrounds of black students enrolled in various types of colleges and universities. The papers in this section provide a history and a profile of blacks in higher education.

The chapter by John Fleming gives an account of the participation of blacks in higher education up to 1954. Fleming documents the effect of slavery on the education of blacks and the racial conflict and resolutions involved in the struggle of blacks for access to higher education. The second chapter by James Mingle begins with the end of legal segregation and describes the initial opening of Southern and Northern white colleges to black students. The role of racial conflict and black student protest is acknowledged in this paper. In addition, Mingle discusses the impact of financial aid and the establishment of two-year colleges on black enrollment, and the response of whites to the presence of blacks on white campuses.

In the final paper in this introductory section, Helen Astin and Patricia Cross provide a current description of blacks in higher education. A profile of black students enrolled in predominantly black and predominantly white four-year colleges is given with particular attention devoted to students' family backgrounds, high school preparations, educational aspirations and self-concepts, and institutional financial aid.

1
Blacks in Higher Education to 1954:
A Historical Overview

JOHN E. FLEMING

Prior to the Civil War, the institution of slavery dictated the Nation's policy toward black Americans and prescribed the norms and social values which specified "appropriate" and "inappropriate" black behavior. For example, the slave code that developed early in the English colonies prescribed the conditions under which blacks worked and lived. Among the restrictive legislation passed to control the slaves was the prohibition against slaves reading and writing. Because this policy was dominant, particularly throughout the South, it was only under the most exceptional circumstances that blacks were able to create learning opportunities. However, some slaves did learn to read and write in clandestine schools and, in some instances, from their masters. These slaves passed on the knowledge they acquired to other slaves.

In large Southern urban areas like Charleston, South Carolina and New Orleans, free blacks attempted to establish their own schools. However, the existence of these schools often depended upon the capriciousness of whites who were generally opposed to educating people of color. Other educational opportunities for blacks existed on a limited basis. For example, some colonization societies provided training opportunities for blacks on the condition that blacks agreed to emigrate to Liberia or Haiti upon completing their education. But most of these organizational efforts included few blacks and had no general impact.

As the Civil War approached, many blacks had reached the conclusion that their best chance for higher education lay in establishing their own educational institutions. At that time (1850-1856) very few (less than 5 percent) blacks out of a population of 4.5 million could read or write. Lincoln University and Wilberforce College were the only two

black schools established in the 1850s by blacks in their
effort toward self education. The efforts of blacks were
later joined by enthusiastic Northern missionaries. Together,
these groups were able to promote the first massive effort
to educate blacks. The American Missionary Association
established Fisk University and Talladega College in 1865.
Morehouse College, Shaw and Howard University were other
historically black institutions established between 1865 and
1867.

During the Reconstruction Era (1868-1877), interested
blacks and their white allies in the South laid the foundation for universal publicly supported education for both
black and white Americans. During this time, Northern
missionaries, who traveled throughout the South, publicized
their belief that emancipated slaves were fully capable of
benefiting from higher education. Unlike Northern missionaries who advocated a **liberal** arts education for the free man,
General S.C. Armstrong, founder of Hampton Institute (1868),
held and promoted the belief that blacks were less competent
than whites, and that blacks should be granted a separate
education that was of a lower calibre (Bullock, 1967).
Southerners showed increasing acceptance of Armstrong's
philosophy. In addition, the political climate of the era
in most states was conducive to such a philosophy. Separate
development for the races received the support of the federal
government when the Supreme Court upheld the doctrine of
"separate but equal" some twenty years later in Plessy v.
Ferguson (1896).

The Plessy decision became the basis for a plethora of
Jim Crow legislation and an increase in violence toward
blacks. The "separate but equal" doctrine was even advocated
in the federal government by President Woodrow Wilson who
permitted increased segregation in governmental offices
(Logan, 1970). During the Jim Crow Era, Booker T. Washington,
a major advocate of segregation, gained prominence among
whites. In his "Atlanta Compromise" speech at the Atlanta
Cotton Exposition in 1895, Washington noted that the development of separate institutions for blacks and whites was the
road to peace and harmony in the South (Logan, 1970). In
addition, Washington urged blacks to cultivate friendly
relations with Southern whites and urged whites to help the
nonviolent blacks who labored for them. Washington also
promoted the belief that blacks should devote themselves to
learning agriculture, mechanics, commerce, and domestic
services.

Encouraged by the Armstrong and Washington philosophies, Southern whites operated on the assumption that blacks should do no more than obtain an education that would prepare them for lower status positions in society. This assumption became apparent in the varied amounts of educational funds that were allocated to black public educational institutions in comparison to white institutions. For example, in one county in Alabama, secondary school officials paid salaries of $3,940 to black teachers who taught 10,745 black students and $28,108 to white teachers who taught 2,285 students (Logan, 1965).

Black colleges made great strides under very difficult circumstances. Of the 88 historically black four-year colleges which survive today (Turner and Michael 1978), forty private and 17 public institutions were established between 1865 and 1890. These institutions were mainly primary and secondary schools, but gradually they developed normal schools and college programs for the education of black teachers. The teachers were able to substantially reduce the illiteracy rate among blacks throughout the South. Nevertheless, white state and educational officials conveniently reasoned that the lower quality schooling that blacks needed required less expenses than the higher quality education that was necessary for white students. This type of logic was also extended to public higher education when the Second Morrill Act of 1890 was passed to include the establishment of black land-grant colleges where states maintained a public policy of segregated education. The colleges that were developed for blacks were of poor quality with inadequately trained teachers and teaching facilities. Moreover, these institutions were initially non-degree-granting agricultural, mechanical, and industrial schools. None of the 17 black land-grant colleges offered a liberal arts education prior to 1916., although one or two institutions offered a four-year degree program   (Holmes, 1934; Bowles and DeCosta, 1971).

After his death in 1915, the influence of Booker T. Washington gradually declined and blacks increasingly demanded a liberal arts education for their children. In addition, blacks realized that "special education", as advanced by Washington, was inadequate to meet their needs as the demand for agriculture decreased and new jobs in manufacturing, trade, and industry appeared. This recognition was especially applicable to blacks who had migrated from rural areas into developing industrial urban centers. The burden of providing blacks with a liberal arts and more relevant education was then assumed by the private black colleges established after the Civil War by Northern mission-

aries. Although these institutions were also forced initially to provide blacks with elementary and secondary education,
by 1928 most of them had eliminated these elementary and secondary departments and were able to concentrate on college
level curriculums. By 1930, black educators had persuaded
the Southern Association of Colleges and Secondary Schools to
include black colleges in its accreditation process; but because of segregation, black colleges could not achieve full
membership. In 1933, black educators formed the Association
of Colleges and Secondary Schools for Negroes whose purpose
was to promote the upgrading and improvement of black
colleges.

By 1930 approximately 19,000 students were enrolled in
black colleges (Aptheker, 1973). In addition, the rate of
illiteracy among blacks had been reduced from 60 percent in
1895 to 25 percent by 1930. In 1939, 119 doctoral degrees
had been awarded to blacks by the leading white colleges and
universities. Most of these recipients had obtained their
undergraduate training from the black colleges. W.E.B. Du-
Bois was one such recipient who had received his college
training at Fisk University and had obtained his Ph.D. from
Harvard University.

Many blacks took pride in the accomplishments of the
private black colleges and in blacks who had successfully
advanced in higher education. However, DuBois, along with
other civil rights leaders and concerned blacks quickly came
to the conclusion that the doctrine of "separate but equal"
was a major inhibiting force to the further progress of
blacks in higher education. During this time, black colleges
were still receiving unequal and discriminatory treatment
through state and federal support and technical assistance.

In response to the position of blacks, the National Association for the Advancement of Colored People (NAACP)
spearheaded the assault on the doctrine and separate development in the federal courts. In 1935, Donald G. Murray was
unsuccessful in his attempt to enter the University of Maryland's segregated school of law. Murray's failure stimulated
a class action suit by the NAACP charging the University of
Maryland with discrimination and in violation of the 14th
Amendment to the Constitution. In 1936, the Court ordered
the University of Maryland to admit Murray to its school of
law. The Murray decision was followed by four additional
NAACP suits which attacked the doctrine of "separate but
equal" in higher education: Missouri ex rel Gaines v.
Canada (1938); Sipuel v. Board of Regents (1948); Sweatt v.
Painter (1950) and McLaurin v. Oklahoma State Board of
Regents (1950).

Based on the Court's ruling in Murray and the later four cases, the NAACP had established a successful attack on the doctrine of "separate but equal." The suit in Gaines was filed after the University of Missouri School of Law denied Lloyd Gaines (a black graduate of Lincoln University) admission to its Law School. The Supreme Court held that Gaines was entitled to equal protection of the law and that the state of Missouri was obligated to provide him with a legal education substantially equal to that offered whites. The Court's ruling in Gaines (1938) established the principle that if states did not provide educational facilities for blacks equivalent to that provided for whites, then blacks had to be admitted to white institutions (Haynes, 1978). Sipuel (1948) and Sweatt (1950) also involved the refusal of white state law schools to admit blacks to their programs. Sipuel reinforced the precedent established in Gaines that blacks had to be admitted to white graduate and professional schools if no black institutions existed. The ruling in Sweatt constituted the first time that the Supreme Court ordered admission of a black student to a white institution on the grounds that the black law school established by the State of Texas (Prairie View) failed to offer blacks equality of educational opportunity (Haynes, 1978). The McLaurin (1950) case involved a black student who was admitted to the University of Oklahoma's graduate school but who was required to eat and sit apart from his white classmates. The Supreme Court ruled that such discriminatory treatment violated McLaurin's constitutional rights and that McLaurin was entitled to the same treatment within the graduate school as his white classmates.

The Court's posture in McLaurin, Sweatt, and the previous cases paved the way for the landmark ruling in Brown v. Board of Education of Topeka (1954). The Supreme Court consolidated the Brown case with four similar cases in the District of Columbia, Delaware, Virginia and South Carolina. In response to Brown and these four cases, the Supreme Court unanimously held that the doctrine of "separate but equal" was unconstitutional and violated the Equal Protection Clause of the Fourteenth Amendment. Chief Justice Earl Warren, who delivered the Court's opinion, held that "enforced school segregation imposed an inferior status on the Negro children". Although the ruling in Brown was aimed at elementary and secondary education, it had broad consequences and implications for higher education which were articulated almost a decade and a half later in Adams v. Richardson (1973), when the Supreme Court ruled that states had to dismantle their dual system of higher education for blacks and whites.

References

Adams v. Richardson.   480 f.2d 1159 (D.C. Cir. 1973).

Aptheker, H.
    1973   The Education of Black People: Ten Critiques,
            1906-1960. Amherst: The University of
            Massachusetts Press.

Bowles, F. and F.H. DeCosta
    1971   Between Two Worlds: A Profile of Negro Higher
            Education. New York: McGraw-Hill.

Bullock, H.A.
    1967   A History of Negro Education in the South From
            1619 to the Present. New York: Praeger.

Brown v. Board of Education of Topeka 347 U.S. 483 (1954).

Fleming, J.E.
    1976   The Lengthening Shadow of Slavery: An Historical
            Justification for Affirmative Action for Blacks
            in Higher Education. Washington, D.C.: Howard
            University Press.

Haynes, III, L.
    1978   A Critical Examination of the Adams Case: A
            Source Book. Washington, D. C.: Institute for
            Services to Education.

Holmes, D.O.W.
    1969   The Evolution of the Negro College. New York:
            Arno Press and the New York Times.

Logan,R.W.
    1965   The Betrayal of the Negro from Rutherford B. Hayes
            to Woodrow Wilson. New York: Collier Books.

    1970   The Negro in the United States. New York:
            Van Nostrand Reinhold Co.

McLaurin v. Oklahoma State Regents 339 U.S. 637 (1950).

Missouri ex. rel. Gaines v. Canada 305 U.S. 337 (1938).

Murray v. Maryland 182 A 590 (1935):169 Md 478 (1937)

Plessy v. Ferguson 163 U.S. 537 (1896)

Sipuel v. Board of Regents of University of Oklahoma 322
        U.S. 631 (1948).

Sweatt v. Painter 339 U.S. 629 (1950).

Turner, W.H. and J.A. Michael
    1978   Traditionally Black Institutions of Higher
            Education: Their Identification and Selected
            Characteristics. Washington, D.C.: National
            Center for Educational Statistics, U.S. DHEW.

2

The Opening of White Colleges and Universities to Black Students

JAMES R. MINGLE

Introduction

The end of legal segregation in Southern white institutions and the opening of colleges and universities in other parts of the country to increasing numbers of black students has produced extraordinary changes in higher education over the last three decades. Of the approximately 45,000 black students enrolled in higher education at the beginning of World War II, only about one in ten was enrolled in a predominantly white college or university. In 1978, of the over one million black students enrolled, seven of ten could be found in white institutions (Arce, 1976; Mingle,1978a;1980) This chapter reviews the historical process of this change in both the North and the South and some of the reasons for it.

Blacks in White Four-Year Colleges in the South

As Fleming (1981) noted, at the end of World War II, blacks accelerated their aggressive and ultimately successful strategy to end segregation in southern colleges. From a handful of blacks in the 1940s, black enrollment in southern white institutions increased to a few hundred by the early 1950s. Johnson (1954) estimated that the total black enrollment for the 1952-53 academic year was 453 students in twenty-two historically white public institutions in the South. However, through legal efforts and some voluntary action, segregation barriers fell following the famous ruling in Brown (1954), and desegregation in the South accelerated. Oklahoma's undergraduate schools desegregated in 1955; all but 10 of the public colleges in Tennessee had desegregated by 1956, and 10 of the 15 colleges and universities in Missouri had done so by this time. (Bullock, 1967:262-267).

Despite the increase in desegregation efforts after
Brown, the Southern Education Reporting Service (1965) estimated that only 17 percent of the public institutions in the
Deep South had admitted blacks by 1961 and that the desegregation of these white institutions had little impact on the
total number of blacks attending white institutions in the
South. As indicated in Table 1, in 1960, 96 percent of all
black students in the region were still enrolled in the
traditionally black institutions.

For the most part, the desegregation of the Southern
white colleges proceeded without the delaying tactics, rancor,
and violence sometimes associated with integrating the public
schools. However, three incidents in the South drew national
attention: Autherine Lucy was driven by campus rioting from
the University of Alabama in 1956; George Wallace's stand
in the school-house door" occurred seven years later at the
same institution; and James Meredith's admission to the
University of Mississippi in 1962 which focused national
attention on the integration of the Southern colleges.

During the first half of the 1960s the number of blacks
attending white colleges in the South steadily increased,
rising from 3,000 in 1960 to 24,000 in 1965 and to 98,000 in
1970 (See Table 1). From 1965 to 1970 black enrollment in
the predominantly white institutions of the South more than
tripled. As a result of increasing black access to predominantly white institutions, the percentage of black enrollment in the predominantly black institutions dropped from 82
to 60 percent from 1965 to 1970 and from 60 to 40 percent
from 1970 to 1978 (Table 1). The predominance of this enrollment in 1978 was found in public institutions. Private
white colleges in the South enrolled only 6 percent of all
black students in the region, while private black colleges
enrolled another 12.5 percent.

Partly, because of the substantial growth of white student enrollment and the steady out-migration of blacks from
the South from 1950 to 1970, the black share of total enrollment in the South declined during the fifties and then stabilized during the first half of the sixties. By 1976, the
442,000 blacks enrolled in the South represented 15 percent
of total enrollment--up from 10 percent in 1965 (See Table 1).
This percentage, however, was still below their 19 percent
representation in the college aged population.

Blacks in the White Colleges of the North

Although there was no legal segregation in the colleges
of the North and West, the level of black enrollment out-

Table 1

Total Black Student Enrollment in the South, 1952-1976

Year	Total	Predominantly White Institutions	Predominantly Black Institutions	Percent of Total Enrollment Black	Percent of Black Enrollment in Predominantly Black Institutions	Percent of Total Black Enrollment in the South
1952	63,000	--	63,000	13%	100%	70%
1960	84,000	3,000	81,000	10	96	50
1965	134,000	24,000	110,000	10	82	49
1970	245,000	98,000	147,000	12	60	47
1976	426,000	243,000	183,000	15	43	41
1978	442,000	266,000	176,000	15	40	42

Sources: Estimates of black student enrollment in predominantly white colleges and universities for the years 1960 and 1965 are taken from those made by the Southern Education Reporting Service. Enrollment in traditionally black institutions for 1952, 1960, 1965 are derived from School Enrollment Reports of the U.S. Bureau of the Census, Current Population Reports (Series P-20), and the U.S. Office for Civil Rights, Racial and Ethnic Enrollment in Higher Education, 1970. Figures for 1976 and 1978 are from the Fall Enrollment and Compliance Report, of the Higher Education General Information Survey (HEGIS). Predominantly black institutions are those with greater than 50 percent black enrollment. Taken from James R. Mingle, Black Enrollment in Higher Education: Trends in the Nation and the South (Atlanta: Southern Regional Education Board, 1978a), p. 8., and Minority Enrollment: 1978 (Atlanta: Southern Regional Education Board, 1980).

20

side the South on the eve of World War II was minuscule.
Carlos Arce (1976) estimated that slightly over 5,000 black
students were in white colleges outside the South in 1939.
This represented five tenths of a percent of total enrollments
in the North, and about half of these students were concentrated in fewer than two dozen institutions.

Black migration northward and the GI Bill for veterans
substantially accelerated black enrollment after World War II.
From 1940 to 1950, the percentage of the black population
residing outside the South increased from 23 to 32 percent.[1]
Arce estimated that black enrollment in white colleges outside the South in 1947 was 61,000, which was about 47 percent of all black enrollment but only 3 percent of the total
enrollment in these colleges. Black enrollment nationwide
represented 6 percent of total enrollment that year, a high
point which would not be reached again until 1967 (Arce,1976).

In 1967, black enrollment experienced a dramatic increase. It reached 8.4 percent of all enrollment in 1971,
paused at that level for two years, then increased again
annually from 1974 to 1977. The U.S. Bureau of the Census
reported that black college enrollment in October 1977 accounted for 10.8 percent of the total college enrollment.
Blacks in 1976 made up 12.6 percent of the Nation's 18 to 24
year old college-age population (U.S. Bureau of the Census,
1978).

These enrollment increases were due primarily to the
dramatic rise in the number of blacks in predominantly white
institutions in the North, as opposed to the steady but substantially lower growth rates of the traditionally black institutions of the South. Arce's (1976) study revealed that
black enrollment in white institutions increased 160 percent
from 1967 to 1974, compared to a 34 percent increase in the
black enrollment of traditionally black colleges and a 33
percent increase in total enrollment.

Private colleges such as Oberlin have a history of enrolling black students. In addition,other prestigious institutions such as Northwestern, Carleton, and Macalester
launched aggrevise recruitment campaigns for blacks in the
1960's. However, the greatest numerical growth in black
enrollment has occurred in Northern public colleges. Nationwide, 13 percent of all black students in 1978 were enrolled
in private white colleges,with another 7 percent in private
black colleges. Twenty-two percent of all white students
were enrolled in private institutions in 1978 (Mingle, 1980).

Weinberg (1977) reported that the aftermath of <u>Brown</u> and an increase in black enrollment in predominantly white institutions did not automatically end discrimination on Southern or Northern white campuses. As late as the 1960s, official housing discrimination existed in northern universities (Meier and Rudwick, 1973). However, student protests terminated these practices. Similarly, racial restrictions on black student participation in athletics and campus activities on Southern and Northern campuses were eliminated in the early sixties as a result of Civil Rights pressure and student protest. Despite these victories, blacks still experienced a sense of estrangement on white Southern and Northern campuses throughout the sixties (Bindman, 1965).

Factors Influencing the Growth of Black Enrollment

The Federal Government and Financial Aid. To a large extent, the growth of black enrollment in higher education in the post-World War II period is attributable to the intervention of the federal government. Apart from legal imperatives, the increase in black enrollment at white colleges and universities was greatly aided by the provision of Federal financial aid to students and institutions. Policy makers who were interested in increasing black student enrollment immediately recognized the importance of financial aid as a critical resource. In the 1950s, the National Scholarship Service and Fund for Negro Students (NSSFNS) recruited blacks from segregated high schools to attend white colleges. Later this modest program was supplemented by the National Defense Student Loan Program in 1958 and the National Achievement Program in 1964 (Bowles and DeCosta, 1971).

The significant increase in black enrollment beginning in 1967 was preceded by the Higher Education Act of 1965, which greatly expanded available financial aid through the College Work Study Program, Educational Opportunity Grants, and the Guaranteed Student Loan Program. These programs were followed by the Basic Educational Opportunity Grant Program (BEOG), established in 1972. BEOG provided grants, based on need, which students could carry to the institutions of their choice. BEOG's have had an extraordinary impact on levels of black enrollment in all colleges and universities. In 1976-77, 1.5 billion dollars in BEOG's were awarded nationwide to nearly 2 million students. In addition, approximately 1 billion dollars in other federal funds were provided through other need-based programs. These federal dollars were supplemented by 746 million dollars in state aid programs in 1977-78 (Mingle, 1978a).[2]

The Growth of State Systems. While federal government
programs were a major stimulus for black enrollment, state
governments responded to the demands for increased access
by greatly expanding the size and scope of public education
in the 1960s. Much of this expansion occurred in the growth
of the two-year college sector. In 1961, there were 593
two-year community colleges nationwide; but by 1976 the number of community colleges had grown to 1,147 (Mingle, 1978b)
with only 16 of them being traditionally black institutions
(Turner and Michael, 1978). Black students were attracted to
the public two-year colleges because of their proximity, low
tuition and open admissions policies. By the Fall of 1976,
black enrollment in two-year colleges totaled 429,293, which
represented 41.5 percent of all black students enrolled in
higher education at that time (Mingle, 1978a). Both blacks
and other minorities are disproportionately represented in
two-year colleges as opposed to four-year colleges and
universities (Goodrich, Laziotte and Welch, 1973; Astin,
1977).

The role of state funding formulas for higher education
has often been overlooked as an explanatory factor in increasing the enrollment of blacks and other "new students"
in higher education. With state dollars tied to enrollment
levels, public institutions have had strong incentives to
maximize enrollment and oppose state-mandated enrollment
ceilings. In recent years, as the market for traditional
college students (who in the past were predominantly white
males age 18-21) has stabilized, institutions have actively
pursued new groups of students--blacks, other minorities,
women, and older students, in order to sustain institutional
growth.

Expansion of the High School Pool. Obviously, the
expansion of the available pool of black high school
graduates was an important prerequisite for increased black
student enrollment. But this pool had significantly
expanded in the fifties and sixties well before the large
increases in college enrollment. While the percentage of
20 to 24 year old blacks with a high school diploma increased
from 25 percent in 1950 to 42 percent in 1960 and then to 62
percent in 1970, black enrollment as noted did not begin its
dramatic climb until the late sixties, when white colleges
began actively recruiting black students (Mingle, 1978a). In
the 1970s, the high school graduation rates of blacks continued to grow, increasing to 75 percent of the 20 to 24

year old population in 1977 (compared to 85 percent of whites in this age group). This contributed further to the growth of black enrollment in higher education.

Black Student Activism and Institutional Response. Civil rights activity and protest movements also contributed to the growth of black student enrollment. By 1967 and 1968, the activism of blacks was beginning to significantly affect the recruitment and support efforts of white colleges. A University of Michigan study found that a number of institutions initiated or accelerated their efforts in the months following the assassination of Dr. Martin Luther King, Jr. in the Spring of 1968 (Peterson et al., 1978).

The Michigan study examined institutional responses to increased black enrollment in thirteen predominantly white colleges of the North and Midwest during the 1968-1972 period, when these institutions were experiencing significant increases in black enrollment. Early success in recruiting black students and developing special programs to meet their needs depended on the interaction of a number of external and internal factors: access to a "convenient" source of black students; early involvement in such programs as Upward Bound, Talent Search, and foundation-sponsored high school preparatory programs; aggressive leadership from institutional presidents and other administrators; contingents of liberal faculty; or contact and exchange programs with black colleges. Also, the Michigan study noted that increases in black enrollment often ran parallel to other major changes--declining white enrollments, shifts from private to public control, secularization of religious institutions, and transformation of an institution from a teachers college to a broader comprehensive university, which meant increases in offerings, staff, and definition of service region. All these changes tended to facilitate increased black enrollments in the institutions.

Conflict was also an important factor, and most of the institutions in the Michigan study experienced at least one major racial incident involving building takeovers, presentation of a list of demands, and/or other confrontation tactics. Initial institutional responses--often recruiting efforts and special support and academic programs--were usually criticized as being too little too late. Occupying of buildings and threats of violence sometimes followed, and so did additional institutional responses. While the perception of the role of confrontation varied within the institutions, the Michigan team of investigators concluded that conflict in most cases "was effective in keeping the institution's focus on their original commitments and was

often influential in speeding up the rate of enrollment
increase and program development" (Peterson et al., 1978:160).

The Future of Black Enrollment in White Institutions.
Current trends indicate that predominantly white institutions
can expect to enroll a growing percentage of all black students in higher education in the future. The competitive
forces operating among higher education institutions will
certainly serve as a motivating force for white colleges to
continue to recruit black students. As the total student
pool becomes smaller (and blacks become a larger share of
that pool due to higher birth rates), more and more institutions will look to blacks and other minorities as their "new
market." In the South, the continuing litigation surrounding the Adams case, insofar as it establishes numerical
goals for levels of black enrollment in white institutions,
will be a stimulus for growth. This latter factor, however,
may mean that black colleges with limited resources and program offerings will find it difficult to compete for quality
black students. In addition, two-year colleges, because of
their low cost, are expected to continue to attract black
students, thus posing another source of drain on black
enrollment in black colleges. Spence (1977) has noted that
two-year public colleges will claim a growing part of
college enrollment in the decade of the eighties in general
because of the growing shift of undergraduates from four-year
to two-year colleges and because of the increase in older
students in the latter institutions.

Increases in black enrollment during the 1980s will not,
however, be of the same magnitude as those experienced in
the 1970s. First, total higher education enrollment between
1980 and 1985 is expected to decrease nationwide Spence
(1977). Second, white colleges increased their black enrollment in the 1970s in large part by recruiting and admitting
18 and 19 year old black high school graduates for their
freshman classes. These groups now enroll in college at
about the same rate as do whites (U.S. Bureau of the Census,
1979a). Levels of educational attainment among blacks
continue to lag behind those of whites, but this is due to
lower rates of high school graduation and persistence at the
college level among blacks. While freshman levels of black
enrollment nationwide generally approximated levels of black
population by the mid-1970s, blacks remained considerably
underrepresented in graduate and professional programs.
Higher education administrators have found retention of students to higher levels to be a far more difficult issue than
freshman admission policies.

The competency-based examinations that are being increasingly administered in many states as a requirement for high school graduation could also have negative effects on the available pool of black high school graduates. However, if the long-term potential of these exams is to make public school systems more accountable through the use of evaluative testing, these exams could have a positive effect on the quality of black students in higher education.

A critical factor in future levels of black enrollment will be the availability of financial resources. The prospects for the growth of federal financial aid dollars at the same magnitude as experienced in the 1970s are not great, however. Federal and state programs will do well to maintain their current level of dollar support after accounting for inflation. Thus it is likely that blacks will increasingly be forced to continue their college education on a part-time basis and will seek enrollment in institutions that provide programs for part-timers.

The level of black enrollment in white institutions will also depend heavily on the receptivity of white institutions to that enrollment and on the ability of students and institutions to overcome the skill deficiencies which many black and white students bring to higher education. Thus far, the success of compensatory education efforts at the collegiate level have not been great.

Finally, the future level of black enrollment in white and black institutions will depend heavily on the higher educational aspirations of students themselves. Although a college education is still a goal of many young American students, the college-going rates of the population as a whole leveled off in the 1970s. Part of this leveling off is attributed to students' perceptions of their returns from having invested in a college education. Unless students perceive such returns as rewarding, white colleges and other higher educational institutions can expect significant declines in black and white college enrollments.

References

Arce, C. H.
    1976 Historical, Institutional and Contextual Determinants of Black Enrollment. Doctoral dissertation: University of Michigan.

Astin, A.W.
    1977 "Equal access to postsecondary education: myth

or reality?" UCLA Educator 19:8-17.

Bindman, A.
    1965   Participation of Negro Students in an Intergrated
           University. Doctoral dissertation: University
           of Illinois.

Bowles, F. and F.A. DeCosta
    1971   Between Two Worlds: A Profile of Negro Higher
           Education. New York: McGraw Hill.

Brown v. Board of Education of Topeka.   347 U.S. 483; (1954).

Bullock, H.A.
    1967   A History of Negro Education in the South From 1619
           to the Present. Cambridge: Harvard University
           Press.

Fleming, J.E.
    1981   "Blacks in higher education to 1954: An historical
           overview." Pp. 7-13 in G. Thomas (ed.), Black Stu-
           dents in Higher Education: Conditions and Experi-
           ences in the 1970s. Westport, Connecticut: Green-
           wood Press.

Goodrich, A.L., L.W. Laziotte and J.A. Welch
    1973   "Minorities in two-year colleges: a survey."
           Community and Junior College Journal 43:29-31.

Johnson, G.B.
    1954   "Racial intergration in public higher education in
           the South." Journal of Negro Education 23:317-329.

Meier, A. and E. Rudwick
    1973   CORE: A Study in the Civil Rights Movements 1942-
           1968. New York: Oxford University Press.

Mingle, J.R.
    1978a Black Enrollment in Higher Education: Trends in the
           Nation and the South. Atlanta: Southern Regional
           Education Board.

    1978b Fact Book on Higher Education in the South, 1977 and
           1978. Atlanta: Southern Regional Education Board.

    1980   Minority Enrollment: 1978. Atlanta: Southern
           Regional Education Board.

Peterson, M.W., R.T. Blackburn, Z.F. Gamson, C.H. Arce,
        W. Davenport, and J.R. Mingle
    1978   Black Students on White Campuses: The Impacts of
            Increased Black Enrollments. Ann Arbor: Institute
            for Social Research.

Southern Education Reporting Service
    1965   Statistical Summary, 1964-65. Nashville, Tenn.

Spence, D.S.
    1977   A Profile of Higher Education in the South in
            1985. Atlanta: Southern Regional Education Board.

Turner, W.H. and J.A. Michael
    1978   A Definitive List of Traditionally Black Insti-
            tutions. Washington, D.C.: National Center for
            Education Statistics.

U.S. Bureau of the Census
    1950   Census of the Population. Characteristics of the
            Population. Volume 1. Washington, D.C.: U.S.
            Government Printing Office.

    1960   Census of the Population. Characteristics of the
            Population. Volume 1. Washington, D.C.: U.S.
            Government Printing Office.

    1970   Census of the Population. Characteristics of the
            Population. Volume 1. Washington, D.C.: U.S.
            Government Printing Office.

    1978   Current Population Reports, Series P-32, No. 73.
            Washington, D.C.: U.S. Government Printing Office.

    1979a   Current Population Reports, Series P-20, No. 333.
            Washington, D.C.: U.S. Government Printing Office.

    1979b   Current Population Reports, Series P-20, No. 335.
            Washington, D.C.: U.S. Government Printing Office.

Weinberg, M.
    1977   Minority Students: A Research Appraisal. Wash-
            ington, D.C.: U.S. Government Printing Office.

Footnotes

1. Arce also notes that black migration northward was an im-
    portant demographic factor in the increases from 1950 to 1970.
    From 1950 to 1960, the percentage of the black population
    outside the South increased from 32 to 40 percent, and from
    1960 to 1970 from 40 to 48 percent (1976:23).   Larry H. Long
    concluded in a U.S. Bureau of the Census report (1978b) that
    sometime between 1967 and 1976, the South switched from
    being an exporter of low-income persons to being an importer,
    primarily as the result of retaining blacks and whites below
    the poverty level rather than attracting immigrants.

2. The importance of financial aid to levels of black enroll-
    ment is supported by the decline of black enrollment experi-
    enced in Fall 1978, which was 7.5 percent less than in 1977
    (U.S. Bureau of the Census, 1979b).   This decline may be in
    part attributable to the increased audit activity by the
    federal government of BEOG applications in 1978.

3

Black Students in Black and White Institutions

HELEN S. ASTIN and PATRICIA H. CROSS

Introduction

Blacks constitute about 9 percent of college enrollments. About two-thirds attend white institutions, and the rest are enrolled in predominantly black institutions (Astin and Cross, 1979). In recent months renewed interest and debate have centered on questions of the survival of the historically black institutions, the role these institutions have played in the educational and occupational development of black youth, and the characteristics of blacks attending black institutions, especially as compared with black students attending white institutions. Even though one-third of all black full-time, first-time freshmen are in predominantly black institutions (Astin and Cross, 1979), only 13 percent of the highly able blacks--as defined by scores of 1000 or higher on the combined verbal and mathematics subtests of the Scholastic Aptitude Test (SAT)--were enrolled in black institutions in the fall of 1975 (Astin and Scherrei, 1979).

This chapter gives a descriptive profile of black students enrolled in these two types of institutions. By examining the high school preparation and performance as well as the aspirations of black students, we hope to identify their academic strengths and weaknesses. Such information can help institutions provide the kind of educational environment that maximizes benefits to the students. When one is concerned with issues of access, a number of questions that need to be answered are: Do students apply to a variety of institutions? Are they accepted by a similar variety of institutions? Are they accepted by their first-choice institutions? Are they financially able and willing to go away from home to attend college? The data presented here deal with some of these questions. Parental education and income, as well as the student's ability to get financial aid, are important determinants of a student's decision to attend

college and the type of college attended. In this profile
of black students, the above questions were examined along
with the degree plans and intended majors of black students,
their self-concepts, and their values.

Data

For this analysis, we used data collected by the Cooperative Institutional Research Program (CIRP) in the fall of
1976. The analyses for this chapter are based on questionnaire responses of a 10 percent random subsample of first-
time, full-time freshmen enrolling in a representative sample
of 393 institutions, including 29 black institutions. The
data were weighted to correct for sampling bias and to
reflect the actual population of first-time, full-time
freshmen.[1]

The weighted Ns used in these analyses are as follows:
Black men in black institutions = 23,300; black women in
black institutions = 24,830; black men in white institutions
= 25,360; and black women in white institutions = 27,700.

Findings

High School Preparation and Applications to College

Respondents to the CIRP freshman questionnaire were
asked to indicate the type of preparation they had in high
school. Seventy-eight percent of men and women attending
black institutions indicated having completed a college
preparatory program while in high school. In predominantly
white institutions, however, 81 percent of the black men,
compared with 78 percent of the women, said that they
completed a college preparatory curriculum. A higher proportion of white students (95%) indicated that they were in
a college preparatory high school program.

The survey administered to freshmen entering in 1976
asked them about their specific preparation in high school
courses, vocational skills, and study habits. Blacks in
black institutions felt better prepared than black students
attending white institutions on all of these measures except
study habits. But a higher proportion of black women attending white institutions than those attending black schools
indicated that they were well-prepared in science. Comparing
black and white students, we find that whites felt better
prepared in mathematics and science, whereas black students

were more comfortable about their preparation in reading
and composition and in the social sciences. Further, a
higher proportion of blacks than whites believed that they
had acquired vocational skills and were better prepared in
music and the arts.

Another measure of preparation is the student's actual
performance in high school as measured by grades. Table 1
lists the proportions of students with different average
high school grades. Both black men and women attending white
institutions had higher average high school grades than those
attending predominantly black institutions. For example,
about 8 percent of black men and 16 percent of black women
attending white institutions had a grade average of A- or
better, compared with 4 percent of the men and 9 percent of
the women attending black institutions. Among both blacks
and whites, women entering college made better grades in high
school than did men. At white institutions, the proportions
of white men with A- or better grades was 25 percent,
compared with 8 percent of the black men.

The number of college applications and acceptances
depends on the student's past academic performance and on
his/her financial resources, especially if a student is to
attend college away from home. Close to one-half of all
entering freshmen said that the college they were attending
was the only one to which they had applied.

Table 1

DISTRIBUTION OF STUDENTS BY HIGH SCHOOL GRADES
(Percentages)

High School Grades	Blacks in Black Institutions		Blacks in White Institutions	
	Men	Women	Men	Women
A/A+	1.5	4.3	3.3	5.3
A-	2.5	4.9	5.1	10.4
B+	7.6	16.6	16.2	19.6
B	27.1	23.6	22.0	29.9
B-	14.7	17.2	17.0	13.8
C+	24.1	18.5	25.1	12.7
C	21.6	13.4	9.7	8.3
D	0.9	1.5	1.7	0

Table 2 reports the number of applications and acceptances for blacks. A slightly higher proportion of blacks
in black institutions than blacks in white institutions had
not applied to institutions other than those in which they
were enrolled. With respect to acceptances, about 76 percent
of blacks in white institutions indicated that they had been
accepted by one or more other schools as opposed to about
74 percent of the blacks in black institutions. We do not
know, however, whether these other applications and acceptances involved were at black or white institutions. Over
65 percent of black men and women in both types of institutions indicated that the institution they were attending was
their first choice. About 90 percent indicated that they had
enrolled in either their first- or second-choice institution.

A critical issue with respect to access is whether
students are willing and financially able to attend an institution that is some distance from their homes. The proportion of black students attending white institutions who came
from a 50-mile radius was somewhat higher (about 40 percent
of the men and 45 percent of the women) than the proportion
of blacks enrolled in black colleges (36 percent of the men
and 39 percent of the women). Among white students, 36 percent of the men and 38 percent of the women attended a
college within 50 miles of their homes. Over one-third of
all students were within commuting distance of their colleges.
A somewhat higher proportion of men than of women went to a
college that was a distance 500 miles or more from their
homes. Further, blacks in black institutions tended to go to
a college farther away than blacks in white institutions.

Going to college serves a variety of purposes, and
different students attend for different reasons. The different reasons students attend college are listed in Table 3.
A higher proportion of black men and women attending black
institutions than those attending white institutions endorsed
each reason listed as being very important in their decision
to go to college. Black men and women differed, however,
with respect to their three most important reasons. For
example, independent of the type of institution, the three
most important reasons given by black men for going to college
in rank order, were, "to be able to get a better job," "to be
able to make more money," and "to learn more about things
that interest me." For black women, in addition to being
able to get a better job, "getting a general education " and
"learning more about things that interest me" were the two
other very important reasons. Thus, while black men were
motivated primarily by financial reasons, black women were

Table 2

DISTRIBUTION OF STUDENTS BY NUMBER OF
COLLEGES APPLIED TO AND ACCEPTED BY
(Percentages)

Number of Other Colleges	Blacks in Black Institutions				Blacks in White Institutions			
	Men		Women		Men		Women	
	Applied	Accepted	Applied	Accepted	Applied	Accepted	Applied	Accepted
None	35.3	28.9	33.4	22.3	26.6	24.4	24.8	24.4
One	15.9	23.9	21.3	33.3	14.7	22.4	25.2	34.4
Two	17.1	22.5	18.9	21.0	20.7	25.4	18.6	15.8
Three	18.6	15.6	16.2	15.4	17.9	13.7	12.5	14.3
Four	7.9	7.4	6.6	4.9	6.4	5.1	5.7	5.5
Five	2.6	0.9	2.6	2.6	6.0	2.7	8.2	3.6
Six or More	2.6	0.8	1.3	0.5	7.7	6.3	4.9	2.0

Table 3

DISTRIBUTION OF STUDENTS BY REASONS FOR ATTENDING COLLEGE

Reason	Blacks in Black Institutions		Blacks in White Institutions	
	Men	Women	Men	Women
My parents wanted me to go	46.5[a]	49.9	44.9	37.8
I could not find a job	12.0	13.5	12.3	10.5
I wanted to get away from home	17.4	12.6	15.8	11.9
To be able to get a better job	82.8	86.3	78.3	77.6
To gain a general education and appreciation of ideas	70.6	83.3	66.4	72.9
To improve my reading and study skills	57.4	56.3	51.4	50.0
There was nothing better to do	7.2	6.6	4.4	2.5
To make me a more cultured person	55.6	61.4	38.9	46.1
To be able to make more money	79.1	73.0	71.0	64.6
To learn more about things that interest me	76.5	81.4	70.3	78.7
To meet new and interesting people	59.0	61.8	55.5	54.6
To prepare myself for graduate or professional school	61.0	69.8	58.9	65.5

[a]Percentages represent the proportion of students who checked the response category "very important."

more likely to indicate a stronger interest in the learning process and in becoming better educated. The same differences have been found among white men and women (Astin, 1979).

Examining the students' reasons for attending a particular institution can give some insight as to the types of factors considered by black students who choose to apply at and enroll in a black institution as compared with those who elect to attend a white institution. Table 4 presents these results. As Table 4 shows, relatives, teachers, and friends were relatively important influences on students attending black institutions. In addition, it shows that black students in white institutions were more likely to report that the availability of financial aid was a strong determinant of their decision to attend a white institution or that the college actively recruited them.

Family Background

Parents' education and income are important correlates of a student's educational progress and attainment. To succeed, the student should receive both emotional and financial support from his parents. As is well known, underrepresented minorities are generally disadvantaged with respect to parents' formal education and income. For instance, in our sample, over 40 percent of the fathers of black students had less than a high school education, while only about 13 percent of the fathers of white students were not high school graduates. By the same token, about 15 percent of the black students' fathers had a baccalaureate or higher degree, compared with about 45 percent of the white students' fathers. There were, however, some interesting differences between blacks attending black institutions and those at white colleges in that the former tended to have somewhat better educated fathers than the latter. Although the fathers of white women had about the same education as the fathers of white men, black women tended to have somewhat less educated fathers than did black men.

The patterns with respect to mother's education were similar. The mothers of black women tended to be somewhat less educated than the mothers of black men. In addition, the mothers of black men and women attending black schools tended to be better educated than the mothers of blacks at white institutions. The mothers of both sexes were in general better educated than the fathers.

Table 4

DISTRIBUTION OF STUDENTS BY
REASONS FOR ATTENDING THIS PARTICULAR COLLEGE

	Blacks in Black Institutions		Blacks in White Institutions	
Reason	Men	Women	Men	Women
My relatives wanted me to come here	15.8[a]	13.6	9.3	8.6
My teacher advised me	10.9	4.3	5.0	8.4
This college has a very good academic reputation	51.6	56.4	48.3	59.1
I was offered financial assistance	28.0	24.5	32.1	34.1
I was not accepted anywhere else	5.3	3.3	2.9	2.4
Someone who had been here before advised me to go	20.7	18.5	12.8	10.1
This college offers special educational programs	35.0	30.1	25.6	33.7
This college has low tuition	18.2	12.6	10.8	16.2
My guidance counselor advised me	11.7	8.8	9.8	12.1
I wanted to live at home	11.5	11.8	7.3	4.0
A friend suggested attending	12.6	10.5	7.7	4.2
A college representative recruited me	10.0	7.1	15.1	9.2

[a]Percentages represent the proportion of students who checked
the response category "very important."

The findings with respect to parents' income parallel the findings for educational attainment. Black women tended to come from poorer families than black men.
The parental income level of blacks at the black institutions, however, was similar to that of blacks at white
institutions. For example, 37 percent of black men in
black institutions reported parental incomes of $6,000
or less and 14 percent reported incomes of $20,000 or
more. The comparable figures for black men at white colleges were 36 percent and 15 percent respectively.

Student Financial Status

An individual's ability to finance a college education is an important consideration not only in the initial decision to pursue a postsecondary education at all
but also in further decision about where to go to college.
Black entering freshmen were much more concerned than
were their white counterparts about their ability to finance college.[2] Whereas 56 percent of black students said
that their parents had a low income and thus could not
help them with college, the comparable figure for whites
was only 19 percent. Moreover, 16 percent of black students were heads of households or single parents, compared to 4 percent of whites. By the same token almost
90 percent of black students received financial aid, compared with 55 percent of whites. The amount of aid varied,
however, depending on the type of institution attended.
For example, in 1976-77, blacks attending black institutions received an average of $1,851, per student, in
aid whereas blacks attending white universities received
$3,116, per student.

Degree Plans and Intended Majors

Students' degree plans often reflect their commitment to higher education, a demonstration of both interest and motivation. Table 5 shows that black men and
women, independent of the type of college they attended,
had very high degree aspirations. Over 30 percent of
both sexes at both white and black institutions planned
to get a doctorate or a professional degree such as an
M.D. or an LL.B. Blacks in black institutions tended to

Table 5

DISTRIBUTION OF STUDENTS BY
HIGHEST DEGREE PLANNED
(Percentages)

Degree	Blacks in Black Institutions		Blacks in White Institutions	
	Men	Women	Men	Women
None	7.7	2.9	4.4	1.9
A.A.	2.0	2.7	1.0	3.2
B.A.	22.3	23.4	28.8	24.2
Master's	31.4	35.8	26.3	31.5
Ph.D., Ed.D.	16.3	18.0	12.7	14.9
M.D., D.O., D.D.	9.1	7.5	10.5	10.2
LL.B., J.D.	5.6	5.4	8.0	9.1
B.D., M.Div.	0	0.9	2.8	1.8
Other	5.6	3.4	5.5	3.2

aspire to the Ph.D. or Ed.D. more often, whereas blacks
in white institutions aspired to professional degrees.
Black women in white institutions were generally the most
highly motivated to get these advanced degrees. White
men had similarly high aspirations, but that was not
the case with white women, a little fewer than 20 percent
of whom had plans for the Ph.D., the M.D., or the LL.B.

With respect to probable major fields of study, some
interesting differences between blacks in the two types of
institutions, as well as between blacks and whites, are
shown in Table 6. Black men in black institutions tended
to favor business, and technical fields (such as data
processing, computer programming, and drafting), while
blacks in white institutions tended to select health fields,
social science, and math and statistics more often. Fewer
white men than black men chose education as a major. The
biological and physical sciences were named more often
by white men than by black men.

Black women in black colleges chose business, education, and the humanities in greater numbers, whereas
black women in white institutions tended to select biology, english, engineering, history, and political science
more often. White women tended to be more traditional in
their choice of field, naming education and health fields
more often than did black women.

Self-Concept and Values

Students were asked to rate themselves on a number of
intellectual and personal/social traits. Black men in white
schools gave themselves high ratings on athletic ability and
on popularity with the opposite sex. Both sexes in both
types of institutions tended to rate themselves high on all
dimensions except academic ability and mathematical ability.
Even though smaller proportions of blacks than whites rated
themselves high on these traits, blacks nonetheless saw themselves as being intellectually self-confident. It is possible that their reference group differs for the two types of
rating. They may use the "majority" student as a reference
point with respect to academic ability, but they may compare
themselves with their peers--primarily other blacks in high
school--on intellectual self-confidence.

In addition to self-ratings, students also rated the
importance of a number of life goals. Blacks at black institutions were more likely to value societal goals and contributions, whereas blacks at white institutions gave higher
priority to personal gain. For example, "influencing the

Table 6

DISTRIBUTION OF STUDENTS
BY PROBABLE MAJOR FIELD
(Percentages)

Probable Major Field	Blacks in Black Institutions		Blacks in White Institutions	
	Men	Women	Men	Women
Agriculture	1.3	0.2	0	0.1
Biological science	6.5	6.2	6.5	8.1
Business	27.3	20.5	19.6	13.1
Education	8.8	15.4	8.4	12.5
Engineering	12.8	1.3	12.8	2.6
English	0.6	0.7	0.4	2.1
Health professional	6.7	6.1	11.3	5.0
History/political science	3.9	12.6	2.3	15.6
Humanities	4.9	5.1	4.6	3.6
Fine Arts	1.2	0.6	0.8	1.2
Mathematics/statistics	0.9	0.8	2.9	0.5
Physical science	2.0	1.6	2.6	0.7
Social science	4.9	12.2	9.0	13.2
Other fields (technical)	6.2	5.3	3.1	7.7
Other fields (nontechnical)	9.0	9.3	11.6	10.5
Undecided	3.1	2.0	4.1	3.7

political structure," "making a theoretical contribution to science," and "participating in a community action program," were goals endorsed more often by blacks in black institutions; in contrast blacks at white institutions valued "receiving recognition from others," "becoming financially well-off," and 'succeeding in business."

Summary

A number of interesting differences emerged between blacks attending black institutions and those attending white institutions.

Blacks at white institutions tended to have made better grades in high school and to have applied to and been accepted by more postsecondary institutions.

Blacks at black institutions were more likely to attend a college that was a greater distance from their homes.

With respect to reasons for going to college, the sexes differed more than did students attending the two types of institutions. Black men at both types of institutions were strongly motivated by occupational considerations (e.g., "to be able to get a better job"), whereas women said they were more interested in the pursuit of knowledge for its own sake. Black women in black institutions, however, were more likely to value the vocational aspects of a college education than were their counterparts at white institutions.

Reasons for choosing a particular college differed. Blacks at black institutions were more likely to say that relatives, teachers, and friends were influential in their decision; those at white institutions were more likely to report that receiving financial aid and being actively recruited were important reasons.

Black college women came from poorer and less educated families than the black men. Blacks in black institutions tended to have better educated parents than blacks in white institutions.

Higher proportions of blacks in white schools than in black schools received financial aid, and the amounts of aid were larger.

Blacks had very high educational aspirations generally; there were interesting differences by type of institution attended. Blacks in black schools aspired more

often to the Ph.D. or Ed.D., whereas blacks in white
schools planned on getting professional degrees.

Blacks in white schools gave themselves very high
ratings on athletic and interpersonal dimensions;
blacks at both types of institutions were more likely
than whites to rate themselves high on all traits
except academic ability and mathematical ability.

In their values and goals, blacks in black institutions
were more concerned about the political structure and
community action, whereas those attending white institutions gave higher priority to financial and status
goals.

Conclusion

The civil rights movement, as well as campus unrest in
the 1960's, generated greater efforts to enroll blacks in
white institutions. These efforts were in large part
successful, and that success has prompted questions about
the legitimacy of maintaining separate institutions for
blacks. Do black colleges offer students unique experiences
that are important to their educational and personal development? Do some black students want or need to attend a black
institution before they are ready to compete in the corporate
and professional world? Can racially separate institutions
provide "equal" opportunities and educational experiences?
These are some of the major questions surrounding the debate
about black colleges. Answers, however, are not readily
available.

A profile of blacks in black and in white institutions
should be maintained because it offers important information
for future college-bound blacks. Often the college-educated
parents of this new generation are the alumni of these black
colleges. They value their college experiences, and they
want their children to have the same experiences.

Young blacks with a strong social conscience tend to
gravitate toward the black colleges, believing perhaps that
in such an atmosphere they can more meaningfully explore and
debate the racial and societal issues that confront this
nation, free of the constraints that may be inevitable in a
predominantly white institution. Blacks who go to white
institutions, on the other hand, tend to have better academic
records and a higher opinion of their own athletic ability
and popularity with their peers. Thus, they have the self-
confidence that may be required to survive in the competitive
environment in which they find themselves.

One crucial question not answered by our analyses is
whether differences in student characteristics are in part
attributable to regional differences. Therefore future
investigations need to consider regional differences.
In addition, more research needs to be done on the special
features of black colleges and on the contributions they
can continue to make toward the development of black students.

References

Astin, A.W., M.R. King, and G.T. Richardson
     1976   The American Freshman: National Norms for
             Fall 1976. Washington and Los Angeles:
             Cooperative Institutional Research Program,
             American Council on Education and University
             of California at Los Angeles.

Astin, H.S.
     1979   "Patterns of women's occupations." Pp. 28-37
             in Julia Sherman and Florence Denmark (eds.),
             The Psychology of Women. New York:
             Psychological Dimensions.

Astin, H.S. and P.H. Cross
     1979   The Impact of Financial Aid on Student Persis-
             tence in College. Final Report to the Office
             of Planning and Evaluation (Department of
             Health, Education and Welfare). Los Angeles:
             Higher Education Research Institute.

Astin, H.S. and R. Scherrei
     1979   Do Highly Able Minority Women Have Adequate
             Access to Higher Education? Unpublished
             manuscript. Los Angeles: Higher Education
             Research Institute.

Footnotes

1. For a detailed discussion of the sampling of institutions
    and the weighting procedures, see Astin, King and
    Richardson, 1976.

2. This brief profile on the financial situation of blacks
    is abstracted from data presented in a final report to
    the United States Office of Education on a study of
    The Impact of Financial Aid on Student Persistence in
    College, by H.S. Astin and P.H. Cross.

Section II

Academic Admissions Requirements and Financial Resources as Contingencies for Black Access and Persistence: Overview

Section II of the volume evaluates the roles of academic admissions requirements and financial resources (e.g., personal and institutional) in the higher educational entry and retention process for blacks. Vigorous debate concerning the utility and predictability of standardized testing and the extent to which they pose a liability for black access to higher education exists. Nevertheless, these tests continue to be used by colleges and universities as a major criterion in the selection process (Institute for the Study of Educational Policy, 1976).

As a result, it has been suggested that less effort be devoted to debating the issue and more attention be given to teaching blacks and other minorities how to perform more effectively on these exams (Bernal, 1975). Others argue for the increased use of open and special admissions programs as alternatives to standardized testing.

The impact of family background and financial aid in higher education also remains an important issue for blacks. This is particularly true at the graduate and professional levels where Federal and State support has been much lower than support at the undergraduate level (Mendal and Tabb, 1977). Howard University researchers (Institute for the Study of Educational Policy) noted that the negative impact of family income on the status of blacks in higher education was greatest at the graduate and professional levels where the likelihood of entering at these advance levels was directly related to parents' ability to pay. Jencks, et. al. (1979) recently reaffirmed the importance of family background on students' schooling and subsequent attainment. These authors noted that family background exerts a stronger influence in the status attainment process than past research has indicated. In addition, they confirmed that being white, having parents with extensive schooling, high status jobs and high income enhances son's or daughter's attainment.

The chapters in this section evaluate institutional usage of standardized tests, the impact of testing and family background on college access and persistence and the effects of alternative admissions criteria on black access to higher education. The first chapter by Gail Thomas examines the actual and projected impact of family background and standardized test performance on the college enrollment status of blacks relative to whites. The second chapter by Lorenzo Morris raises the question of how institutions use test data and describes how students are sorted and channeled into various types of colleges based on their test performance. The third chapter by Patricia Cross and Helen Astin discusses the impact of financial aid on the persistence of blacks in four-year colleges. In the final chapter, Virginia Calkins and Lee Willoughby describe the impact of nontraditional admissions criteria on the access of blacks to medical school.

References

Bernal, E.M., Jr.
    1975   "A response to educational use of tests with
            disadvantaged students." American Psychologist.
            30:90-92.

Institute for the Study of Educational Policy
    1976   Equal Educational Opportunity for Blacks in U.S.
            Higher Education. Washington, D.C.: Howard
            University Press.

Jencks, C., S. Bartlett, M.Corcoran, J. Crouse,
D. Eaglesfield, G. Jackson, K. McClelland, P. Muerer,
M. Olneck, J. Schwartz, S. Ward and J. Williams
    1979   Who Gets Ahead? The Determinants of Economic
            Success in America. New York: Basic Books.

Mendal, R.W. and W.G. Tabb
    1977   "Problems in admissions in U.S. dental schools."
            College and University. 3(Summer):298-317.

4

The Effects of Standardized Achievement Test Performance and Family Status on Black-White College Access*

GAIL E. THOMAS

Introduction

One of the continuing concerns among blacks is the impact of conventional college admissions criteria and financial aid on black access to higher education. The salience of this issue has increased as a result of the Bakke decision and other events which have been perceived by many blacks as a threat to special admissions programs and affirmative action efforts. No comprehensive evaluations exist on the impact of affirmative action programs on minority access to higher education. However, it is generally assumed that these programs have played a major role in increasing the presence of blacks in higher education. Two decades ago, when affirmative action programs were nonexistent, education beyond high school was primarily a privilege of white middle class students. However, during the initial existence of these programs (1968-72) black college enrollment doubled, with a large portion of the enrollment consisting of disadvantaged students. Black students now number approximately one half million in U.S. colleges and universities.

National data are employed in this chapter to examine the impact of standardized achievement test performance and family status on the college entry of blacks and whites. The college enrollment status of students is evaluated for blacks and whites in the aggregate and with statistical controls for standardized test performance and family status. In addition, projected rates of college enrollment are presented for blacks and whites when the latter background variables are the major determinants of college access.

*This research was supported by the United States National Institute of Education, Department of Education.

The Impact of Standardized Test Performance on Schooling

Researchers have consistently observed that standardized achievement test performance exerts a major influence on postsecondary education access (Sewell and Shah, 1967; Havighurst and Neugarten, 1967; Jencks et.al., 1972). Although some studies show that a sizeable proportion of students who perform successfully on standardized tests do not enter college (Havighurst and Neugarten, 1967; Peng et.al. 1977), most studies show that students with high test scores are more likely to further their education than students with low test scores (Sewell, Haller and Portes, 1969; Sewell, Haller and Ohlendorf, 1970; Thomas, Alexander and Eckland, 1979).

Black students score an average of 15 points below the white mean on traditional standardized tests (Jencks, 1972). The low test performance of blacks creates an access barrier to undergraduate, graduate, and professional school access. This in turn hinders blacks from becoming full members in professions (e.g., law and medicine) that require the passing of standardized tests as a part of their licensing procedure (Hall, 1970; Odegaard, 1977; Evans, 1976). Jencks (1972) noted that about a quarter of the correlation between test scores and educational access and attainment is explained by the fact that students with high test scores generally come from economically successful families. The College Entrance Examination Board (CEEB, 1974), similarly reported that the average family income for students who scores between 750-800 points on the SAT was $24,124 while students in the lowest SAT score range (200-249) had a mean family income of $8,639. To some extent, the low performance of blacks on standardized achievement tests has been compensated for by special admissions programs which have permitted blacks and other disadvantaged students higher education access despite their lower test performance. However, the current decline in support for affirmative action programs (in comparison to the late 60s and early 70s) and the increase in "reverse discrimination" suits may offset the remaining influence of these programs.

The Impact of Family Status on Schooling

Upper-middle class children average approximately four more years of schooling than children from lower status family backgrounds. Jencks et.al. (1972) estimated that less than ten percent of the overall effects of family status on children's educational attainment can be explained by the fact that economically upper and middle class children have superior IQ genotypes. Instead, a greater portion of the variance is attributed to the fact that middle and

upper class parents are able to provide their offspring with
the type of skills, values, and cultural and social experiences that schools value and subsequently reward (Jencks et.
al. 1972). Also, many middle and upper class families have
the money and/or influence to assure their children entry into higher education. The ability of families to finance
their children's education is especially crucial today given
the increasing cost of higher education and the decreasing
availability of federal and state funds to support higher
education, particularly at the graduate and professional
levels (Mendal and Tabb, 1977; Kloberg e.a., 1977).

Bayer (1972) reported that black freshmen had fewer
family financial resources than whites. In 1972, over one-
half of the black freshmen in the ACE survey were from
families with incomes of $7,999 or less compared to over one-
half of the white freshmen who were from families with incomes of $15,000 or greater. In addition, Howard University
researchers (Institute for the Study of Educational Policy
1976) noted that low income blacks were more likely to attend low-cost colleges regardless of their ability, and that
a significantly greater porportion of low income white freshmen were enrolled in public universities than were low income
black freshmen. These researchers also observed that black
freshmen at all income levels were enrolled more often in
four-year colleges (including the traditionally black colleges), while white freshmen at all income levels were enrolled in universities.

Method

Data

The data for this analysis are from a subsample of
14,009 black and white males and females (1,904 blacks,
12,105 whites) who participated in the 1972 Base Year and
1973 First Year Follow-Up study of the National Longitudinal
Study (NLS) of the High School Senior Class of 1972. The
survey was sponsored by the National Center for Education
Statistics (NCES) and conducted by the Educational Testing
Service and Research Triangle Institute.

The project employed a two-stage probability sample
with schools as first-stage sampling units and students as
second-stage units. The original sample involved a representative sample of approximately 21,600 twelfth grade males and
females who were enrolled in approximately 1,200 public, private and church affiliated secondary schools within the fifty states of the United States and the District of Columbia.

Within each participating school, a random sample of eighteen twelfth graders was drawn from senior class rosters. Participating students completed questionnaires which inquired about students' post-high school plans, aspirations, family background, and previous educational experiences. These students were also administered a standardized achievement test which was constructed by Educational Testing Services. The test measured students' verbal and nonverbal skills.

Variables

College enrollment is defined as entrance in either a two-year or four-year college academic program in October of 1972 or 1973. Respondents who were enrolled in vocational programs after high school in October 1972 or 1973 or who did not pursue any type of postsecondary education during either time period are considered non-college enrollees.

Race, family status (SES), and achievement test constitute the remaining variables. The family status and achievement test score measures employed are trichotomous indices that were developed by the Research Triangle Institute (RTI). The measures consist of upper and lower quartiles with the middle two quartiles combined.[1] The family status composite included five variables (father's education, mother's education, father's occupation, parental income and a household index) which were weighted, standardized, and summed over non-missing components. The standardized achievement test measure is an equally factor-weighted linear composite of four standardized subtests that were administered to students during the initial Base-Year (1972) survey.

Findings

Table 1 presents the distributions of family background, test performance, and college entry by race.

An immediate observation here concerns the disproportionate representation of blacks in the low family status and low achievement test categories. Sixty-six percent of the blacks are from low family status backgrounds as compared to only 22 percent of the whites; and 68 percent of the blacks scored low on the achievement test measure compared to 21 percent of the whites. In addition, Table 1 shows that in the aggregate, a higher percentage of the NLS whites (40%) entered college between 1972 and 1973 than did blacks (31%).

Table 1

Percentage Distribution for Family Background,
Test Performance and College Entry by Race

	Blacks (1)	Whites (2)
Family Background	(N=1,883)	(N=12,065)
Low (1)	66.4	22.4
Medium (2)	28.2	51.1
High (3)	5.4	26.5
(Total N missing =61)		
Test Performance	(N=1,904)	(N=12,105)
Low (1)	68.3	20.9
Medium (2)	28.2	48.2
High (3)	3.5	30.9
(Total N missing = 0)		
College Entry	(N=1,898)	(N=12,094)
No college (1)	69.2	60.1
College (2)	30.8	39.9
(Total N missing = 17)		

Data Source: National Longitudinal Survey of the High School
Senior Class of 1972 sponsored by the National Center
for Education Statistics.

Table 2 shows the percentage of blacks and whites entering
college when family status and test performance are controlled. The middle and high level categories of both of
the latter variables have been combined because of the small
number of blacks in the high family status and high test
score categories. Therefore, family status and test performance are presently dichotomous measures (i.e., low vs. high).

Here it can be seen that the previous finding in Table 1
of a higher enrollment of whites in postsecondary institutions does not hold when blacks and whites are compared within family status and test performance categories. Instead,
when controlling for these background variables, a higher
percentage of blacks enter college than whites. Portes and
Wilson (1976) reported similar findings from their study
of black and white males. However, the resulting taus in
Table 2 show that racial differences in college enrollment
favoring blacks are primarily among students who are low on
both or either family status and standardized test performance. Among students who are high on both variables,
racial differences in college enrollment are far less significant.[2] Sixty-four percent of the high family status, high
test performing blacks attend college versus 54 percent of
the whites in these categories. However, 17 percent of the
low family status, low achieving blacks attend college versus
only 6 percent of the whites of comparable status. Similarly, 31 percent of the high status, low achieving NLS blacks
entered college in 1972-73 compared to 15 percent of the
whites in these categories. Among low family status, high
achieving students, the black-white percentages are 44 and
25 respectively.[3]

The results in Table 2 are somewhat surprising, particularly when compared with Table 1. One hypothesis that may
be drawn from Table 2 is that blacks with low educational resources (e.g., test scores and/or family status) were better
able to capitalized on special admissions and financial aid
programs than their white counterparts in 1972-73. The
extent to which special programs were available to low status
whites at that time is unknown. However, in the recent

Table 2

Percentage College Entry by Race,[a]
Family Background and Test Performance[b]

	Low Status Low Performance	High Status Low Performance	Low Status High Performance	High Status High Performance	N
Blacks (1)	16.7	30.7	43.9	63.8	
	(N = 936)[c]	(N = 341)	(N = 310)	(N = 290)	1877
Whites (2)	6.4	14.9	24.8	54.5	
	(N = 949)	(N = 1550)	(N - 1748)	(N = 7807)	12,054
taus:[b]	-.160[d]	-.160	-.153	-.042	

Data Source: National Longitudinal Survey of the High School Senior Class of 1972 sponsored
by the National Center for Education Statistics.

Note: Total N missing = 78

[a]The actual number of blacks and whites who entered college are as follows: 1) Low Status-Low Performance--Blacks = 156, Whites = 61; High Status-Low Performance--Blacks = 105, Whites = 231; Low Status-High Performance--Blacks = 136, Whites = 433; High Status-High Performance--Blacks = 185, Whites = 4,097.

[b]Due to the small number of blacks in the high SES and high test performance categories, the high and middle level categories for both variables have been combined here.

[c]Figures in parentheses below percentages are base N's.

[d]All taus are significant at the .01 level.

Bakke suit, it was reported that the University of California at Davis did admit 16 disadvantaged whites under its special admissions program in addition to disadvantaged blacks (Hartnett and Payton, 1977). Also, Lavin, Alba, and Silberstein recently noted that many colleges and universities are now attempting to make their affirmative action programs equally available to disadvantaged whites as well as blacks and other racial minorities.

The advantage for low ability and/or low family status blacks shown in Table 2 might also be attributed to the high educational aspirations and expectations that blacks hold (Portes and Wilson, 1976; Thomas, 1979). These psychological assets may help blacks counteract, to some extent, the negative effects of low family status and low test performance. Finally, the catering of two-year colleges and the traditionally black colleges to black and disadvantaged students may also explain the higher college enrollment of blacks than whites indicated in Table 2.

The final table, Table 3, is intended to show more clearly the role of family status and standardized test performance on the college access of blacks and whites. The specific question addressed here is: What would have been the college enrollment rates of NLS blacks and whites in 1972-73 if family status and/or standardized test performance were the sole determinants of college entry? Calculations in Table 3 are based on the number of blacks and whites who attended college in 1972-73. Projected rates of black-white enrollment are shown when: (a) high family status, (b) high standardized test performance, and (c) high family status and high standardized test performance are the criteria for college entry. The high categories for family status and test scores entail the middle and high categories of the original trichotomous measures combined. The last column of Table 3 reproduces the previous rates of college enrollment for NLS respondents given in Table 1. These latter rates provide a basis for comparing the projected rates of black-white enrollment given in the first three columns.

First it can be seen that if the college enrollment of students was totally a function of high family background status, only 16 percent of the blacks would attend college as opposed to the original 31 percent; and 36 percent of the whites would attend college instead of 41 percent. Secondly, if high test scores were the sole basis of college entry, only 17 percent of the blacks would attend college rather than 31 percent; and 39 percent of the whites would attend

Table 3

Predicted Rates of College Entry for Blacks and
Whites Given High Family Status and
High Test Performance Requirements

	High Status	High Test Performance	High Status and Test Performance	Current Rates of Black-White Entry
Blacks (1)	15.5%[a]	17.1%	9.9%	31.0%
	(290/1877)	(321/1877)	(185/1877)	(582/1877)
Whites (2)	35.9%	38.9%	35.3%	41.3%
	(4328/12054)	(4530/12054)	(4097/12054)	(4822/12054)

Data Source: National Longitudinal Survey of the High School Senior Class of 1972 sponsored by
the National Center for Education Statistics.

[a] The percentages given for each group are based on the number of students in each category attending
college divided by the total number of respondents (i.e., those attending and not attending college).

instead of 40 percent. Therefore, disparities between the
actual and projected rates of attendance are slightly greater
when high family status is the major contingency for college
entry than when high test scores is the major criterion.
When high family status and high test scores are both a prime
basis for college entry, racial disparities between the
actual and projected rates of enrollment are even greater
than when either factor is an individual determinant of
college entry. This is especially true for blacks. Given
both variables as the criteria for college entry, only 9.9
percent of the NLS blacks who entered college in 1972-73
would have attended as opposed to 31 percent, and 35 percent
of the whites would have attended instead of 41 percent.

Summary and Conclusion

The data presented in this chapter clearly indicate
that family status and standardized test performance still
constitute important contingencies for blacks and whites in
the college entry process. When NLS blacks and whites were
examined in the aggregate without regard to these background
variables, the college enrollment rate was higher for whites
than for blacks. However, when both background variables
were controlled and blacks and whites were compared within
family status and test performance categories, blacks
exceeded whites in college enrollment, particularly blacks
who were low on either or both background variables.
A major inference drawn was that low family status and/or
test-performing blacks were more successful than whites in
capitalizing on affirmative action and financial aid programs
that were available in 1972-73. In addition, the need for
these programs to continue to assist low status whites as
well as blacks and other disadvantaged students was noted.

Data were also presented which showed what the projected
rates of black-white college enrollment would have been for
students who entered college in 1972-73 if the ability of
families to finance their children's education and standardized test performance were the primary criteria for college
entry. The results illustrated that under such conditions,
the rate of college enrollment for both blacks and whites
would decline, with the decline being substantially greater
for blacks than for whites. Consequently, the black-white
gap in college entry would be greatly increased. The projected drastic decline in black college enrollment indicated
by these projected rates may become an increasing reality as
the cost of postsecondary schooling and the emphasis on
standardized testing increase and as the support for affirmative action and student aid programs decreases (National
Advisory Committee on Black Higher Education, 1979).

Morris, 1979). These results, while speculative, clearly imply the continued need for federal and statewide efforts to assist all disadvantaged students in gaining access to college and subsequent higher education.

The data in this chapter were restricted to college enrollment. Therefore, no conclusions can be drawn concerning the advantages and disadvantages that blacks and whites experience in higher education beyond the point of college entry. However, other studies (Institute for the Study of Educational Policy, 1976; Johnson et.al., 1975) and more recent analyses by the author (Thomas, 1980) indicate that black students persist at a lower rate than whites in four-year colleges. Other work presented elsewhere in this volume shows that black students are still underrepresented in graduate and professional schools (Thomas et.al., 1981; Blackwell, 1981; Morris, 1979). Racial data beyond the point of college entry are therefore needed to address the nature of black underrepresentation at the graduate and professional levels. Data are also needed on the extent to which blacks who do gain access at various levels of higher education persist towards degree completion and obtain marketable employment. Finally, systematic evaluation of the affects of affirmative action efforts on minority access and the need for such efforts by various disadvantaged groups including whites is needed. An assessment of these and similar issues noted here should provide greater knowledge about the effects of family status and standardized achievement performance on higher educational access and the extent to which blacks and other disadvantaged groups have progressed toward equality of educational opportunity.

References

Bayer, A.E.
   1972   The Black College Freshman: Characteristics
          and Recent Trends. Washington, D.C.: American
          Council of Education.

Blackwell, J.E.
   1981   "The access of black students to medical and law
          schools: trends and Bakke implications."
          Pp. 189-202 in G. Thomas (ed.), Black Students in
          Higher Education: Conditions and Experiences in
          the 1970s. Westport, Connecticut: Greenwood Press.

College Entrance Examination Board
   1974   College-Bound Seniors, 1973-74. New York:
          College Entrance Examination Board.

Evans, F.R.
    1976   Applications and Admissions to ABA Accredited Law
            Schools: An Analysis of National Data for the
            Class Entering in the Fall of 1976. Law School
            Admissions Council, 1977.

Ferguson, G.A.
    1959   Statistical Analysis in Psychology and Education.
            New York: McGraw-Hill.

Goodman, L.
    1973   "Causal analysis of data from panel studies and
            other kinds of surveys." American Journal of
            Sociology 78 (March): 1135-1191.

Hartnett, R. and B.F. Payton
    1977   Minority Admissions and Performance in Graduate
            Study. New York: Ford Foundation.

Havighurst, R.L. and B.L. Neugarten
    1967   Society and Education. Boston: Allyn and Bacon.

Hall, W.F. IV
    1970   Higher Education in Black Atypical Students.
            University Park, Pa.: Penn State University.

Institute for the Study of Educational Policy
    1976   Equal Educational Opportunity for Blacks in U.S.
            Higher Education: An Assessment. Washington, D.C.
            Institute for the Study of Educational Policy,
            Howard University.

Jencks, C., M. Smith, H. Acland, M.J. Bane, D. Cohen,
    H. Gintis and B. Heyns
    1972   Inequality: A Reassessment of the Effect of Family
            and Schooling in America. New York: Harper and
            Row.

Johnson, D.G., V.C. Smith, Jr. and S.L. Tarnoff
    1975   "Recruitment and progress of minority medical
            school entrants 1970-72." Journal of Medical
            Education 50 (July 1975): 713-755.

Kloberg E.J.V. III, A. Robinson and G. Read
    1977   "Financing graduate students." College and
            University 3 (Summer): 488-497.

Lavin, D.E., R.D. Alba and R. Silberstein
    1979   "Open admissions and equal access: a study of
            ethnic groups in the City University of New York."
            Harvard Educational Review 49 (February) 53-92.

Mendel, R.W. and W.G. Tabb
   1977   "Problems in admissions in U.S. dental schools."
           College and University 3 (Summer): 298-317.

Morris, L.
   1979   Elusive Equality: The Status of Black Americans
           in Higher Education. Washington, D.C.: Howard
           University Press.

National Advisory Committee on Black Higher Education
   1979   Access of Black Americans to Higher Education:
           How Open is the Door? Washington, D.C.: U.S.
           Government Printing Office.

Odegaard, C.E.
   1977   Minorities in Medicine. New York. The Josiah
           Macy, Jr. Foundation.

Peng, S., J. Bailey and B.K. Eckland
   1977   "Access to higher education: results from the
           national logitudinal study of the high school
           class of 1972." Educational Researcher 6:3-7.

Portes, A. and K. Wilson
   1976   "Black-white differences in educational attain-
           ment." American Sociological Review 41:414-431.

Sewell, William H. and Vimah P. Shah
   1967   "Socioeconomic status intelligence and the attain-
           ment of higher education." Sociology of Educa-
           tion 40:559-572

Sewell, W.H., A.D. Haller and A. Portes
   1969   "The educational and early occupational attainment
           process." American Sociological Review, 34:82-92.

Sewell, W.H., Haller, A.D. and G.W. Ohlendorf
   1970   "The educational and early occupational attainment
           process: replication and revisions. American
           Sociological Review 35:1014-1027.

Thomas, G.E.
   1975   Race and Sex Effects in the Process of Educational
           Achievement. Chapel Hill. University of North
           Carolina (Unpublished Dissertation).

Thomas, G.E.
   1977   Family Status and Standardized Achievement Tests As
           Contingencies for Black and White College Entry. Re-

port No. 239. Baltimore: Center for Social
Organization of Schools, Johns Hopkins University.

Thomas, G.E., K.L. Alexander and B.K. Eckland
   1979 "Access to higher education: the importance of
         race, sex, social class and academic credentials."
         School Review 87:133-156.

Thomas, G.E.
   1979 "The influence of ascription achievement and
         educational expectations on black-white post-
         secondary enrollment." The Sociological
         Quarterly 20 (Spring): 209-222.

   1980 The Impact of Schooling and Student Characteristics
         on the Four-Year College Graduation of Race and
         Sex Groups. Baltimore, Maryland. Center for
         Social Organization of Schools. Johns Hopkins
         University.

Thomas, G.E., J.R. Mingle and J.M. McPartland
   1981 "Recent trends in racial enrollment, segregation
         and degree attainment in higher education."
         Pp. 107-125 in G. Thomas (ed.), Black Students in
         Higher Education: Conditions and Experiences in
         the 1970s. Westport, Connecticut: Greenwood
         Press.

Footnotes

1. See Thomas (1975; Appendix B) for a detailed discussion
    of the procedures and assumptions regarding the construc-
    tion of the family status and achievement test composites.

2. A test of the second order interaction in Table 2 is
    significant according to Goodman's (1973) test for inter-
    action.

3. A test (Ferguson, 1959) for significant differences
    between the cell proportions in Table 2 was performed
    and presented elsewhere (Thomas, 1977). The results
    showed that all cells were significant with the least
    significant difference in college entry rates among
    high family status/high standardized test performing
    blacks and whites.

5

The Role of Testing in Institutional Selectivity and Black Access to Higher Education

LORENZO MORRIS

Introduction

With the expanding of standardized achievement tests in higher education, their role in determining access to selective institutions has become pivotal despite continuing critcism of cultural bias and psychometric deficiencies in these tests. In 1970, the Association of Black Psychologists called for a moratorium on standardized testing, arguing that their cultural/psychometric limitations invalidated their prediction of the performance levels of blacks. This criticism has been reiterated by various groups, but to no great avail.

As we move to the 1980s, the power of these tests over all students, and over blacks in particular, continues. But this does not mean that the black psychologist and similar critics should be ignored; rather it may be that their criticisms are incomplete. What has not been evaluated, nor fully examined, are the questions of who decides to use the tests, why they use them, and under what conditions. The unabated increases in institutional reliance on standardized testing may not be conditioned as much by a belief in the accuracy of the tests as by the institutional traditions to which these tests conform. Terms like "cultural bias" and "prediction" involve a relational concept of student and institution, but the institutional aspect has rarely been examined. This chapter examines the hypothesis that cultural bias and similar problems related to testing are as much the result of institutional predispositions as they are the consequence of psychometric deficiency.

Reliance on Standardized Tests in Undergraduate Admissions

The majority of four-year colleges and universities require that applicants take standardized achievement tests

(Wesman, 1968), but only a few of these institutions rely extensively on these for purposes other than admissions. Preliminary findings from a pilot survey of colleges and universities administered in 1976 by the Institute for the Study of Educational Policy (ISEP) tended to support this conclusion. The survey was administered to affirmative action officers at a representative sample of 100 four-year colleges and universities across the country with a 25 percent response rate. The institute (ISEP) was informed through prior contacts with these institutions that affirmative action officers were very knowledgeable of minority student statuses concerning entry test score and subsequent academic performance. In addition, these individuals were said to know how the test scores of minorities were used and evaluated relative to other students. Despite this optimistic information only 25 of the 100 respondents provided information. All participants were assured a high degree of confidentiality. However, the low response rate suggested that institutions were still reluctant to provide information concerning their use of standardized test results. Therefore, the results presently reported are used in a limited manner to describe tendencies and directions of institutional behavior regarding their use of standardized tests.

Responses from the survey indicated that 82 percent of the responding institutions require their freshmen applicants to take the SAT or the ACT test. However, only two of the respondents indicated that their schools had a minimum test score requirement for entering freshmen. Yet, almost all respondents noted that their institutions gave weight to test scores in the admissions process.

When asked whether their minimum test performance requirements were different for minority students than for majority students, the two institutions with these standards responded no. Only forty percent of the respondents noted that tests results were used, to some extent, to counsel and place students within classes and fields of study. Three of the respondents indicated that they relied more heavily on the tests to counsel minority students that to counsel majority students. Almost none of the respondents indicated distinct usage of standardized testing by their institution apart from the admissions function and, in a few instances, a counseling function.

These results represent a pilot effort and should not be generalized. However, replication of similar results on a wider basis would certainly question the current major emphasis on standardized testing. For example, one popular

belief is that the SAT is a prime predictor of college
success (McClelland, 1976). But apart from a partial correlation (e.g., between test performance and first year college
GPA), it is difficult to determine the practical utility of
these tests in predicting college outcome if their usage by
colleges and universities is in fact minimal.

Institutional Variations in the Use of Standardized Achievement Tests

Reliance on achievement test scores cannot be meaningfully estimated without taking into account institutional
differences. Astin (1977) has noted that higher educational
institutions vary extensively in their standards of admission
and that variability in their test requirements may be explained by the type of institutions and their degree of
selectivity. In addition, a recent study by Bailey (1978)
noted that the main difference in admissions between institutions of lower and higher selectivity lies in the level of
SAT scores required.

Table 1 shows how public and private four-year and two-
year colleges vary regarding SAT and ACT scores. Here we
see that universities and four-year colleges have higher
average SAT scores than two year colleges. Private institutions have higher test scores than public institutions
except for two-year colleges where the mean SAT scores for
the student body are higher in public than in private two-
year colleges. The standard deviations shown in Table 1
indicate that the test scores of the average student in the
least selective type of college is within the normal range
of students in the most selective type of institution. The
lower end of the normal range at private four-year colleges
is 656 (912 $\overline{X}$ SAT - 256 SD = 656), which is 24 to 76 points
below the average level of two-year colleges. Therefore,
the "average" student in the least selective type of college
could be expected to perform within the normal range of
student performance in the most selective type of institutions.

Unless more than a third of students in the highly
selective colleges leave because of personal academic
deficiencies (and this generally does not happen), the
average student from the least selective college could be
qualified to graduate from the most selective college. Thus,
the use of traditional standardized tests can serve to
characterize and distinguish institutions hierarchically
but, given the fact that even the most select institutions
admit low test-performing students, these tests do not

Table 1

Mean and Standard Deviations of the Scholastic Aptitude
Test (SAT), Scholastic Aptitude Math Subtest (SAT-M)
and American College Test (ACT) by
Institutional Type and Control, 1974-1975

	SAT	SAT-M	ACT
Private University			
$\overline{X}$	850	435	19.0
SD	438	223	9.9
Public University			
$\overline{X}$	835	445	18.6
SD	330	174	7.5
Private 4 Year			
$\overline{X}$	912	469	20.4
SD	256	129	5.9
Public 4 Year			
$\overline{X}$	849	451	18.6
SD	203	106	5.0
Private 2 Year			
$\overline{X}$	680	326	15.0
SD	356	188	7.9
Public 2 Year			
$\overline{X}$	732	383	16.2
SD	305	164	6.8

Source: Lorenzo Morris, Elusive Equality: The Status of
Black Americans in Higher Education Washington, D.C.
Howard University Press, 1979. Based on unpublished
data from the College Entrance Examination Board and
the American Council on Education.

guarantee that even the most select institutions will not admit low test performing students. However, to the extent that these tests are primary in selective admissions, institutions are more likely to exclude a student because he or she does not meet the desired test criterion rather than because his/her scores are below the range of a capable student. Many students whose test scores indicate they could "make it" in college are excluded because their scores would detract from the institution's "average" and presumably from its image. Thus, many qualified students are denied access to the most selective institutions.

The Use of Test Data by Black Institutions

The role of testing with respect to minority students may be further explored by examining how black institutions use test data. A study by the American College Testing Program (1978) concluded that, in general, standardized tests are more a part of the admissions process at traditionally black colleges than at predominantly white colleges and other universities. However, this study did not take into account the fact that black institutions had lower test score entry requirements than other institutions.

Boyd's (1977) study showed that the average ACT, SAT-Verbal, and SAT-Math scores for traditionally black institutions were 12,336, and 349 respectively, while the corresponding scores for non-black institutions were 20, 474, and 502 respectively. Black institutions may in fact rely on standardized tests as often as or to a larger extent than other institutions. However, studies indicate that they rely less on these tests as a basis for denying students access and rely more on high school GPA (Morris, 1979). As a result, these institutions accept many students who are likely to be denied admission by other institutions with higher test score requirements.

In addition, black institutions retain and graduate a higher percentage of black students than non-black institutions (ISEP, 1976; Thomas, 1980). The higher attrition rate of blacks in white institutions has been said to be a function of the higher academic standards of white institutions, and by implication. However, this may not be the only reliable explanation since the attrition rate of black students in two-year colleges is higher than black attrition in black or white four-year colleges (Kolstad, 1977).

Institutional Selectivity and the Role of Testing

In describing variations in the accessibility of higher educational institutions, Astin (1977) has argued that there are distinct hierarchical relationships among institutions that have been consciously developed. He observed:

It is possible to argue that higher education in the United States has evolved into a highly refined institutional status hierarchy. Like most status systems, it comprises a few elite and widely known institutions, a substantial middle class, and a large number of relatively unknown institutions. While most people are familiar with the hierarchical nature of private higher education--with a few prestigious private universities occupying the top positions--it is not always recognized that a similar hierarchy exists within many public systems. Unlike the private hierarchy, which evolved more or less by historical accident, the hierarchies within the public system were developed as part of a conscious plan.

If the higher education hierarchy which Astin describes has been consciously developed, then the question of what role testing serves becomes important. Bailey (1978) has argued that standardized tests are often used as a screening device to control higher education and to preserve the higher education hierarchy. He further noted that some institutions view the test scores of entering freshmen as a reflection of the institution's worth or "perceived" quality. Therefore those institutions which are most selective may occasionally reject applicants with superior records and routinely accept only applicants that are in the top 5 to 10 percentile rank of their classes and who score well above 600 on the SAT. However, Hawes (1966) noted that the personal qualities and characteristics of students are factors that the highly selective institutions also take into consideration when evaluating applicants. Astin and Henson (1977) found that more selective institutions charge higher tuition, pay higher faculty salaries, and spend more on student educational expenditures. Table 2 lends some support to Astin's (1977) observation that students' standardized test performance corresponds to socioeconomic status and other non-academic characteristics of the institutions. The results in Table 2 show that the average institutional SAT and ACT scores do not directly correspond to the cost of attending the institution. Institutions which cost less

Table 2

Mean SAT and ACT-Composite Scores
By Cost To Attend Higher Educational Institution, 1974

Institutional Costs	$\overline{X}$ SAT-V	$\overline{X}$ SAT-M	$\overline{X}$ ACT
Less than $2,200	402	209	8.9
2,201 - 3,300	728	379	16.2
3,301 - 4,400	817	419	18.3
4,401 and above	662	334	14.8

Source: Reanalysis of unpublished data from the College
          Entrance Examination Board.

than $2,200 have an average SAT-Verbal score of 402, an
average SAT-Math score of 209, and an average ACT score of
8.9. However, institutions that cost $4,400 and above have
an average SAT-Verbal of 662, an average SAT-Math of 334,
and an average ACT of 14.8. Assuming that the results in
Table 2 are representative and that institutional selectivity
is equated with an institution's status or quality, it
should be understandable to some extent that highly selective institutions would have a vested interest in maintaining
high test scores for their incoming students.

    The final results presented in Table 3 suggest that in
addition to students' test score performance, students'
ability to finance their education also determines their
location in the higher education hierarchy. Table 3 shows
that the family income of students in universities is consistently higher than the family income of students in four-
year and two-year colleges. It is also clear that black
and other minority students are disproportionately distributed in two-year colleges as opposed to selective four-year
colleges and universities (National Center for Education
Statistics, 1978). The reason is partly due to the low cost
of two-year colleges, which blacks can more readily afford
than the costs required for four-year colleges and universities. This explanation and the present findings lend
support to Astin's (1977) observation of a consciously
maintained stratification system among higher educational
institutions. Nevertheless, findings throughout this chapter
suggest that there is a direct relationship between a
student's standardized test score and the non-academic

Table 3

Family Incomes of Students by Higher Educational Type, 1972-1976
(Dollars in Thousands)

Institutional Type	Total Percent	<$4	$4-9.9	$10-14.9	$15-19.9	$20-24.9	$25+	Median Income Constant $ current/constant
1972								
Two-Year	100.0	11.6	30.2	31.5	12.6	6.3	7.9	11,126/11,126
Four-Year	100.0	7.0	22.5	29.4	15.7	9.5	14.9	13,153/13,153
University	100.0	3.4	17.6	29.5	17.0	12.2	20.3	14,908/14,908
1974								
Two-Year	100.0	9.1	22.8	31.5	14.3	10.3	12.2	13,031/11,056
Four-Year	100.0	6.8	18.8	26.4	15.6	11.9	20.4	14,802/12,559
University	100.0	3.6	14.0	26.2	17.0	14.0	25.2	16,994/14,419
1976								
Two-Year	100.0	8.3	18.5	26.3	17.3	12.4	17.1	14,475/10,635
Four-Year	100.0	5.9	14.8	14.8	22.3	17.1	13.7	16,025/11,777
University	100.0	3.2	9.8	18.9	17.2	15.6	35.3	20,290/14,911

Source: Reanalysis of unpublished data from the American Council on Education.

attributes associated with the type and quality of college that he/she ultimately attends.

If blacks and other minorities were to score higher on standardized achievement tests than upper income whites, then the current socioeconomic stratification of institutions might be threatened. These poorer students could conceivably be awarded enough scholarships to tip the enrollment racial/ ethnic balance toward black and other minorities, but such a massive inversion of score distribution has never happened. Consequently, testing has not opened up educational opportunities for any economically disadvantaged group. In fact, traditional standardized tests add very little to meritocratic selection and nothing to equality of educational opportunity for minorities.

Conclusion

Whether or not standardized tests predict the college performance of black students, the location of these students in higher educational institutions appears to correspond more closely to the socioeconomic status and quality of the institution than to the students' test-predicted levels of performance. Unfortunately, data are not available to determine exactly how the admission process works in terms of the weight given to students' test results. However, it is clear that testing has a negative effect on black admissions at most colleges and universities. Also, the limited exploratory survey data initially presented suggest that admissions officers do not use minority students' test results to help these students improve their deficiencies as measured by these tests. More importantly, the use of these tests by institutions has not been evaluated to determine their effect on equality of higher educational opportunity. This effect may vary according to the racial composition of the school. For example, although the predominantly black institutions make greater use of standardized test data than white institutions (Boyd, 1977), these institutions place a greater emphasis on high school GPA than test scores. In addition, these institutions have lower entry requirements than most white institutions. Therefore, black colleges may offer minorities greater educational opportunity than white colleges.

The racial composition of a college or university is not the only parameter that may make for differences in the admissions process. The type and quality of colleges and universities are also important variables that operate in the admissions process. In fact, these variables appear to operate in a manner which sorts and places blacks independent of their test performance. Therefore, as suggested by Bailey (1978) and others, the use of standardized tests may simply be a support or formal prop for maintaining the status quo of higher educational institutions.

In response to the question initially raised in this chapter about how the use of standardized achievement testing affects social and racial inequality in higher education, the answer is three-fold. First, heavy reliance on such testing places blacks at a disadvantage, but there is no clear standard for the appropriate level of reliance on these tests and thus no clear level of black disadvantage. The strongest grounds for the failure of higher education to carefully examine and justify the extent to which tests are used grows out of the recognition that testing is not a unique disadvantage for black applicants. Because scores correspond to a range of socioeconomic and academic disadvantage of blacks, the marginal impediment created by admissions testing has generated much discussion but little analysis and less specific action by college administrators. Second, the setting of admissions standards in higher education is treated the private right of institutions and the exercise of that right essentially corresponds to the structural characteristics of institutions. Third, the use of achievement tests in higher education seems to accomodate the social and racial inequalities among institutions rather than rectify such inequalities.

More importantly, one can arbitrarily assume that standardized tests are culturally neutral and objective measures of potential and/or achievement, and still not justify their use in selection procedures. Once the grounds for justification move beyond claims of institutional convenience to the claim of improving meritocracy, the demonstrated value of testing disappears. The students who gain access to selective institutions through testing are virtually the same ones whose race and socioeconomic status would otherwise assure them access. A close look at the histories of selective institutions (Wright, 1976) demonstrates that the expansion of testing in admissions has done little or nothing to contribute to the educational opportunities of blacks, who by all other standards "merit" them. Consequently, achievement testing appears to have had the effect on blacks of standardizing inequalities rather than creating objectivity in the admissions process.

References

American College Testing
   1978   Unpublished Report to the National Advisory
           Committee on Blacks in Higher Education,
           Washington, D.C.

Astin, A.W. and B. Henson
   1977   "New measures of college selectivity." Research
           in Higher Education 6:1-9.

Astin, A.W.
   1977   "Equal access to postsecondary education: myth or
           reality?" UCLA 19:8-17.

Bailey, R.L.
   1978   Minority Admissions. Lexington, Mass. and Canada:
           Lexington Books (D.C. Heath and Company).

Boyd, W.
   1977   "SAT's and minorities: the dangers of under-
           prediction." Change Nov.: 64.

Hawes, G.R.
   1966   The New American Guide to Colleges. New York:
           Columbia University Press.

Institute of the Study of Educational Policy
   1976   Equal Education Opportunity for Blacks in U.S.
           Higher Education An Assessment. Washington,
           D.C.: Howard University Press.

Kolstad, A.
   1977   Attrition from Colleges: The Class of 1972
           Two and One Half Years after High School
           Graduation. HEW: Government Printing Office.

McClelland, D.C.
   1976   "Testing for competence rather than for intelli-
           gence." Pp. 12-24 in N.J. Block and Gerald
           Dworkin (eds.), The I.Q. Controversy. New York:
           Panteheon Press.

Morris, L.
   1979   Elusive Equality: The Status of Black Americans
           in Higher Education. Washington, D.C.: Howard
           University Press.

National Center for Education Status
    1978   The Condition of Education. Washington, D.C.:
             U.S. Government Printing Office.

Thomas, G.E.
    1980   The Impact of College Racial Composition on the
             Four-Year College Graduation of Black Students.
             Baltimore, Maryland: Center for Social Organiza-
             tion of Schools. Johns Hopkins University.

Wesman, A.
    1968   "Intelligence testing." American Psychologist
             23:267-74.

Wright, S.
    1976   "The black college in historical perspective."
             In Phillip Jones (ed.) Historical Perspectives
             on the Development of Equal Opportunity in Higher
             Education, ACT Special Report #22, Iowa City:
             ACT Publications.

6

Factors Affecting Black Students' Persistence in College

PATRICIA H.CROSS and HELEN S. ASTIN

Introduction

Student persistence in higher education is a subject of growing concern, particularly as it relates to members of ethnic minority groups. Open admissions and equal access do not guarantee equal opportunity until students complete their undergraduate careers or otherwise fulfill their educational goals.

Previous research has found that student persistence is related to a number of complex variables including demographic characteristics, socio-economic status, academic ability, motivation, degree aspirations, personal values and attitudes, and the environmental characteristics of the college a student attends. Financial factors also play an important role (Pantages and Creedon, 1978). Knowledge of how all these factors affect the persistence in college of minority group students is badly needed.

Among recent efforts to widen access to college, probably the most important are federal and state commitments to remove existing financial barriers by helping pay for needy students' college education through various kinds of aid programs. This chapter examines the types and amount of financial aid received by black students in order to determine how that aid affects their persistence in college.

Sample and Research Design

During fall, 1975, approximately 186,000 first-time, full-time freshmen entering 366 colleges and universities completed the Student Information Form (SIF), which is administered every year by the Cooperative Institutional Research Program (CIRP).

The SIF asks students about their family background, their high school preparation and grades, the financial aid they expect to receive, their aspirations, values and attitudes, as well as some of their demographic characteristics. Approximately 40,000 of the students were followed up in the fall of 1977 according to a stratified design which oversampled low-income and minority students and students from large institutions. A total of 16,657 students returned usable questionnaires. After 4,052 students whose questionnaires were nondeliverable were excluded from the statistical procedure, which has been used successfully with other CIRP data and follow-ups (See H. Astin and Cross, 1979), was employed to weight the data to represent all students who enrolled for the first time in American colleges in fall, 1975.[1]

A variable describing student persistence was developed on the basis of responses to a number of questionnaire items: (1) the student's initial degree aspirations at the time of college entry in 1975; (2) the student's enrollment status as reported for each month of the academic years 1975-76 and 1976-77; (3) the student's enrollment status in the fall of 1977; and (4) the student's degree attainment by the fall of 1977. Using these four groups of responses, we placed most students into one of four criterion groups: (1) full-time persisters: students who attended college full-time during the two academic years under study and who were enrolled in the fall of 1977; (2) erratic persisters: students whose attendance shifted between full-time and part-time but who never actually withdrew from school; (3) stop-outs: students who had dropped out of school at some point during the two academic years under study but who were enrolled in fall, 1977; and (4) withdrawals: students who had dropped out of school and not re-enrolled by fall, 1977.

Excluded from the analyses were those students who said as freshmen that they had planned to go no further than an associate degree, who had completed that degree by the time of the follow-up, and who were not enrolled in the fall of 1977 because they had achieved their degree goal.

Method of Analysis

The three main questions examined in this study were as follows: (1) When important predictors of full-time persistence are controlled, what is the effect of the

student's race (black or white) on persistence? (2) Are
students able to persist longer in some types of educational
environments than others? (3) Holding other factors constant, what effect does financial aid have on student persistence?

We chose our criterion variable of full-time persistence
as opposed to all other attendance patterns (erratic, stop-
out and withdrawal) because we believe that full-time
persistence has important economic and educational implications for both students and institutions. Therefore, we
decided to examine the variables and factors that encourage
it.

Regression Procedures

The research design consisted of two stepwise multiple
regression procedures performed on two groups. Group one
consisted of a random sample of one-third of the white and
black students combined (N=3,863) and group two was composed of all black respondents (N=3,514). The regression
model was essentially the same for both groups, consisting
of the following three sets of predictor variables:

1. Background and personal variables: sex, age,
father's education, mother's education, parental income,
degree of financial concern about ability to finance education, religion, marital status, type of high school preparation, high school grades, SAT scores, freshman degree
aspirations, and seven expectations at the time of college
entry: that the respondent will earn at least a B average
in college, have to work at an outside job during college,
obtain a bachelor's degree, drop out permanently, seek
individual counseling on personal problems, be satisfied
with college, and get married while in college.

2. Institutional and environmental variables: size
of college enrollment, selectivity of the institution, distance in miles from home to college, type of control (private or public), institutional type (university, 4-year
college, or 2-year college), geographical region, and cost
of tuition and fees. In addition, two other variables that
had been found to be significant predictors of persistence
in other studies were also used (Astin, A., King and
Richardson, 1975): (a) the type of residence in which the
student lives during college, and (b) the student's pattern
of employment. The employment variables included whether the
student worked (either as part of the college work-study
program or in any other paid employment), whether he/she
worked on or off campus, the number of hours worked, and

whether the job was related to the student's field of study.

3.   Financial aid variables: received financial aid, received financial support from parents, total amount of aid, total amount of grants, loans and work-study, ten dichotomous variables describing various types of aid packages and the net cost of college to the student and his family (tuition and fees minus grants).

In each of the three sets of variables, each variable was allowed to enter freely in a stepwise fashion, provided it reached statistical significance at the .05 level.

4.   College experiences and attitude variables: a fourth set of variables included the student's values and attitudes, college experiences and behavior. These variables were not allowed to enter the regression equation because they were based on data collected in 1977 and may thus represent outcome rather than input variables. However, we wanted to examine the relationship of these variables to the criterion variables, so we retained them in the regression model and reported the partial r's for all those which were significant at the .01 level. These variables included college grades, five statements describing possible financial situations, self-ratings of academic ability, work and career values, why the student enrolled in college, college experiences and the types of campus activities in which the student participated.

Findings

Overview

Overall, our data show that whites were more likely than blacks to persist in college full-time through the beginning of their junior year (65 percent vs. 60 percent) while blacks were more likely to withdraw (21 percent vs. 18 percent for whites). The two races differed little in their chances of becoming either erratic persisters (about 12 percent) or stopouts (5 percent).

Blacks were far more likely than whites to receive aid and to get larger amounts of financial aid (Table 1). These differences undoubtedly reflect differences in the parental incomes of the two groups: 68.3 percent of the blacks reparental incomes of less that $10,000, compared to only 17.1 percent of the whites.

Both whites and blacks were likely to receive all their financial aid in the form of grants, but whites were

Table 1

Type of Aid Received, by Institutional Type and Race/Ethnicity
(Percentages of Aided Students)

Form of Aid[a] 1975-76	Public University		Private University		Public 4-Year		Private 4-Year		Two-Year		Predominantly Black[b]	
	White	Black	White	Black	White	Black	White	Black	White	Black	White[b]	Black
Grant only	58.2	43.8	48.4	23.3	50.8	40.9	34.5	26.1	60.4	66.7		37.6
Loan only	9.6	6.4	8.6	6.0	12.1	3.0	5.5	2.5	8.0	1.3		2.1
Work only	3.1	.3	2.3	0	3.7	0	4.7	2.6	1.2	1.2		.5
Large grant, loan & work-study	.9	2.7	2.9	10.4	.2	4.5	4.9	10.5	.5	1.4		3.7
Small grant, loan & work-study	3.6	8.6	6.4	8.2	3.7	11.6	15.7	22.0	4.1	3.2		14.6
Large grant & loan	3.7	5.7	8.9	19.8	4.4	15.2	4.6	11.0	2.6	5.2		9.7
Small grant & loan	16.5	15.5	18.3	25.5	14.5	15.6	18.9	5.2	13.6	6.6		10.3
Large grant & work-study	1.1	5.6	1.2	4.4	3.5	1.4	4.4	9.3	2.4	4.8		9.4
Small grant & work-study	2.1	11.0	2.3	2.4	5.9	7.5	5.7	9.9	6.7	9.6		10.9
Loan & work-study	1.2	.3	.7	0	1.3	.4	1.3	.9	.5	0		1.3
Mean aid	$1376	1854	2257	3152	1410	1906	2133	2701	1263	1246		1846
Percentage with aid	37.7	85.1	63.1	91.8	56.4	89.9	63.0	95.3	59.1	87.1		92.9

Table 1 Continued

a/Seven mutually exclusive dichotomous variables were created describing various possible financial aid "packages." For those packages which contained a grant, an attempt was made to distinguish between whether that grant constituted a substantial part of the package or not. Thus, the designation "large" grant does not refer to the size of the grant but indicates that most of the total value of the package was in grant form. Likewise, "small" grant means that the grant component is less substantial.

b/There were no white students attending the predominantly black institution in our sample.

considerably more likely than blacks to get <u>one</u> type of aid
only, while blacks were more likely to get a "package"
combining grant, loan and work-study aid. The smallest
differences in type of aid received between these black
and white students attending predominantly white two-year
colleges.

Persistence of Blacks and Whites Combined

Table 2 shows the results of the regression analysis
designed to identify the variables that predict full-time
persistence for white and black students combined. For
this analysis, race (black vs. white) was allowed to enter
as an independent variable, along with all other variables
in the first three sets: background and personal variables,
institutional and environmental variables and financial
aid variables. Of the 69 potential predictors, 17 entered
the regression equation with a statistically significant
weight, producing a multiple correlation coefficient ($\underline{R}$) of
.34.

The most significant positive predictors of full-time
persistence were the student's past academic achievement as
measured by high school grades, SAT score and having been
in a college preparatory curriculum in high school; attending
either a university or a four-year college was also a strong
positive predictor. The most significant negative predictor
was being employed 21 or more hours per week while attending
college. These findings are consistent with those of past
research (A. Astin et.al., 1975); Pantages and Creedon, 1978).

However, some other findings are quite surprising,
particularly those whose beta weights had signs different
from those of the zero-order correlation and which contradict
past research findings. One such finding is that being
black entered the regression equation as a positive predictor
of full-time persistence; blacks who are similar to whites
on the significant predictor variables are somewhat more
likely than white students to persist full-time. Peng and
Fetters (1978) have reported similar results.

Another finding is that parental income entered the
equation with a negative weight, despite the positive zero-
order correlation between parental income and full-time
persistence. Possibly the "middle income squeeze" has made
children of middle income parents less eligible than others
for financial aid, causing some of them to drop out of
school. Or perhaps middle income students may drop out in
response to current job market conditions and the widespread
publicity about the declining value of a college degree,

Table 2

Predictors of Full-Time Persistence
For White and Black Students Combined
(R=.34)

Variables	Standarized Beta Coefficient	Zero-Order Correlation	$F^{a/}$ Ratio
Personal and Background Variables			
High school grades	.11	.18	34.17
SAT score	.10	.15	15.27
Religion: affiliated (yes/no)	-.05	-.04	-11.38
Freshman expectation: get a BA	.05	.16	10.29
Freshman expectation: get married while in college	-.05	-.06	9.58
High school program: college preparatory	.05	.11	8.73
Freshman expectation: drop out permanently	-.04	-.06	7.27
Race: black	.05	-.01	6.27
Parental income	-.04	.05	5.18
Marital status: single	-.03	.02	4.11
Environmental & Institutional Variables			
Institutional type: university	.32	.14	96.00
Institutional type: 4-year college	.27	-.00	82.11
Worked 21 hours or more per week	-.11	-.15	50.25
Institutional selectivity	-.09	.12	12.89
Region: West/Nonwest	-.03	-.05	4.57
Financial Aid Variables			
Type of financial aid: small grant & work-study	-.05	-.05	9.47
Type of financial aid: small grant, loan & work-study	-.04	-.02	6.09

a/
$F > 3.84 = p < 0.05$; $F > 6.64 = p < 0.01$; $F > 10.83 = p < 0.001$

while low income students tend to persist because they believe that education, despite the poor current job market, is their only real hope for long term upward mobility.

The financial variables were allowed to enter the equation only after the personal and institutional ones had entered because we considered it important to assess the independent contribution of financial aid to persistence only after we had controlled for the important known predictors such as past academic achievement and type of college attended.

Only two of the financial aid variables entered the regression, both with significant negative weights. They each involved aid in the form of a package including both a loan and a small grant which perhaps means that unless the grant is a large portion of a student's financial aid package, the effect may be to hinder, rather than help, the recipient persist in college.

Table 3 lists for the total black-white sample, the significant partial correlations between the criterion variable and the student's college experiences and behavior after controlling for all three sets (personal, institutional, and financial) of independent variables. The two most sifnificant variables proved to be (a) the student's degree of involvement in campus life, and (b) the grades he/she received in the first two years of college. Table 4 presents similar partial correlations for blacks only. It also shows degree of involvement in campus activities, college GPA in addition to parents' willingness to help finance students' education as the most significant correlates of persistence.

Black Persistence

We next conducted an identical analysis using the sample of black students only. The student's race variable used in the first analysis was omitted, and the racial composition of the college's student body (i.e. whether or not it was predominantly black) was added (Table 5). Comparing the results of this analysis to those of the previous one, we found that high school grades and being employed 21 hours or more per week while attending college were again two of the most significant predictors of persistence for blacks. Of particular interest was the finding that the most significant institutional predictor of full-time persistence proved to be the institution's racial composition. Attending a predominantly black institution positively predicted full-time persistence. This is a particularly striking finding since the correlation between attending a

Table 3

Significant Correlates of 1977 Follow-Up
Data with Full-Time Persistence for
Black and White Students Combined

Variables	Zero-Order Correlation	Partial r [a]
Involvement in college activities	.21	.13
College GPA	.17	.11
Work values: chance to use training	.09	.10
Lonely in college	-.09	-.08
Bored in college	-.10	-.08
Contribute to support of parents	-.07	-.05
Parents not willing to help financially	-.08	-.04
Work values: be helpful to others	.04	.04
Dissatisfied with college	-.06	-.04
Social activities overemphasized	.07	.04
Head of household/single parent	-.06	-.04

[a]
The partial r is a correlation between each variable and full-time persistence, after control of all predictor variables in Phase I. All partial r's are significant at the .01 level.

Table 4

Significant Correlates of 1977
Follow-Up Data with Full-Time
Persistence for Black Students Only

Variables	Zero-Order Correlation	Partial r [a]
Involvement in college activities	.02	.13
Parents not willing to help financially	-.14	-.12
College GPA	.19	.12
Bored in college	-.08	-.07
Self-rating: academic ability	.15	.07
Contribute to support of parents	-.09	-.06
Work values: be helpful to others	.06	.05
Have major debts or expenses	-.04	-.04
Reason for going to college: contribute to the community	.06	.04
Lonely in college	-.04	-.04

[a]
The partial r is a correlation between each variable and full-time persistence, after control of all predictor variables in Phase I. All partial r's are significant at the .01 level.

Table 5

Predictors of Full-Time Persistence
for Black Students Only

Variables	Beta Coefficient	Zero-Order Correlation	$F^{a/}$ Ratio
Background and Personal Variables			
High school grades	.13	.17	47.80
SAT score	.07	.16	12.99
Degree plans: MA	.05	.07	10.16
High School program: college preparatory	.05	.11	9.20
Age	-.05	-.12	8.60
Freshman expectation: drop out permanently	-.05	-.08	8.50
Freshman expectation: get a BA	.04	.11	6.96
Freshman expectation: seek counseling for personal problems	.04	.03	6.03
Religion: Protestant	.04	.03	4.89
Sex: Female	-.03	.02	4.05
Environmental and Institutional Variables			
Predominantly black institution	.19	.10	49.41
Worked 21 hours or more per week	-.10	-.13	35.43
Institutional control: private	-.11	.02	13.29
Worked on campus	.05	.06	9.18
Tuition and fees	.09	.08	6.36
Live off campus but not with parents	-.04	-.09	5.42
Financial Aid Variables			
Amount of loan	-.05	-.03	8.39
R^2		.33	

a/

  $F > 3.84 = p < 0.05$; $F > 6.64 = p < 0.01$; $F > 10.83 = p < 0.001$

predominantly black college and full-time persistence increases as student input variables are controlled, providing strong evidence that predominantly black colleges do indeed have a positive impact on student persistence (A. Astin, 1970). But attending a black private college negatively affects the persistence of black students after attendance at a predominantly black college is controlled for. This is somewhat puzzling, because earlier research on undergraduate students in general has consistently shown that attending a private college increases students' persistence (A. Astin et.al., 1975;1977). Possibly, because the nation's private black colleges are currently in dire financial straits, they cannot offer their students the types of financial aid and student support services that the public black colleges can.

Only one financial aid variable (amount of loan) entered the equation for blacks with a significant weight; the larger their educational loan, the more likely were students to drop out. Apparently being burdened with a large debt has more serious consequences for the presistence of black than of white students, probably because blacks are worse off economically. Previous research has found that loans have a strong negative effect on persistence among low income students (A. Astin, 1975; H. Astin and Cross, 1979). Since black students as a group come from families with much lower incomes than do white students, it is not surprising that the variable measuring the amount of loan should enter the regression equation for black students with a negative weight. Why large loans would have greater negative effects for low income or black students than for others is not clear. Possibly low income or black students are not confident, based on their family experience, that they will be able to repay the loan, and they are greatly burdened psychologically by large loans. Or else low income students may need money so badly that when they receive their loan at the semester's start they may spend it all immediately and find themselves, later on, without the funds to continue in school.

Students' degree of involvement in campus life, as mentioned, correlated highly with full-time persistence. Most of the other variables which remained significantly related to full-time persistence after controlling for the three sets of input variables were the same for both groups of students, although their degree of significance changed somewhat. The perception that parents are unwilling rather than unable to help pay for college expenses seems to affect blacks' persistence more adversely than that of whites. For both groups, perceived financial pressures of various kinds

and feelings of loneliness and boredom in college were
negatively related to persistence, whereas aspiring to a
career in which one can be helpful to others was positively
related.   In addition, for black students, self-confidence
in their academic ability was important.

For both black and white students, factors such as past
academic achievement the type of college the student attends, the expectations he or she enters college with, and
the number of hours the student is employed per week appear
to play a more important role than financial aid in predicting whether the student will remain in college full time.
However, this interpretation may not reflect the true importance of financial aid, especially for black students,
because this study lacks a real control group of black
students who received no financial aid.   Since about 90
percent of our sample's black students receive some kind of
aid, there is too little variability to test whether financial aid -- as opposed to no financial aid -- encourages
students to stay in college. However, since 2 in 3 blacks
students reported parental incomes of less than $10,000, it
appears likely that having aid does play a positive and
probably essential role in the students' ability to persist
in college. What we can test is whether some forms of
financial aid variables that entered one or both regression equations involved either a "package" amount of the
loan component or the actual amount of the loan, there is
some evidence that loans have a negative impact on student
persistence.   The policy implication of this finding is that
students' financial aid should be limited to grants and work-
study funds, particularly in the case of low income students.

Besides the findings on financial aid, the analysis did
reveal that the type of institution a student attends does
play a significant role in his or her persistence. Black
students with approximately the same input characteristics
(academic achievement, freshman expectations, number of hours
employed while in college, etc.) are considerably more likely
to persist full-time in college if they attend predominantly
black institutions rather than predominantly white ones.
Possibly, further research can identify the particular qualities of black colleges which create this positive climate.
Predominantly white colleges and universities might benefit
from this knowledge in seeking to create an environment
which has positive affects on the persistence of black
students.

References

Astin, A.W.
  1970   The Methodology of Research on College Impact,
          Part One. Sociology of Education 43 (Summer):
          223-254.

Astin, A.W., M.R. King, and G.T. Richardson
  1975   The American Freshman: National Norms for
          Fall 1975. Washington and Los Angeles:
          Cooperative Institutional Research Program,
          American Council on Education and University
          of California at Los Angeles.

Astin, A.W.
  1977   Four Critical Years. San Francisco: Jossey-Bass.

Astin, H.S. and P.H. Cross
  1979   The Impact of Financial Aid on Student Persistence
          in College. Final Report to the Office of Plan-
          ning, Budgeting and Education (Department of
          Health, Education and Welfare). Los Angeles:
          Higher Education Research Institute.

Pantages, T.J. and C.F. Creedon
  1978   "Studies of college attrition: 1950-1975."
          Review of Educational Research 48 (Winter): 49-101.

Peng, S.S. and W.B. Fetters
  1978   "Variables involved in withdrawal during the first
          two years of college: preliminary findings from
          the National Longitudinal Study of the High School
          Class of 1972." American Educational Research
          Journal 15 (Summer): 361-372.

7

Impact of an Innovative Selection Procedure on Medical School Admissions: Implications for Black Students

VIRGINIA CALKINS and T. LEE WILLOUGHBY

Introduction

In the Fall of 1972, the University of Missouri-Kansas City (UMKC) School of Medicine initiated a change in selection procedures which has been followed in succeeding years. The school, which enrolled its charter class in 1970, offers a six-year combined Arts and Sciences School of Medicine program which is entered directly from high school. Students are enrolled concurrently in liberal arts and medical school courses. During the first two years, approximately three-fourths of a student's curriculum time is spent in Arts and Sciences and one-fourth in Medicine; whereas, in years 3 through 6, one-fourth of the program is devoted to Arts and Sciences and three-fourths to Medicine. An entering student is at a patient's bedside the first day of college. Students participate in a multidisciplinary health care team for three months each year during years 3 through 6. They are enrolled in school year-round with one month of vacation.

The Council on Selection is charged with identifying those applicants who are most suited to a patient-centered curriculum. A primary criterion for identification is that students have the potential to be both competent and caring physicians. The intent of the Council is to select students who can meet the academic demands of the six-year program and become action-oriented problem solvers. This philosophy of selection has not been easy to implement based on the traditional admission criteria of academic achievement and standardized test scores. In addition, it has been a challenge to select high school youngsters and predict their performance six years hence.

Previous research on selection and prediction clearly indicates that grades and test scores correlate poorly with performance in the clinical years of medical education

(Schwartzman, Hunter and Lohrenz, 1962; Burgess, 1972;
Gough and Hall, 1975; Murden, et.al., 1978) and even less
with success as an intern or practicing physician (Richards,
Taylor and Price, 1962; Wingard and Williamson, 1973).
Recent research here at UMKC suggests that clinical performance is composed of elements unrelated to measures of
cognitive achievement (Willoughby, Gammon and Jones, 1979).
Holland and others (Holland, 1967; Holland and Nichols, 1964;
Holland and Richards, 1965; Richards et.al., 1962) have
repeatedly pointed out that academic talent is only one of
several human talents. When selection is carried out on the
basis of increasingly high academic aptitude, persons who are
selected may be quite incompetent in other areas (Gough,1967).
Moreover, Linn (1973) and D'Costa et.al., (1974) emphasized
the difficulties inherent in achieving cultural fairness in
any test.

The widespread use of interviews in the selection of
students for medical school recognizes the importance of
non-academic factors in the selection process (Wilson, 1974;
Char, et.al., 1975; Poorman, 1975). Burgess, Calkins, and
Richards (1972) reported on the use of a structured interview
as a selection device, and Calkins, Willoughby and Smith,
(1976) and Murden, et.al. (1978) indicated that the interview
and other non-cognitive variables were significant predictors
of performance in medicine.

The Selection Process

The Council on Selection at the University of Missouri-
Kansas City School of Medicine is a diverse group. It consists of four physicians (two of whom practice in the
community and two of whom are full time at the School of
Medicine), two basic scientists, one liberal arts representative, two student physicians, a faculty member from the
Office of Medical Education, and (since 1974) a community
representative. These representatives are (except for the
latter two) elected by their respective peers to the Council
on Selection.

This group agreed to de-emphasize the importance of high
school academic performance beginning with candidates who
would be considered for the 1973 entering class. Specifically,
it was agreed that all students above a certain cutting score
on "academic potential" (as defined by the Director of Admissions) would be considered for admission but that the actual
high school subject grades and college admission test scores
would not be a part of the application material available
to interviewers nor considered by the Council on Selection.

Other aspects of the admission process (e.g. reliance on extensive biographical and interview data) remained the same as in prior selection years.

To implement their decision to de-emphasize high school academic performance, the Council on Selection sought assurance from the University's Director of Admissions and Registrar (DAR) that an applicant above the cutting "academic potential" score could satisfy requirements of the program. All candidates predicted by the Director of Admissions and Registrar to have a reasonable chance to succeed academically were identified as "academically qualified" (Categories A and B below) and were considered for a place in the Fall 1973 class. The Director of Admissions' projection was based on a four-point scale: (1) A-high school rank of 90th percentile and higher with aptitude scores 70th percentile and higher, with 80 to 99 percent chance of success in the freshman year; (2) B-high school rank 80th to 89th percentile with aptitude scores 60th percentile and higher, and a 50 to 79 percent chance of success in the freshman year; (3) C-high school rank 50th to 79th percentile with aptitude scores below 50 percentile, and a 25 to 49 percent chance of success in the freshman year; and (4) D-high school rank below 50th percentile, and 1 to 24 percent chance of success in the freshman year.

Students who were judged "not academically qualified" were rejected without further consideration. All academically qualified candidates were subsequently invited to the campus for interviews. Each candidate had two interviews, one with a physician and one with a non-physician. The interviewers (not all of whom were members of the Council on Selection) were invited to the Council meeting when the applicants whom they had interviewed were discussed and voted upon.

In discussing and evaluating applicants, the Council considered work experiences, accomplishments outside the classroom, and evaluations of applicants provided by high school references. These measures, along with the structured interview, were presumed to assess characteristics such as initiative, persistence, leadership, and inter-personal competency, all of which were thought to be related to clinical success (Price, et.al., 1971; Murden et.al., 1978).

A decision regarding an applicant was made in the following manner. Interviewers reported the results of their interviews (including the total rating points) and made recommendations based on their evaluations of the candidates. They responded to any questions posed by Council members.

All pertinent application information was available and discussed. However, a student's class rank, admission test
scores, and DAR category were not made known to Council
members (this information was available to members prior to
1973). Following discussion of applicants, each member of
the Council rated each applicant on a five-point scale. The
individual ratings were averaged to form a Council Index.

Results of the Selection Procedure

Product-moment intercorrelations were computed on selection variables and the Council Index for the 162 applicants
in 1972 and the 241 applicants in 1973. Table 1 shows the
results for the 1972 applicants. For these applicants, selection data that correlate significantly with the Council
Index in order of magnitude, are: admission test score (.58),
DAR category (.50), reference ratings (.38), and race, which
was negatively correlated with the Council Index (-.30).
The intercorrelations presented in Table 2 for 1973 applicants, who were evaluated according to the new selection
policy, differed in several respects from the 1972 data.

The admissions test score correlated .18 with the Council Index for 1973 applicants, whereas it correlated .58 (the
highest correlation) for the 1972 applicants. For the 1973
applicants, the physician and non-physician interviewers'
recommendations (.67 and .64) and ratings (.57 and .59) were
the highest correlations, followed by reference ratings (.38)
and extracurricular achievement (.33). Lastly, the significant negative correlation between race and the Council Index
(which suggests discrimination toward minorities) that was
present in 1972 was negligible (.06) in 1973. The Council,
therefore, agreed to select students for the first-year class
entering in the Fall of 1974 in the same manner, setting a
minimum cutting score on academic potential and eliminating
specific academic information from a candidate's application
materials presented and discussed at meetings of the Council
on Selection.

The results of the 1974 selection process are presented
in Table 3. The interviews by both physician and non-physician continued to have the highest correlation with the
Council Index (.63 and .57). Next in order of importance
was prior academic performance as represented by DAR category
(.41) followed by class rank (.34). The non-academic criteria of reference ratings, extracurricular achievement, and
health-related job experience also correlated significantly
with Council Index score for the 1974 applicants. Admission
scores (a second component of DAR category) showed a higher

Table 1

Intercorrelations of Selection Variables and Council Index: 1972 Applicants (N = 162)

	1	2	3	4	5	6	7	8	9	10	11	12	13	14	15	16	17	18
1 Sex																		
2 Race	-.20																	
3 F.E.	.17	-.29																
4 M.E.	-.02	-.17	.42															
5 Out Org	.08	-.02	-.02	-.04														
6 Sci/H	.04	-.12	.00	.06	.19													
7 N-Ach	.20	-.13	.09	.02	.04	.21												
8 H. Job	-.15	-.20	.05	.16	-.02	.32	.09											
9 C.R.	-.15	-.17	-.23	-.18	.13	-.01	.11	-.06										
10 No. HS	-.03	-.08	-.03	-.04	.11	-.12	-.27	-.04	.24									
11 A.T.S.	.24	-.50	-.15	.07	.05	.17	.03	.10	.11	.19								
12 R.R.	.08	-.12	-.14	-.05	.04	-.04	.11	-.02	.26	.02	.26							
13 DAR	-.07	-.41	-.12	-.07	.07	.09	.06	.07	.75	.20	.52	.30						
14 PIR	-.05	-.02	-.12	.10	.03	.16	-.01	.19	.10	.17	.08	.17	.15					
15 PID	-.06	-.05	.00	.07	.08	.07	-.01	.10	.20	.26	.15	.18	.26	.53				
16 NPIR	.02	-.20	.07	.15	.13	.26	.23	.18	.16	.17	.26	.16	.36	.09	.09			
17 NPID	.05	-.14	-.01	.04	.03	.16	.15	.11	.17	.12	.20	.30	.35	.14	.19	.56		
18 No.CMV	.04	-.04	.02	.00	-.06	-.03	.02	.04	-.03	-.03	-.15	-.12	-.14	-.03	-.04	-.07	-.14	
19 CI	.14	-.30	.07	.11	.10	.27	.18	.18	.19	.29	.58	.38	.50	.50	.52	.50	.54	-.10

.18 = p ≤ .05.   .27 = p ≤ .01.

1. Sex = (Male=1; female=2); 2. Race (White=0, Other=1); 3. F.E.=Father's Education; 4. M.E.= Mother's Education; 5. Out Org= No. of Outside Organizations; 6. Sci/H=No. of Science/Health Projects; 7. N-Ach=Non Academic Achievement; 8. H Job=Health-related Job Experience; 9. C.R.= Rank in Class; 10. No H.S.= No. in High School Class; 11. A.T.S.=Admission Test Score; 12. R.R.= Reference Ratings; 13. DAR =DAR Category; 14. PIR= Physician Interview Ratings; 15. PID=Physician Interview Decision; 16. NPIR=Non-physic. Interview Ratings; 17. NPID=Non-physic. Interview Decision; 18. No. CMV= No. of Council Members Voting; 19. CI=Council Index.

Table 2

Intercorrelations of Selection Variables and Council Index: 1973 Applicants (N = 241)

	1	2	3	4	5	6	7	8	9	10	11	12	13	14	15	16	17	18
1 Sex																		
2 Race	-.19																	
3 F.E.	.14	-.09																
4 M.E.	-.01	-.09	.55															
5 Out Org	-.04	-.01	.18	.20														
6 Sci/H	.02	.00	.13	.10	.08													
7 N-Ach	-.05	-.03	.16	.15	.14	.09												
8 H. Job	-.33	-.16	.12	.16	.06	.02	.06											
9 C.R.	-.17	-.06	-.19	-.06	.08	-.02	-.15	-.04										
10 No. HS	.07	-.15	.19	.20	.15	.01	-.18	.02	.04									
11 A.T.S.	.18	-.32	.18	.21	.12	-.07	.06	.03	.14	.21								
12 R.R.	-.10	.05	.08	.07	.07	.08	.24	.10	.18	-.14	.14							
13 DAR	-.01	-.20	-.17	.00	.09	-.02	-.13	-.05	.75	.09	.37	.16						
14 PIR	-.04	-.06	.04	.08	.13	-.01	.13	.16	.07	-.09	.18	.24	.09					
15 PID	-.10	-.01	.00	.02	.04	.02	.03	.11	.14	-.05	.14	.08	.11	.61				
16 NPIR	-.12	-.09	.09	.21	.13	.14	.26	.21	.18	.00	.20	.39	.16	.29	.24			
17 NPID	-.11	-.01	.05	.14	.13	.11	.26	.16	.22	-.01	.16	.44	.25	.27	.24	.74		
18 No. CMV	.05	.00	.02	.05	.02	.05	-.06	-.10	.05	.00	-.03	.09	.03	.12	-.01	.15	.06	
19 CI	-.14	.06	.06	.14	.13	.07	.33	.18	.18	-.08	.18	.38	.22	.57	.65	.59	.64	.05

.13 = $p < .05$ .18 = $p < .01$

1. Sex=(Male=1, Female=0); 2. Race (White=0, Other=1); 3. F.E.=Father's Education; 4. M.E. = Mother's Education; 5. Out Org= No. of Outside Organizations; 6. Sci/H=No. of Science/Health Projects; 7. N-Ach=Non Academic Achievement; 8. H Job= Health-related Job Experience; 9. C.R.= Rank in Class; 10. No. HS= No. in High School Class; 11. A.T.S.=Admission Test Score; 12. R.R.= Reference Ratings; 13. DAR = DAR Category; 14. PIR=Physician Interview Ratings;
15. PID= Physician Interview Decision; 16. NPIR=Non-physic. Interview Ratings;
17. NPID=Non-physic. Interview Decision; 18. No. CMV=No. of Council Members Voting;
19. CI=Council Index.

Table 3

Intercorrelations of Selection Variables and Council Index: 1974 Applicants (N = 335)

	1	2	3	4	5	6	7	8	9	10	11	12	13	14	15	16	17	18
1 Sex																		
2 Race	-.09																	
3 F.E.	.08	.04																
4 M.E.	.03	.08	.51															
5 Out Org	-.06	-.03	.20	.18														
6 Sci/H	.04	-.04	.04	.00	.07													
7 N-Ach	-.04	-.15	.05	.04	.20	.22												
8 H. Job	-.34	-.08	.13	.06	.11	.01	.08											
9 C.R.	-.12	-.05	-.16	-.12	.10	.07	.22	.02										
10 No. HS	.09	-.08	-.08	-.07	.08	-.05	-.13	-.01	.18									
11 A.T.S.	.08	-.32	.19	.07	.09	.03	.13	.12	.22	.13								
12 R.R.	.08	-.09	.03	-.01	.06	.04	.15	.05	.27	.11	.16							
13 R.R.D.	-.04	.00	.12	-.06	.02	.01	.12	.05	.13	.03	.13	.50						
14 DAR	-.06	-.14	-.03	-.05	.14	.10	.26	.09	.80	.09	.42	.31	.19					
15 PIR	-.15	-.03	.13	.06	.11	.12	.15	.23	.13	.04	.19	.16	.13	.21				
16 PID	-.06	-.09	.16	.06	.09	.12	.18	.21	.18	.09	.25	.20	.16	.25	.79			
17 NPIR	-.21	-.05	.16	.13	.17	.04	.25	.23	.08	.01	.20	.16	.11	.14	.37	.36		
18 NPID	-.16	-.02	.14	.11	.09	.04	.18	.18	.08	.02	.18	.19	.13	.14	.38	.38	.76	
19 CI	-.14	.02	.13	.09	.17	.09	.24	.22	.34	.03	.30	.28	.24	.41	.63	.68	.57	.57

.11 = p < .05   .14 = p < .01.

1. Sex=(Male=1, Female=0);   2. Race=(White=0, Others=1);   3. F.E.=Father's Education;   4. M.E.= Mother's Education;   5. Out Org=No. of Outside Organizations;   6. Sci/H=No. of Science/Health Projects;   7. N-Achi=Non-academic Achievement;   8. H.Job=Health-related Job Experience; 9. C.R.= Rank in Class;   10. No. HS=No. in High School Class;   11. A.T.S.=Admission Test Score; 12. R.R.=Reference Ratings;   13. R.R.D.=Reference Rec. Decision;   14. DAR=DAR Category; 15. PIR=Physician Interview Ratings;   16. PID=Physician Interview Decision;   17. NPIR= Non-physic. Interview Ratings;   18. NPID=Non-physic. Interview Decision;   19. CI-Council Index.

97

correlation in 1974 than in 1973, but they remained in approximately the same relative position.

The significant correlation of Council Index and race, which was present in 1972 but not in 1973, was again a negligible factor (.02). However, the intercorrelation matrix for the 1972, 1973, and 1974 applicants shows a significant correlation between race and admission test score (r = -.50, -.32 and -.32). Whether this finding indicates that the tests are culturally biased or that the applicant pool is a biased sample of the high school population is unclear. However, it seems that the minority applicant's opportunity for selection is jeopardized when admission test data are included in the information discussed by the Council on Selection at the time of vote.

Before the 1975 selection year, Council members reviewed the selection goals for the University of Missouri-Kansas City School of Medicine. In addition to selecting candidates who demonstrated competency and qualities of a caring physician, the Council decided to also consider, as a priority, students who were members of groups underrepresented in the medical profession or who were from areas under-served by the medical profession. Reviewing the experiences of the three prior years (1972, 1973, 1974) showed that eliminating a potential bias (aptitude test scores in the case of black applicants) was not sufficient to markedly increase the number of black students accepted into the UMKC School of Medicine. In 1972, there had been 20 black applicants in a total pool of 346 (5.8 percent). In 1973, there were 26 of 375 (6.9 percent), and in 1974, 27 of 427 (6.3 percent). The acceptance rate improved slightly from 5 blacks in a class of 72 (6.9%) in 1972 to 6 blacks in a class of 72 (8.3%) in 1973, and 7 blacks in a class of 72 (9.7%) in 1974 (See Table 4). Clearly, some type of affirmative action program was required if greater numbers of blacks were to gain admission.

The Council on Selection first agreed to continue the practice of interviewing all applicants in DAR categories A and B and removing the specific course grades and test score data from the application folders prior to interview. In addition, an actuarial formula was developed by the staff members of the Office of Medical Education which gave weight to those selection variables which were found to have predictive validity for performance in the UMKC program. The formula included variables from the physician and non-physician interviews, references, non-academic achievement and job experience. Weight was also given to minority

Table 4

Numbers of Blacks Applying and Admitted to the University of Missouri-Kansas City School of Medicine

Year	Applicants		Accepted	
	N	Percent	N	Percent
1972	20	5.8	5	5.9
1973	26	6.9	6	8.3
1974	27	6.3	7	9.7
1975	32	7.0	9	12.5
1976	35	8.5	12	15.0

status (blacks, Mexican-Americans, and American Indians but
not Asians) and student residency in a non-metropolitan
county (by Census Bureau definition). The overall weight
amounted to 10 percent of the possible total score, but was
not expected to allow admission to unqualified applicants,
especially in view of the fact that only DAR category A and
B candidates were considered. Following interviews, appropriate application data were quantified, the weighted formula
was applied to the data, and resulting scores were rank
ordered to select the 1975 class. No meetings were held with
interviewers. These new procedures resulted in an acceptance
rate for black applicants of 12.5% (9 in a class of 72).
There were 32 black applicants in the pool of 455, or 7.8%
in 1975.

To select the class to enter in the Fall of 1976, the
Council returned to the practice of having interviewers
attend meetings at which applicants were reviewed and voted
upon. A small weighting factor was then added to the Council
Index score of all minority and rural applicants who received
a Council Index of 4.0 or higher (on the scale of 1 to 5).
There were 12 blacks offered admission to a class of 80,
or 15 percent in 1976. The 1976 applicant pool had 35 blacks
in the total group of 413, or 8.5%. Data for 1972-1976 are
given in Table 4. In 1975, there was a single-order correlation of .10 between race and Council Index, mildly favoring
non-whites. In 1976, this single-order correlation between
race and Council Index was .01. The most significant correlation with the Council Index continued to be the two interviews, both ratings and recommended decisions, closely
followed by references and non-academic achievement. This
pattern has been constant since 1973.

Conclusion

To offer admission to those high school graduates deem-
ed most suited for the program of medical education at the
University of Missouri-Kansas City, the school's Council on
Selection initiated a policy change in its admissions procedure beginning with the 1973 entering class. The Council set
a minimum cutting score on high school rank in class and admission test scores to determine those applicants who would
be interviewed and considered for a place in the entering
class. A candidate's academic achievement was not revealed
to the members of the selection group as they interviewed,
discussed, and voted upon each applicant. Instead, evidence
of leadership, motivation for entering medicine, range of
interests, and interpersonal skills were given serious
consideration.

This policy change clearly resulted in admission to the University's Medical program of students who received high-ratings on non-academic criteria. Evaluation of the new admissions policy found that discrimination against non-whites in the admission process, which was present in 1972, was not a factor in subsequent years in which the new policy approach was implemented. A third, and perhaps most important, conclusion is that eliminating discrimination was a necessary but not a sufficient method to bring about a substantial increase in the number of blacks admitted to this school of medicine. To further accomplish this goal, it is also necessary to take specific affirmative action; namely, weighting for minority status.

The authors recently discussed the UMKC admission procedure described here with admissions officers at Howard University College of Medicine and Meharry Medical College. We sought to learn if these schools had considered or implemented a similar policy of emphasizing non-cognitive characteristics of applicants. We learned that in both institutions admission policies follow traditional lines, in that the criteria of undergraduate grade point averages and scores on the Medical College Admission Test are heavily weighted. Although all students invited for interviews to these medical schools have met and agreed upon level of prior academic performance that was thought to be compatible with success in the program, their specific course grades and scores on the MCAT are included in the application information provided interviewers and admission committee members. We would urge these and other institutions to consider the policy followed at the University of Missouri-Kansas City School of Medicine.

References

Burgess, M. M.
  1972   "Predicting performance in the first year of a six-year medical school program." Journal of Medical Education 47:968-969.

Burgess, M.M., E.V. Calkins and J.M. Richards Jr.
  1972   "The structured interview: a selection device." Psychological Reports 31:867-877.

Calkins, E.V., T.L. Willoughby and C.L. Smith
  1976   "Non-cognitive selection variables as predictors of student performance in a combined baccalaureate-medical program." Paper presented at the annual meeting of AERA, San Francisco, California.

Char, W.F., J.F. McDermott Jr., W.F. Hansen and J.M. Hansen
    1975   "Interviewing, motivation and clinical judgment."
            Journal of Medical Education 50:192-194.

D'Costa, A., P. Bashook, P. Elliot, R. Jarecky, W. Leavell,
D. Prieto and W. Sedlacek
    1974   Simulated Minority Admissions Exercise: Partici-
            pants Workbook. Washington, D.C.: Association
            of Medical Colleges.

Gough, H.G.
    1967   "Non-intellectual factors in the selection and
            evaluation of medical students." Journal of
            Medical Education 42:642-649.

Gough, H.G. and W.B. Hall
    1975   "The prediction of academic and clinical perfor-
            mance in medical school." Research in Higher
            Education 3:301-313.

Holland, J.L.
    1967   "The prediction of academic and non-academic
            accomplishment," in Proceedings of the Invita-
            tional Conference on Testing Problems 44-51.
            Princeton, N.J.: Educational Testing Service.

Holland, J.L. and R.C. Nichols
    1964   "Prediction of academic and extracurricular
            achievements in college." Journal of Educa-
            tional Psychology 55:55-65.

Holland, J.L. and J.M. Richards, Jr.
    1965   "Academic and non-academic accomplishment corre-
            lated?" Journal of Educational Psychology. 56:
            164-174.

Linn, R.L.
    1973   "Fair test use in selection." Review of Educa-
            tional research. 43:139-161.

Murden, R., G.M. Galloway, J.C. Reid and J.M. Colwill
    1978   "Academic and personal predictors of clinical
            success in medical school." Journal of Medical
            Education 53:711-719.

Poorman, D.H.
    1975   "Medical school applicant: a study of the admis-
            sions interview." Journal of the Kansas Medical
            Society 76:298-301.

Price, P.B., E.G. Lewis, G.C. Loughmiller, D.E. Nelson,
S.L. Murray and C.W. Taylor
    1971   "Attributes of a good practicing physician."
           Journal of Medical Education. 46:229-146.

Richards, J.M. Jr., C.W. Taylor and P.B. Price
    1962   "The prediction of medical intern performance."
           Journal of Applied Psychology 46:142-146.

Schwartzman, A.E., R.C. Hunter and J.G. Lohrenz
    1962   "Factors related to medical school achievement."
           Journal of Medical Education 37:749-759.

Willoughby, T.L., L. Gammon and H.J. Jones
    1979   "Correlates of clinical performance in medical
           schools." Journal of Medical Education 54:453-
           460.

Wilson, V.L.
    1974   Medical School Admission Requirements 1975-1976.
           Washington, D.C.: Association of American
           Medical Colleges.

Wingard, J.R. and J.W. Williamson
    1973   "Grades as predictors of physicians' career per-
           formance: an evaluative literature review."
           Journal of Medical Education 48:311-322.

Section III
Institutional Enrollment Statuses, Academic Experiences, and Career Aspirations of Blacks in Higher Education: Overview

Section III of the volume focuses on the current status of black enrollment in various types of institutions, their degree attainment, academic experiences and **career** aspirations. The future needs and direction of blacks in higher education cannot be determined without some knowledge of their current conditions and experiences. The first chapter by Gail Thomas, James Mingle and James McPartland gives a descriptive trend analysis of the enrollment, segregation and degree attainment statuses of blacks at various levels of higher education. The next two chapters by Walter Allen and William Boyd examine the academic achievement, aspirations and social experiences of black students in predominantly white institutions. Very little is known about the internal conditions of minorities in higher education; these chapters help narrow the void.

The fourth chapter by James Tschechtelin also addresses a critical topic--the experiences of blacks in community colleges. Extensive research is needed on blacks in community colleges, given their high enrollment. Tschechtelin focuses on the community college system in the state of Maryland and the matriculation and experiences of blacks and whites in these institutions. The last chapter in this section by Jomills Braddock, investigates the relationship between black and white students' career orientations and their potential occupational payoffs.

8

Recent Trends in Racial Enrollment, Segregation, and Degree Attainment in Higher Education*

GAIL E. THOMAS, JAMES R. MINGLE, and JAMES M. McPARTLAND ⎯⎯⎯⎯⎯⎯⎯⎯

Introduction

Educational researchers and administrators have some knowledge about the access of blacks to undergraduate institutions and factors which affect their transition from high school to college. Studies by Alexander Astin (1975; 1977) and Howard University researchers (Institute for the Study of Educational Policy, 1976) clearly show that black students are disproportionately overrepresented in two-year colleges and underrepresented in major four-year colleges and universities. Also, investigations of factors affecting the access of blacks to college have identified student educational expectations, high school grades and class rank, curriculum placement, family status and standardized test performance as important variables influencing the access of blacks to college. Less is known about the access of blacks to graduate and professional schools and the extent to which they are successful in completing their schooling at various levels in higher education. Also limited knowledge exists on the extent to which blacks and whites remain segregated in higher education after the Adams decision which held that segregation in public higher education is unconstitutional.

Higher education segregation, black participation and degree attainment status are important issues in evaluating the extent to which blacks have achieved equality of opportunity in higher education. This chapter describes recent trends in black-white enrollment, segregation and degree attainment in undergraduate, graduate and professional institutions. Data reported are from the Office of Civil Rights 1972, 1974, and 1976 surveys of student racial enrollment data

* This research was supported by the United States National Institute of Education, Department of Education and the Southern Regional Educational Board, Atlanta, Georgia.

from all U.S. federally funded colleges and universities,
and from the U.S. Office of Education Higher Education
General Information Survey of degrees conferred in 1976-
1977.

Findings

Table 1 presents the total full-time enrollment of
blacks and whites in undergraduate, graduate and professional
institutions for the nation and for the four major geographic
regions of the country. At the national level, black undergraduate enrollment experienced a consistent increase from
1972 to 1976, with 327,498 full-time students enrolled in
1972, 349,698 in 1974 and 394,719 in 1976. Over the same
perios, white undergraduate full-time enrollment experienced
a small decrease, going from 3,758,777 in 1972 to 3,675,117
in 1974 and 3,627,184 in 1976.

At the graduate level, blacks also experienced an
increase in their share of the enrollment between 1972 and
1976, as the number of blacks enrolled increased slightly
and the number of whites enrolled decreased somewhat. At
professional institutions, both blacks and whites increased
their numbers enrolled from 1972 through 1976 with the rates
of black to white enrollment at the professional level
remaining about the same over the period.

Racial distributions across the geographic regions shown
in Table 1 indicate that blacks continue to be enrolled in
large proportions in the South, especially at the undergraduate level where more than half of the black student
enrollment is concentrated. These percentages of black
undergraduates enrolled in the South are close to the population proportion of school-aged blacks residing in the South;
in 1972, 54.3 percent of the black elementary and secondary
school students lived in the South (U.S. Bureau of the Census,
1976, Table 217). The proportion of black graduate and professional students in the South is somewhat smaller, reach-
ing about 42 percent in each year for graduate students and
between 39 and 41 percent for professional students.

Table 2 presents trends in segregation, or the extent of
racial isolation that existed between blacks and white full-
time students in four-year colleges and graduate and professional institutions in 1972, 1974 and 1976.

The segregation index employed measures the degree of
racial separation among students, standardized for the
availability of minority and white students in a given region
and postsecondary level. The index consists of two compo-

Table 1

Percentage Distribution of Full-Time
Enrollment of Blacks and Whites in
Undergraduate, Graduate and Professional
Institutions by Region, 1972-1976

Four-Year

Region	1972 Blk.	1972 Wht.	1974 Blk.	1974 Wht.	1976 Blk.	1976 Wht.
NE[a]	17.2	24.5	18.2	25.9	16.9	24.9
MW	20.3	31.7	20.8	29.5	20.4	29.9
S	55.7	28.2	53.7	27.6	55.8	28.6
W	6.8	15.6	7.3	17.0	6.8	16.3
Nation (100.0% =)	(327,498)	(3,758,777)	(349,698)	(3,675,117)	(394,719)	(3,627,184)

Graduate

Region	1972 Blk.	1972 Wht.	1974 Blk.	1974 Wht.	1976 Blk.	1976 Wht.
NE	21.3	23.7	20.4	26.0	18.8	24.4
MW	22.5	27.9	27.4	30.0	26.8	27.7
S	42.4	27.1	41.5	25.1	42.2	27.0
W	13.8	21.3	10.7	18.9	12.2	21.0
Nation (100.0% =)	(21,548)	(373,109)	(22,091)	(361,605)	(22,084)	(341,971)

Continued

Table 1 Continued

Percentage Distribution of Full-Time
Enrollment of Blacks and Whites in
Undergraduate, Graduate and Professional
Institutions by Region, 1972-1976

Region	Professional					
	1972		1974		1976	
	Blk.	Wht.	Blk.	Wht.	Blk.	Wht.
NE	24.9	24.0	21.8	22.3	21.9	23.2
MW	23.6	32.4	27.3	31.2	26.4	32.3
S	39.8	30.2	38.8	29.9	41.0	29.0
W	11.7	13.4	12.1	16.1	10.7	15.4
Nation (100.0% =)	(8,688)	(166,822)	(9,284)	(174,504)	(10,029)	(198,015)

a
Northeast (NE) = CT, DE, ME, MA, NH, NJ, NY, PA, RI, VT
Midwest (MW) = IL, IN, LA, KS, MI, MN, MO, NE, ND, OH, SD, WI
South   (S) = AL, AR, DC, FL, GA, KY, LA, MD, MS, NC, OK, SC, TN, TX, VA, WV
West   (W) = AK, AZ, CA, CO, HI, ID, MT, NV, NM, OR, VT, WA, WY

nents. The first component is the actual amount of racial
separation experienced by the minority students, or the
"percent white in the school attended by the average minority
student." The second component is the expected racial separation that would be experienced by minority students if the
available minority and white students were randomly distributed among the schools, or the percentage of all students
who are white. These two components are used in the segregation index to measure the extent to which the actual
percentage of white students in the school attended by the
average minority student departs from the percentage expected
if students were randomly distributed.

The index will have a value of 100 whenever white and
minority students attend entirely separate schools; it will
have a value of 0 whenever the actual racial composition of
the schools is the same as a random allocation of the
students would produce. Index values between 0 and 100
measure the degree of segregation for the particular region
and type of school under consideration. The larger the value
of the index, the more segregated or "racially isolated" is
the school population of white and minority students. Additional information concerning the index is presented in a
later chapter by Thomas, McPartland and Daiger.

Table 1 indicated that blacks had gained greater representation in four-year colleges than in graduate and professional institutions. However, despite the greater representation of blacks at the undergraduate level, Table 2 shows
that four-year colleges were more segregated than the nation's
graduate and professional schools in 1972, 1974, and 1976.
Within the nation, Southern public and private institutions
remained more segregated throughout all three time periods
than public and private institutions in the ramaining regions.
However, in the nation as a whole, private colleges and
universities were more segregated in 1972, 1974, and 1976
than public institutions. Regional comparisons in Table 2
show that segregation in the Northeast and West at all levels
of higher education and in Midwestern graduate and professional schools increased between 1972 and 1976. This is
primarily attributed to an increase in segregation in public
institutions in these regions. However, in the South,
segregation in all institutions decreased between these time
periods. Therefore, while the South remained three to four
times as segregated as any other region, it made more progress than other regions in reducing segregation between
1972 and 1976.

Table 2

Segregation Indices for Full-Time Enrollment
in Four-Year Colleges and Graduate and
Professional Institutions by Region and
Control, 1972-1976

Four-Year

Region	1972 Pub.	1972 Pvt.	All	1974 Pub.	1974 Pvt.	All	1976 Pub.	1976 Pvt.	All
NE[a]	14.0	4.7	9.8	12.1	15.3	14.4	23.0	7.3	16.3
MW	10.0	13.7	10.7	12.5	19.7	14.2	11.1	18.7	12.9
S	56.6	68.4	59.7	52.3	61.1	54.6	45.6	61.4	50.0
W	8.0	7.4	7.4	9.3	10.1	9.5	16.8	10.7	16.1
Nation	32.4	35.2	33.0	32.1	32.5	31.9	30.4	33.8	31.3

Graduate - Professional

Region	1972 Pub.	1972 Pvt.	All	1974 Pub.	1974 Pvt.	All	1976 Pub.	1976 Pvt.	All
NE	5.3	2.8	3.8	3.7	5.2	3.8	3.7	2.7,	4.0
MW	1.6	4.3	3.2	4.3	8.0	4.2	2.9	13.4	8.2
S	26.5	42.7	31.7	21.7	36.2	30.8	19.1	29.1	23.3
W	2.7	6.1	3.6	4.0	5.5	3.9	7.2	3.8	6.7
Nation	11.6	16.8	13.7	9.5	18.0	13.6	10.1	13.8	12.0

a/Northeast (NE) = CI, DE, ME, MA, NH, NJ, NY, PA, RI, VT
Midwest (MW) = IL, IN, LA, KS, MI, MN, MO, NE, ND, OH, SD, WI
South (S) = AL, AR, DC, FL, GA, KY, LA, MD, MS, NC, OK, SC, TN, TX, VA, WV
West (W) = AK, AZ, CA, CO, HI, ID, MT, NV, NM, OR, VT, WA, WY

The remaining five tables (3-7) present distributions
showing the degree completion status of blacks at various
levels of higher education and by fields of study in predominantly black and predominantly white institutions. Beginning
with Table 3, we see that in 1976-77 blacks accounted for 6.7
percent of the total associate, bachelor's, master's, first
professional, and doctoral degrees awarded by U.S. colleges
and universities. The degree recipient rate for blacks
during this period was highest at the associate level
(8.3 percent), and lowest at the doctoral level (3.8 percent).
At the baccalaureate level, blacks accounted for 6.3 percent
of all bachelor's degrees received that year. Blacks made
up 11.5 percent of the total population of the U.S. in 1975
and 10.2 percent of the undergraduate enrollment (i.e., two
and four-year colleges) in 1976. In the South the percentage
of degrees received by blacks was higher than for the nation
at all levels. This reflected the higher population level of
blacks (18.8 percent of the total population) and the presence of the predominantly black institutions in the South.

The continuing importance of predominantly black institutions in producing black graduates is further revealed in
Table 4. Predominantly black institutions awarded 39.8 percent of all degrees received by black students in the United
States in 1975-76. These institutions also accounted for a
significant percentage of the master's (24.4 percent) and
first professional degrees (20.4 percent) earned by blacks.
Table 4 also shows that Southern black institutions were
the major producers of black degree recipients at all levels
of higher education. These institutions awarded 69 percent
of the BA degrees, over 40 percent of the MA and first professional degrees, and 8 percent of the doctoral degrees
earned by blacks.

Table 5 presents the level and distribution of blacks
among major fields of study at the baccalaureate and master's
levels. Black representation at the baccalaureate level is
highest in the fields of public affairs (9.7 percent of all
graduates), education (8.9 percent), and social sciences
(8.8 percent). It is lowest in the fields of agriculture
(1.4 percent), theology (2.2 percent), engineering (2.8
percent), foreign languages (3.0 percent), and the physical
sciences (3.1 percent). When the distribution of blacks
among fields is compared to that of whites, it reveals
five fields in which blacks are more likely to enroll
relative to their numbers than whites--business and management, education, psychology, public affairs, and social
sciences.

Table 3

Degrees Awarded to Black Students by Level,
United States and the South
1976-77

| | United States | | | South[a] | | South as a |
	Total	Percent of All Degrees	Total	Percent of All Degrees		Percent of U.S.
Associate[b]	36,409	8.3	12,899	11.4		35.4
Bachelor's	58,700	6.3	28,029	11.2		47.7
Master's	21,041	6.6	9,224	11.4		43.8
First Professional	2,537	3.9	748	4.8		29.5
Doctorate	1,253	3.8	322	4.4		25.9
Grand Total	119,940	6.7	51,222	10.9		42.7

[a]The South includes Alabama, Arkansas, Florida, Georgia, Kentucky, Louisiana, Maryland, Mississippi, North Carolina, South Carolina, Tennessee, Texas, Virginia, and West Virginia.

[b]Associate includes degrees and other formal awards for curriculums of at least two years but less than four years.

Source: Unpublished data from the U.S. Office of Education, Higher Education General Information Survey (HEGIS XII), "Degrees and Other Formal Awards Conferred Between July 1, 1976 and June 30, 1977."

Table 4

Degrees Awarded to Black Students
At Predominantly Black Institutions
And Percent of all Black Degree Recipients,
United States and the South[a]
1975-76

| | United States | | | South | |
	Total Black Degrees in PBIs	Percent of All Black Degrees	Total in PBIs	Percent of All Black Degrees
Bachelor's	23,581	39.8	19,843	69.4
Master's	4,971	24.4	4,265	47.9
First Professional	549	20.4	337	46.6
Doctorate	50	4.1	26	8.1

[a]Predominantly black institutions are those with greater than 50% black enrollment (Total Headcount Fall 1976).

Source: James R. Mingle, Degree Output in the South, 1975-76: Distribution by Race (Atlanta: Southern Regional Education Board, 1978).

Table 5

Bachelor's and Master's Degrees Awarded to Black Students by Field, Percent of Total Degrees, and Percent Distribution Among Fields for U.S. Blacks and Whites, 1976-77

	Bachelor's				Master's			
	Total Awarded Blacks	Percent of Degrees Awarded in Each Field	Percentage Distribution Among Fields Black	Percentage Distribution Among Fields White	Total Awarded Blacks	Percent of Degrees Awarded in Each Field	Percentage Distribution Among Fields Black	Percentage Distribution Among Fields White
Agriculture	309	1.4	.5	2.5	51	1.4	.2	1.1
Architecture	303	3.3	.5	1.0	162	5.0	.8	1.0
Area Studies	97	3.3	.2	.3	55	5.6	.3	.3
Biological Sciences	2,415	4.5	4.1	5.9	206	2.9	1.0	2.3
Business & Management	10,001	6.5	17.0	16.5	1,625	3.5	7.7	14.8
Communications	1,522	6.6	2.6	2.6	167	5.4	.8	1.0
Computer & Information Sciences	361	5.6	.6	.7	67	2.4	.3	.8
Education	12,943	8.9	22.0	15.5	12,700	10.0	60.4	40.3
Engineering	1,385	2.8	2.4	5.2	240	1.5	1.1	4.3
Fine & Applied Arts	1,711	4.1	2.9	4.7	261	3.0	1.2	2.9
Foreign Languages	429	3.0	.7	1.5	99	3.1	.5	1.0
Health Professions	3,136	5.4	5.3	6.4	657	5.0	3.1	4.2
Home Economics	1,054	6.0	1.8	1.9	110	4.7	.5	.8
Law	21	3.8	.0	.1	26	1.7	.1	.5
Letters	2,223	4.7	3.8	5.3	388	3.7	1.8	3.5

Table 5 Continued

Bachelor's and Master's Degrees Awarded to Black Students by Field, Percent of Total Degrees, and Percent Distribution Among Fields for U.S. Blacks and Whites, 1976-77

	Bachelor's				Master's			
	Total Awarded Blacks	Percent of Degrees Awarded in each Field	Percentage Distribution Among Fields		Awarded Blacks	Percent of Degrees Awarded in each Field	Percentage Distribution Among Fields	
			Black	White			Black	White
Library Science	69	8.8	.1	.1	388	5.1	1.8	2.5
Mathematics	712	5.0	1.2	1.6	133	3.6	.6	1.1
Military Science	37	3.7	.1	.1	3	7.0	.0	.0
Physical Sciences	692	3.1	1.2	2.5	94	1.8	.4	1.6
Psychology	3,221	6.7	5.5	5.1	506	6.1	2.4	2.7
Public Affairs	3,582	9.7	6.1	3.8	1,876	9.5	8.9	6.1
Social Sciences	10,360	8.8	17.6	12.4	969	6.3	4.6	4.6
Theology	132	2.2	.2	.7	64	2.0	.3	1.0
Interdisciplinary Studies	1,985	5.9	3.4	3.7	194	4.3	.9	1.5
Totals	58,700	6.3	100.0[a]	100.0	21,041	6.6	100.0	100.0

a/Percentages may not add to 100 due to rounding.

Source: James R. Mingle. Degrees Awarded in the Nation and the South: 1976-77 (Atlanta: Southern Regional Education Board, 1979).

117

The representation of blacks among graduates at the master's level reveals similar patterns to those found at the bachelor's level, but the distribution is overwhelmingly concentrated in a few fields. Only in the fields of education and public affairs did blacks represent close to 10 percent of the graduates in 1976-77. They accounted for less than 2 percent of the graduates in the fields of agriculture, engineering, and the physical sciences. Reflecting past traditional employment opportunities, 60 percent of the black graduates at the master's level received their degrees in the field of education. If we consider three fields--education, public affairs, and business management, nearly 8 out of every 10 black graduates at the master's level are accounted for.

In the 1976-77 academic year, only 1,253 blacks received doctorates nationwide. The predominance of education as a field of study among blacks is evident in Table 6. Approximately 55 percent of all doctorates granted to blacks was in education as compared to 24.6 percent among whites. Psychology and the social sciences were the only two other fields of study where the number of doctorates received by blacks exceeded one hundred. In the field of computer and information sciences, one doctorate was awarded to a black; 10 were awarded in math and 23 in engineering.

Distributions of first professional degrees among fields are also shown in Table 6. As noted previously, blacks accounted for only 3.9 percent of the total first professional degrees granted in 1976-77. Like whites, law was the field of study in which over half of the blacks obtained a professional degree. Blacks represented 5.2 percent of the degrees awarded in medicine, which was the second most important field for blacks. Of the major areas of study at the first professional level (those with greater than a thousand annual graduates) blacks were most underrepresented in veterinary medicine (constituting 1.8 percent of all graduates) than any other fields. Of the 28 graduates receiving the D.V.M. in 1976-77, all but 5 were graduates of Tuskegee Institute, a predominantly black instutution, in Alabama.

In the previous section, the major role of the predominantly black institutions in the production of black graduates (especially for black students in the South) was discussed. Table 7 compares the distribution of black graduates among fields of study in predominantly black institutions and predominantly white institutions.

Table 6

Doctoral and First Professional Degrees Awarded to Black Students by Field,
Percent of Total Degrees, and Percent Distribution Among Fields for
U.S. Blacks and Whites, 1976-77

	Total Awarded Blacks	Percent of All Degrees	Percentage Distribution Among Fields	
			Black	White
Doctoral:				
Agricultural	11	1.2	.9	2.2
Architecture	8	11.0	.6	.2
Area Studies	6	3.9	.5	.5
Biological Sciences	52	1.5	4.2	10.6
Business and Management	13	1.5	1.0	2.5
Communications	1	.6	.1	.5
Computer & Information Sciences	1	.5	.1	.6
Education	685	8.6	54.7	24.6
Engineering	23	.9	1.8	5.8
Fine and Applied Arts	21	3.2	1.7	2.2
Foreign Languages	14	1.9	1.1	2.3
Health Professions	14	2.6	1.1	1.6
Home Economics	6	3.8	.5	.5
Law	2	3.3	.2	.1
Letters	60	2.7	4.8	7.2
Library Science	3	4.0	.2	.2
Mathematics	10	1.2	.8	2.3
Physical Sciences	45	1.3	3.6	9.8
Psychology	105	3.8	8.4	9.2

Continued

119

Table 6 Continued

Doctoral and First Professional Degrees Awarded to Black Students by Field,
Percent of Total Degrees, and Percent Distribution Among Fields for
U.S. Blacks and Whites, 1976-77

	Total Awarded Blacks	Percent of All Degrees	Percentage Distribution Among Fields	
			Blacks	White
Public Affairs	22	6.6	1.8	1.0
Social Sciences	117	3.1	9.3	11.5
Theology	21	2.1	1.7	3.5
Interdisciplinary Studies	13	4.3	1.0	.9
Total	1,253	3.8	100.0a	100.0
First Professional:				
Dentistry	204	3.9	8.0	8.0
Medicine	710	5.2	28.0	20.7
Optometry	15	1.6	0.6	1.5
Osteopathic Medicine	7	0.8	0.3	1.4
Pharmacy	10	1.9	0.4	0.6
Podiatry	11	2.3	0.4	0.8
Veterinary Medicine	28	1.8	1.1	2.6
Chiropractic	2	0.1	0.1	2.1
Law	1,349	3.9	53.2	53.8
Theological Professional-General	200	3.7	7.9	8.5
Other	1	4.3	0.0	0.0
Total	2,537	3.9	100.0	100.0

a/ Percentages may not add to 100 due to rounding.

Source: Unpublished data from the U.S. Office of Education, Higher Education General Information Survey (HEGIS XII), "Degree & Other Formal Awards Conferred Between July 1, 1976 & June 30, 1977."

Table 7

Percentage Distribution of Black Degree Recipients by Field and Level
In Predominantly White and Predominantly Black Institutions, 1975-76

	Bachelor's		Master's & Doctoral	
	White Institutions	Black Institutions	White Institutions	Black Institutions
Agriculture	0.5	0.7	0.3	1.0
Architecture & Design	0.3	0.1	0.4	0.1
Area Studies	0.2	--	--	--
Biological Sciences	3.3	4.3	1.2	1.3
Business & Management	15.2	20.5	4.3	4.1
Communications	2.6	0.9	0.3	0.2
Computer and Information Sciences	0.7	0.5	0.2	0.1
Education	24.9	33.0	70.9	78.7
Engineering	1.8	2.2	0.8	0.2
Fine & Applied Arts	2.9	1.3	0.9	0.3
Foreign Languages	0.7	0.5	0.3	0.3
Health Professions	7.9	2.7	3.1	0.3
Home Economics	2.0	2.1	0.5	0.3
Law	0.1	--	0.1	--
Letters	3.4	3.2	1.4	1.7
Library Science	0.3	0.1	2.0	2.1
Mathematics	1.6	1.8	0.5	0.5
Physical Sciences	1.0	1.2	0.5	1.0
Psychology	4.8	2.9	1.3	0.9
Public Affairs	6.5	3.9	7.0	2.5
Social Sciences	15.8	17.3	3.2	4.2

Continued

Table 7 Continued

Percentage Distribution of Black Degree Recipients by Field and Level
in Predominantly White and Predominantly Black Institutions, 1975-76

| | Bachelor's | | Master's & Doctoral | |
	White Institutions	Black Institutions	White Institutions	Black Institutions
Theology	0.3	0.4	0.3	0.1
Interdisciplinary Studies	3.3	0.4	0.5	--
Total	100.0[a]	100.0	100.0	100.0

a/ Percentages may not add to 100 due to rounding.

Source: James R. Mingle, Degree Output in the South, 1975-76: Distribution by Race
(Atlanta: Southern Regional Education Board, 1978).

A number of observations are important. First, black students in black institutions are more likely to receive their bachelor's degrees in the field of education than blacks in white institutions. This reflects the strong teacher education tradition of the traditionally black institutions. Table 7 also shows that black institutions produce substantially smaller proportions of bachelor's degrees for blacks than do white institutions in the health professions and the public affairs field, but significantly greater percentages in the fields of biological sciences, business and management, engineering, and social sciences.

At the graduate level the higher proportions of black students in black institutions earning degrees in education than their counterparts in white institutions is evident (nearly 8 out of every 10 graduate degrees awarded in black institutions are in the field of education). But, black institutions awarded higher proportions of their graduate degrees to black students in the physical and social sciences than white institutions. As with the bachelor's level, significantly lower percentages of black students in predominantly black institutions are earning graduate degrees in the health professions and the field of public affairs than black students in white institutions.

Summary and Conclusions

For the major part of this decade, black students have approximated parity in higher educational access at the undergraduate level only, not at the graduate and professional levels. Racial isolation of blacks and whites remained quite prevalent between 1972 and 1976, despite the passage of Adams. Segregation was particularly high in four-year colleges where blacks had gained the greatest access. In addition, racial segregation at all levels of higher education was greater in the South than in any other regions in the country. However, the South, having further to come, made more progress in this decade in reducing higher educational segregation than any other region.

Data on degree attainment status indicated that blacks have been primarily recipients of undergraduate degrees as opposed to graduate and professional degrees. The predominantly black institutions, particularly those in the South, continue to play a major role in educating blacks at all levels of higher education. These institutions awarded over one-third of all degrees earned by blacks in the U.S. in 1975-76.

Black representation at the BA and MA level was highest in public affairs, education and the social sciences and lowest in engineering, the physical sciences, foreign language, and agriculture. The high concentration of blacks in education was also evident at the doctoral level where over 50 percent of the degrees earned by blacks was in education, with a disproportionate percentage of these degrees awarded by black institutions.

Overall, the descriptive data in this chapter suggest that greater progress must be made in the decade of the 1980s if blacks are going to achieve the level of parity and diversity of higher educational opportunity anticipated by the drive for equality of educational opportunity and the recent Adams mandate. Higher education administrators and federal and state officials must accelerate their efforts to aid predominantly black and white institutions in achieving not only a greater racial balance among their student bodies, but also in providing all of their students a better quality and more diverse education necessary for today's job market. In addition, greater efforts must be made to increase the access and retention of blacks at the graduate, and particularly at the professional level, where black enrollment has declined. It is indeed these more advanced levels of higher education that constitute the major basis for producing a critical mass of black professionals which has yet to become visible.

References

Astin, A. W.
   1975   Preventing students from Dropping Out.
          San Francisco: Jossey-Bass.

   1977   "Equal access to postsecondary education:
          myth or reality?"   UCLA Educator 19 (Spring),
          8-17.

Institute for the Study of Educational Policy
   1976   Equal Education Opportunity for Blacks in U.S.
          Higher Education An Assessment.   Washington, D.C.:
          Howard University Press.

Mingle, J.R.
    1978   Degree Output in the South, 1975-1976:
            Distribution by Race. Atlanta: Southern
            Regional Education Board.

    1979   Degrees Awarded in the Nation and the South:
            1976-1977. Atlanta: Southern Regional
            Education Board.

U. S. Bureau of the Census
    1976   Statistical Abstract of the U.S.. Washington,
            D.C.: U.S. Government Printing Office.

9

Correlates of Black Student Adjustment, Achievement, and Aspirations at a Predominantly White Southern University *

WALTER R. ALLEN

Introduction

Last year marked the twenty-fifth anniversary of the Supreme Court's historic decision outlawing racial segregation in the nation's public schools. Over the ensuing years, a generation of black students has attended school relieved of the burdens of de jure (if not de facto) segregation. Much has been said and written about these black students' experiences in desegregated schools. For the most part, however, this attention has focused on the elementary and secondary school years. As successive waves of black students have completed their high school education and moved into post-secondary settings, more attention is now focused on post-secondary desegregation processes. While black student experiences and outcomes in desegregated post-secondary institutions have been relatively neglected research topics, research dealing with post-secondary desegregation processes in predominantly white, southern universities is even more rare.

This chapter uses a causal modelling framework to identify factors that influence black students' adjustments, achievements, and aspirations at the University of North Carolina, Chapel Hill. It asks how black students are faring in an institution once among the most racially-exclusionary in the country. Moreover, this question is posed against a backdrop provided by the Department of Health, Education and Welfare's pending litigation charging the University of North Carolina with the continued operation of a racially-segregated system in violation of federal law.

*Helpful comments on early drafts from the following persons are gratefully acknowledged: Bruce Hare, Genna Rae McNeil, Rupert Nacoste, and Clarence Thornton. Kris Anderson assisted with the analysis.

Black Students on White Campuses

Studies of black students attending predominantly white post-secondary institutions commonly incorporate one or a combination of three central concerns regarding black students: 1) their social and economic characteristics, 2) their levels of adjustment in predominantly white institutions, and 3) their academic successes in these institutions. The literature's discussion of these topics implies a causal ordering among factors viewed as having definite implications for the experiences and outcomes of black students in desegregated post-secondary settings. In what is essentially a social-psychological model, student characteristics are assumed to determine student adjustment to the college setting, which in turn influences student performance. It is further assumed that black student academic achievements suffer because of the difficulties they experience adjusting to the foreign environments presented by white colleges. These models also assume that the colleges in question experience commensurate difficulties adjusting their norms, structures, and practices to incorporate black students. A major premise derived from this set of assumptions is that a poor fit exists between black students and predominantly white colleges or universities. Some of the literature on black students in white colleges is useful for determining the extent to which this premise is true.

Black college students are different from their white peers in several respects. The most notable differences are with respect to family backgrounds. On the average, the parents of black students have fewer years of education, earn less and work at lower status jobs than is true for white students (Bayer, 1972; Boyd, 1974). One outgrowth of these socioeconomic status inequities is a more pronounced need among black than white students for college financial aid (Bayer, 1972; Boyd, 1974). Black college students, as a rule, also score lower on college boards and are more often than whites from less academically strong high schools (Institute for the Study of Educational Policy-ISEP, 1976). Despite these social and economic disadvantages, black college students report aspirations that equal or exceed those of white students (Bayer, 1972; Gurin and Epps, 1975; Morris, 1979). Black students however, less often than whites, actually attain their educational and occupational aspirations. In addition, black and white students differ substantially in the types of colleges and major fields entered, with blacks being more heavily concentrated in two-year colleges, traditional major fields (e.g. education and the social sciences), and southern institutions (English and Settle, 1976; Thomas, 1980). Black college students also differ from whites in terms of their cultural orientations, lifestyles, behaviors, and values (Centra, 1970; Ballard, 1973).

Black students attending predominantly white colleges sometimes experience considerable adjustment difficulty. To be sure, many of their adjustment problems are common to all college students (Webster, Sedlacek and Miyares, 1979); but these students also face more specific problems. For instance, black students often find it necessary to create their own social and cultural networks given their exclusion (self- or other-imposed) from the wider university community. Such mechanisms in the form of fraternities/ sororities, friend-kin networks, black student organizations or black dorms perform vital support and mediation roles (Willie and McCord, 1973). The ability of black students to generate their own social activities, support networks, and political mechanisms is limited by scarcity of numbers (Keith, 1972; Reed, 1979). Of all problems faced by blacks on white campuses, the psychosocial ones arising from alienation and a lack of support from the general environment seem to be the most serious (Rosser, 1972). However, adjustment problems are also posed for black students by the academic environments which these schools provide. The usual difficulties associated with movement from high school into college are often amplified for black students by such factors as weak academic backgrounds, poor counseling, poor relationships with faculty, and strong feelings of alienation (Hedegard and Brown, 1969; Will et.al., 1973; Webster et.al., 1979).

Although some blacks at predominantly white colleges do adjust and are academically successful (Ballard, 1973; Boyd, 1977), many of these students are not as academically successful as their white peers. On the average, black students have higher attrition rates (DiCesare, 1972), lower grade point averages (Boyd, 1974), and lower enrollments in postgraduate programs (ISEP, 1976) than whites. These students also report more academic problems than white students (Willie et.al., 1973; Webster et.al., 1979) The academic difficulties of black students on white campuses are often compounded by the absence of remedial/tutorial programs and sufficient information exchange with whites, i.e., faculty and students (Boyd, 1974; Morris, 1979).

A previous study of black students at the University of North Carolina (UNC) suggested that their experiences were comparable to those of black students attending other predominantly white campuses around the nation. These students were dissatisfied with their overall educational experience, troubled by the limited numbers of blacks at all levels in

the university, disappointed by the campus social life,
exposed to racial discrimination, doing less well academically and in general disenchanted with the school (Kleinbaum
and Kleinbaum,1976). The purpose of this research was to
determine whether such conditions persist for black students
currently attending UNC.

Problem, Method and Data

This chapter reports findings from a more recent survey
of black students attending the University of North Carolina,
Chapel Hill. UNC was an ideal site for this study because
of its southern location and recent, rapid growth in black
student enrollments (50 percent increase from 1970 to 1978).
The purpose of the study was to identify and estimate the
relative importance of factors that influence black student
adjustment, achievement, and aspirations. The model which
guides this study is presented in Figure 1. A detailed discussion of variables and measurement is provided in the appendix. Causality flows from left to right in the research
model depicted in Figure 1. Student background variables
(sex, father's occupation, sibling education, mother's education and family structure) appear in the first panel of the
model. The second panel consists of factors related to high
school experience (percent black in high school and high
school grade-point average); and the third panel concerns
the students' perceived college support of black students.
The fourth panel of variables concerns black student interaction and involvement regarding various aspects of the
campus environment (campus race relations, relations with
professors and involvements with campus black support networks). The fifth panel considers student subjective states
(feelings of academic anxiety and alienation); and the final
panel focuses on student outcome variables (college satisfaction, academic performance and occupational aspirations).
The model, therefore, suggests that black student college
satisfaction, academic performance and occupational aspirations are influenced directly, and indirectly, by preceding
variables in the model. Multiple regression analysis is the
procedure used to evaluate the model.

The data for this study are from a Spring 1977 survey
of black undergraduates at the University of North Carolina,
Chapel Hill. One hundred thirty-five questionnaires, representing 16 percent of all black undergraduates enrolled at
that time, form the data base for this study. Access to a
College of Arts and Sciences computerized list of currently-
enrolled black undergraduates insured accurate sampling.
The mailed questionnaire, which took approximately half an

Illustration 1: Correlates of Black Student Adjustment, Achievement and Aspirations

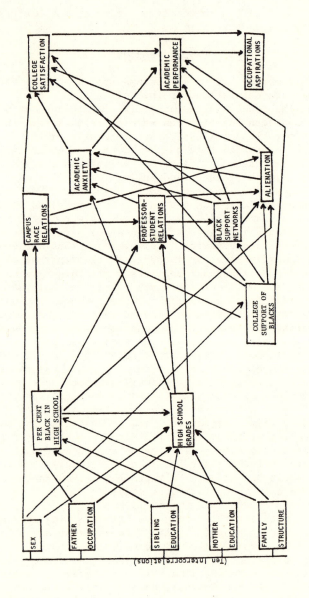

Note: Only the major paths of hypothesized causation are shown.

130

hour to complete, asked questions about student characteristics, problems and needs.

Findings

The correlation matrix displayed in Table 1 reveals
several interesting patterns. For example, occupational
aspirations are significantly higher among students having
better educated mothers, students from high schools with
high percentages of blacks and students with lower academic
anxiety. Student academic performance level is highest
where college satisfaction is high and feelings of alienation and academic anxiety are low. Students who evaluate
campus race relations and UNC's support of black students
positively are also more satisfied with college. On the
other hand, dissatisfaction with college is more common for
students having better-educated siblings, lower high school
GPAs, and who report more feelings of academic anxiety and
alienations.

While high student academic performance is associated
with high college satisfaction, neither variable seems to be
significantly related to student aspirations. As previously
found (Allen, 1978), Table 1 shows that black student
occupational aspirations are strongly related to mother's
educational attainment. Also students who attended high
schools with high percentages of blacks report high
aspirations and academic performance, although interestingly
enough, not high satisfaction with the college experience
at a predominantly white university. Finally, pronounced
feelings of alienation and academic anxiety are generally
detrimental to black student adjustment, achievement and
aspirations.

Other important patterns are also revealed by Table 1.
For instance, alienation is greater among students having
better educated siblings, higher high school grades, more
years in two-parent families and more academic anxiety.
Conversely, alienation is lower among students who have
better-employed fathers and a more positive evaluation of
campus race relations and college support of black students.
Students with less well educated mothers, less well employed
fathers and negative evaluations of UNC's racial atmosphere
and support of black students, report significantly higher
academic anxiety. Contrary to expectations, involvement in
black support networks does not increase among alienated
students. However, there is a slight tendency among students
with negative views of race relations, and a significant
tendency among those reporting negative experiences with
white professors, to be more involved in black support

Table 1
Correlation Matrix for Variables in Model
(N = 135)

	1	2	3	4	5	6	7	8	9	10	11	12	13	14	15
1. OCCASP															
2. ACDPERF	.07														
3. COLSAT	.01	.28*													
4. MED	.26*	.02	.05												
5. STBED	.14	.03	-.24*	.08											
6. FOCCP	.04	.10	-.04	.55*	.09										
7. HSGPA	.04	.12	-.20*	-.12	.14	.02									
8. % BLK	-.22*	.14	-.06	.05	-.16	.08	.17*								
9. FAMSTRUC	.14	.01	-.07	-.14	-.10	-.15	.12	.25*							
10. SEX	.14	.01	.06	-.06	-.19*	-.00	.08	-.01	.07						
11. RESP	.03	.16	.35*	-.23*	-.05	-.19*	-.06	-.14	-.03	.06					
12. RREL	.04	.02	.30*	.15	-.06	.11	-.05	-.15	-.13	.05	.26*				
13. SUPPT	.06	.02	-.12	.07	-.13	.06	.06	-.00	.07	.09	-.03	-.12			
14. ACDANX	-.20*	-.22*	-.37*	-.16*	-.07	-.15	.06	-.11	.08	.09	-.24*	-.16*	.02		
15. ALIEN	-.02	.21*	.30*	.14	-.21*	.20*	-.19*	-.03	-.27*	-.13	.25*	.19*	-.10	-.22	
16. PSREL	-.15	.06	.13	-.06	-.03	-.00	-.09	-.07	.06	-.02	.12	.43*	-.18*	-.10	.19*

*Significant at the .05 level or beyond.

1. OCCASP=Occupational Aspirations, 2. ACDPERF=Academic Performance, 3. COLSAT=College Satisfaction, 4. MED=Mother's Education, 5. SIBED=Sibling's Education, 6. FOCCP=Father's Occupation, 7. HSGPA= High School GPA, 8. % BLK=Percent Black in High School, 9. FAMSTRUC=Family Structure, 10. SEX=Sex, 11. RESP= College's Support of Blacks, 12. RREL= Race Relations, 13. SUPPT=Black Support Networks, 14. ACDANX=Academic Anxiety, 15. ALIEN=Alienation, 16. PSREL=Professor-Student Relations.

networks. Students with negative views of campus race
relations also got along less well with professors and felt
more alienated. No significant sex differences are revealed
in Table 1, although black women expressed stronger feelings
of alienation.

The multiple regression analyses summarized in Table 2
further explicate variable relationships in the model.
Together, the selected variables explained respectively 25%,
19%, and 35% of the variance in black student adjustments,
achievements and aspirations. With controls, mother's
education is the strongest predictor of student occupational
aspirations, and aspirations are higher for students with
better educated mothers. Percent black in high school is a
positive predictor of aspirations and academic performance,
while academic anxiety exerts a negative effect on these
latter variables. The importance of college satisfaction
for academic performance is amplified: contented students
are on the average, better students (or vice versa). The
importance of better educated siblings, better high school
grades, lower levels of alienation and greater percent black
in high school for better black student performance in college is also revealed by Table 2. Student academic anxiety
persists as the major predictor of satisfaction, with more
anxious students being less satisfied. A negative association between college satisfaction and sibling's educational
attainment is also confirmed. Students with positive views
of campus race relations and UNC's support of black students,
also tended to express greater satisfaction with college.

The model accounts for variance among intervening
variables with alternate degrees of success. It explains
sizeable percentages of the variance in feelings of alienation (31%) and professor-student relations (23%); medium
percentages in academic anxiety (17%) and race relations
(14%); and low percentages in involvement with black support
networks, evaluation of university supportive responses to
black students, high school GPA, and high school percent
black.

Table 2 also shows that students with positive views
of the university's support, better employed fathers, less
educated siblings and who are male, feel less alienated;
while students with the most positive views of campus race
relations get along better with their white professors.
Students who view university support of blacks positively
tend to have a positive evaluation of race relations and are
less anxious academically. Students who evaluate campus
race relations and their professors negatively are more
likely to be active in black support. Table 2 further shows

Table 2

Standardized Regression Coefficients for Model of Student
Adjustments, Achievements and Aspirations
(N=135)

Independent[a, b] Variables	Dependent Variables					
	% BLK	HSGPA	RESP	RREL	PSREL	SUPPT.
MED	.04	-.19	-.19	.19	-.16	.10*
SIBED	-.15	.20	-.03	-.09	.02	-.16
FOCCP	.11*	.11*	-.08	.06	.05	.05
FAMSTRUC	.26	.08	-.04	-.07	.12	.09
SEX	-.05	.10	.05	.03	-.05	.06
% BLK		.18	-.11	-.12	-.01	-.09
HSGPA			-.05	.03	-.10*	.07
RESP				.29	-.03	.03
RREL					.48*	-.10*
PSREL						-.15
SUPPT						
ALIEN						
ACDANX						
COLSAT						
ACDPERF						
R^2	.099	.101	.081	.139	.228	.084

* Coefficients twice standard error and larger than .10

[a] See Table 1 for complete variable names.

[b] Standard deviations are not reported for the sake of space but are available upon request.

134

Table 2: (Contined) Standardized Regression
Coefficient for Model of Student
Adjustments, Achievements and Aspirations

Independent[a] Variables	Dependent Variables				
	ALIEN	ACDANX	COLSAT	ACDPERF	OCCASP
MED	.08	-.13	.07	-.04	.29
SIBED	-.27*	-.11	-.21	.15*	.16
FOCCP	.21*	-.07	-.10*	.09	-.15
FAMSTRUC	-.24	.04	.02	.01	.17
SEX	-.16	.06	.07	.03	-.10
% BLK	.03	-.18	-.06	.14*	.21
HSGPA	-.08	.04	-.10*	.16*	-.10
RESP	.28	-.26	.18	.06	.09
RREL	-.04	-.06	.17	-.11	.15
PSREL	.16	-.05	-.06	.07	-.21
SUPPT	-.08	-.02	-.12	.08	.05
ALIEN		-.10*	-.11	.17*	-.00
ACDANX			-.30*	-.05	-.14
COLSAT				-.30*	-.07
ACDPERF					.04
R^2	.312	.167	.349	.194	.252

*Coefficients twice standard error and larger than .1.

[a]See Table 1 for complete variable names.

135

that students with better employed fathers and more years in two-parent households are more likely to have attended a school with a low percentage of blacks and students with better educated siblings and better employed fathers reports better high school GPAs. Finally, Table 2 suggests that UNC females perform better than males academically in high school, but males outperform females in college.

Conclusions

This study attempted to specify important correlates of black student adjustments, achievements and aspirations at a predominantly white, southern university. Several important observations regarding the experiences of black students at this institution were derived. For example, we found that black student satisfaction with the predominantly white college environment and their levels of adjustment were enhanced to the extent that they positively perceived campus race relations and the university's supportive services for black students. In addition, academic performance was higher among black students who were satisfied with UNC's college environment. Academic performance levels were lower for students expressing strong feelings of alienation and academic anxiety. Whether poor academic performance precipitates or arises from dissatisfaction, alienation and anxiety is a moot issue. The point is that together, these factors can, and often do, result in student failure. It is also clear from this data that black student feelings of alienation and academic anxiety (and presumably their negative effects on academic performance) are greatly reduced when black students perceive that the university is committed to providing them with the necessary supportive services.

Much of what this study reveals about black student adjustment, achievements and aspirations at the University of North Carolina-Chapel Hill, is not new. Many of the findings here are conventional wisdom, coming to us through prior research on black students in desegregated settings, as well as by common sense. Yet somehow these findings continue to elude policymakers and others concerned with desegregation in higher education. Feelings of anxiety, unhappiness, and alienation are counterproductive to positive academic outcomes among all students. In addition, no student could be satisfied in an institution perceived as insensitive to their needs and reluctant to incorporate their kind into its structure.

Examinations of how and why black students fare as they do on white campuses are too often distorted by assumptions of egalitarianism. While this assumption is integral to the ideals of American culture, its reality fails to be actualized for blacks in this society. Black students enter white universities as the victims of sustained personal and institutional discriminations. After their entrance, such incidents of discrimination evidently do not cease and black students subsequently experience adjustment and academic performance difficulties. Through some perverse logic, major responsibility for these outcomes are assigned to the students, while in fact, black student outcomes on white campuses result from a combination of personal and institutional factors.

Researchers and policymakers in the area of postsecondary desegregation processes must therefore begin to pay more attention to institutional processes. For the structures, norms, practices and personnel of these schools may ultimately determine whether black student outcomes are positive or negative. To date, white colleges in this nation have failed to consistently create the kinds of environments that would foster positive outcomes for black students. To be sure, some black students at these schools evidence high satisfaction, achievements and aspirations; but such outcomes generally occur in spite of, rather than because of, actions by the colleges.

Faced with an influx of students whose values, skills, and backgrounds do not necessarily insure ease of adjustment to the traditional middle class, white-oriented environment, the responsiveness of these colleges becomes critical (Peterson et.al., 1978). Indeed, the nature of a college's response to large-scale desegregation in all probability determines how well black students will fare at that institution. As American institutions enter the next decade, one hopes their responsiveness to the growing numbers of black, minority and other previously excluded students will improve. Hopefully, higher education will resist the lures of retrenchment and instead recognize its responsibilities to these students. Black students have much to gain from white colleges and universities; they also have much to contribute towards the enrichment of these schools and the larger society. It now remains for institutions of higher education in this country to act affirmatively and create settings more conducive to the positive development of black student potentials.

References

Allen, Walter R.
1978   "Race, family setting and adolescent achievement
        orientation." Journal of Negro Education 47
        (Summer):230-243.

Ballard, A.B.
1973   The Education of Black Folk: The Afro-American
        Struggle for Knowledge in White America.
        New York: Harper Colophon.

Bayer, A.E.
1972   The Black College Freshman: Characteristics and
        Recent Trends. American Council on Education
        Research Reports 7 (October).

Boyd, W.M.
1974   Desegregating America's Colleges: A Nationwide
        Survey of Black Students, 1972-73.
        New York: Praeger.

1977   "Black undergraduates succeed in white colleges."
        Education Record 58 (Summer): 309-315.

Centra, J.A.
1970   "Black students at predominantly white colleges:
        a research description." Sociology of Education
        43 (Summer):325-339.

DiCesare, P.C., W.E. Sedlacek and G.C. Brooks
1972   "Nonintellectual correlates of black student
        attrition." Journal of College Student
        Personnel 13:319-324.

English, R.A. and T.J. Settle
1976   "Minority students in higher education."
        Integrated Education 14:3 (May-June) 48-57.

Gurin, P. and E.G. Epps
1975   Black Consciousness, Identity and Achievement.
        New York: Wiley.

Harper, F.D.
1971   "Media for change: black students in the white
        university." Journal of Negro Education 40:
        (Fall):255-265.

Hedegard, J.M. and D.R. Brown
  1969   "Encounters of Some Negro and White Freshmen
          with a Public Multiversity." Journal of Social
          Issues 25:(Summer):131-144.

Institute for the Study of Educational Policy
  1976   Equal Educational Opportunity for Blacks in U.S.
          Higher Education Washington, D.C.: Howard
          University Press.

Keith, L.
  1972   "Issues facing black students and faculty at
          predominantly white institutions." Journal of
          Afro-American Issues 1 (Summer)69-73.

Kleinbaum, D.G. and A. Kleinbaum
  1976   "The minority experience at a predominantly
          white university: A Report of a 1972 Survey at
          the University of North Carolina at Chapel Hill."
          Journal of Negro Education 45 (Summer):312-328.

Morris, L.
  1979   Elusive Equality. The Status of Black Americans
          in Higher Education. Washington, D.C.: Howard
          University Press.

Peterson, M.W., R.T. Blackburn, Z.F. Gamson, C.H. Arce,
R.W. Davenport, and J.R. Mingle
  1978   Black Students on White Campuses: The Impacts of
          Increased Black Enrollments. Ann Arbor: Survey
          Research Center, University of Michigan.

Reed, R.J.
  1979   "Increasing the opportunities for black students
          in higher education." Journal of Negro Education
          47 (Spring):143-150.

Rosser, J.M.
  1972   "Higher education and the black American: an
          overview." Journal of Afro-American Issues 1
          (Fall):189-203.

Thomas, G.E.
  1980   "Equality of representation of race and sex groups
          in higher education: institutional and program
          enrollment statuses." American Educational Review
          Journal 17 (June).

Webster, D.W., W.E. Sedlacek and J. Miyares
    1979   "A comparison of problems perceived by minority
           and white university students." Journal of
           College Student Personnel 20 (March):165-170.

Willie, C.V. and A.S. McCord
    1973   Black Students at White Colleges.
           New York: Praeger.

Appendix

Variable Measurements

The dependent variables of college satisfaction,
academic performance, and occupational aspirations were
measured respectively by asking: "How would you describe
your general feelings as a student at UNC-CH?" (seven point
scale, ranging from very dissatisfied to very satisfied),
"What is your current Grade Point Average?" (continuous
scale, ranging from 0 to 4.0); and "What occupation would
you like to go into after you finish school?" (occupations
assigned Duncan SEI prestige scores ranging from 0 to 100).
Student academic anxiety and alienation were measured by
asking: "How high would you rate your general anxiety with
regard to academic pressure here at UNC-CH?" (seven point
scale ranging from very low to very high) and "How much do
you personally feel a part of campus life insofar as student
activities and government are concerned?" (seven point
scale ranging from not at all to very much). The nature of
student social interactions was measured by asking about
campus race relations, "How do you perceive the general
racial climate here on campus?" (seven point scale ranging
from very poor to excellent); professor-student relations,
summary index combining responses to "How would you rate
your white professors on the following scales in regard to
their service to black students?: open and willing to give
black students adequate time and attention, have difficulty
communicating with black students (reverse scaled), avoid
black student interaction outside the classroom (reverse
scaled), provide encouragement to continue to study and go on
for an advanced degree, and seem genuinely concerned about
black student welfare." (seven point scales ranging from
never to always); black support networks, summary index
of responses to "To what extent do you participate in the
extra-curricular activities of the Black Student Movement?,
How often do you have an opportunity to interact with other
black students?, and How would you rate the quality of these
interactions?, and How helpful do you find these interactions?" (seven point scales ranging from very negative to

very positive responses), student evaluation of the
adequacy of UNC's support of black students was measured by
a summary index of responses to "How helpful has the
academic advising been which you have received while here?,
How responsive or adequate have campus counseling services
been to your needs?, How adequate to your needs is this
financial aid?, and How responsive are campus tutorial and
remedial academic services to your needs?: (seven point
scale ranging from very negative to very positive responses),
desegregated high school experience is represented by
percentage of high school that was black (six point scale
ranging from 0 to 100%) and high school grade point average
(continuous scale ranging 0 to 4.0). Finally, student background is referenced by sex (female=1; male=0), father's
occupation (Duncan SEI prestige score), mother and oldest
sibling education (eight point scale ranging from some high
school to Ph.D., J.D., or M.D.), and family structure (lived
with both parents 0-7 years and lived with both parents more
than 7 years).

10

The Forgotten Side of the Black Undergraduate: An Assessment of Academic Achievements and Aspirations during the 1970s

WILLIAM M. BOYD II _____

Introduction

Much attention has been devoted to the alleged poor qualifications and alienation of black students at white colleges (Astin, A., 1972; Astin, H. et.al., 1972; Bayer, 1972; Epps, 1972), but their academic accomplishments and other experiences on these campuses have been largely neglected (Brazziel, 1974; Peterson et.al., 1978; Spurlock, 1974). This chapter describes some of the findings from recent surveys of black undergraduates on white campuses. These surveys were conducted by A Better Chance, Inc. (ABC) in 1973, 1975, and 1977.[1,2] Almost 800 black undergraduates at a representative sample of 40 predominantly white, four-year colleges were interviewed during each survey (See Appendix for subsample of colleges).

Stratified random sampling techniques were used to assure that the surveys would provide a valid basis for generalizations. The sampling universe covered all four-year colleges and universities in the United States with 51 percent or more white enrollment. At each institution quotas were established for a minimum number of black respondents

for each college year (freshman, sophomore, etc.).
In addition, interviewers randomly selected students within
class-year strata and sought diversity in sex, college
major, and extracurricular interests in instances where a
list of black students could not be obtained. As a result
of these procedures, a unique data base was developed which
permitted a trend analysis regarding various characteristics
of black students on a number of diverse, predominantly
white, college campuses.

Academic Backgrounds and Performance of Black Students

Our findings show that in 1973 only a small proportion (23%) of black students in white colleges had poor academic backgrounds, and by 1977 this proportion had declined
even further (12%). Also, in 1977 almost twice as many
black students had a college grade point average (GPA) of
"B-" or better as did students in 1973 (44% vs.26%). Not
surprisingly, the proportions of students admitted under
special programs during this period decreased substantially.

One public northeastern college in the sample was a
major exception to our general finding regarding the decline
in the number of black students in white colleges who received special admission. In 1977, all of the black students
at this college were admitted under special programs, and 79
percent were from families where neither parent had attended
college. Thirty-seven percent of these black students in
this college achieved GPAs of "B-" or better, so the institution fell only slightly behind national averages for academic performance. It did, however, vary dramatically from
national averages for proportions of students feeling they
had been victims of racial discrimination (89% vs. 50%
nationally) and proportions participating in black organizations on campus (84% vs.49% nationally).

First College-Generation Black Students

Although many black students in the study whose parents
did not attend college did fare well academically, some of
the stereotypes about first-generation black students were
supported by the present data. For example, the proportion
of first-generation blacks who had excellent academic preparation prior to college was much smaller than the proportion of other black students (9% vs. 20%). Similarly, only 7
percent of the first-generation students had attended private secondary schools as compared to 18 percent of the
other students. Also, three times as many other students

chose college majors in the biological and physical sciences
as did first-generation students (20% vs. 6%). Twice as
many other students were enrolled in select colleges as were
first-generation students. Finally, although first-generation and other students did not differ in their college GPAs
in 1973 (25% vs. 25%), by 1977 only 42 percent of the first-
generation students had obtained this average, versus 52
percent of the second-generation students.

Black Students in
Private Versus Public Colleges[3]

Differences in students' family background often parallel and are reinforced by the different types of colleges
which students attend. Our surveys indicated that although
black students' experiences in public and private white
institutions were very similar in 1973, they had become quite
different by 1977. In 1977, twice as many black students in
private white colleges were graduates of private secondary
institutions as were black students in public white colleges
(20% vs. 10%). Also, more black students in private than
public colleges felt that their academic preparation for
college was good or excellent (60% vs. 50%). Fifty-five
percent of the former students had college GPAs of "B-" or
better as compared to only 40 percent of the students in
public colleges. In addition, twice as many black students
in private colleges majored in math, engineering, and the
biological sciences as did blacks in public white colleges.

An explanation for the better academic experiences of
black students in private colleges can be drawn from other
observations revealed in the study. For example, more than
three fourths (76%) of students in private colleges identified
the academic reputation of the college as an important factor
in their choice of colleges, while only about half the students in public colleges did so. In addition, approximately
70 percent of the black students in private colleges indicated class size as a positive characteristics of their
college, while only 50 percent of blacks at public colleges
indicated this response.

We also found that a majority of black public college
students emphasized proximity to home as an important
influence on their choice of college. Over 80 percent of

these students enrolled at colleges in the same geographic
region as their secondary schools, while only 60 percent
of the black students in private colleges attended secondary
schools in the same region.

Our findings on the experiences of black students in
public versus private colleges suggest that private white
colleges are faring better than public white colleges in recruiting academically prepared blacks who are willing to
participate in their programs and who did so on a successful
basis.

Black Students in
Selective Versus Less Selective Institutions

Highly selective public and private colleges began to
cut back on their black student enrollment several years ago
(Sedlacek et.al., 1974).[4] This disturbing trend continues
today, and it is a rare director of admissions who is not
concerned about it. Rumors about high levels of black undergraduate attrition in selective white colleges have contributed to decreasing interest of blacks in these institutions.
This is paradoxical given that blacks historically place a
high value on a college education.

Our findings show that 36% of black students in highly
selective colleges in 1973 reported that they maintained a
GPA of "B" or better, and by 1977, 60 percent of black
students in highly selective colleges had such averages. The
comparable percentages for students in less selective
colleges were 23 and 39 percent.

Regarding major fields, we found that in 1977, twice as
many blacks in selective institutions majored in the biological sciences, engineering, math, and the physical sciences
as did students in less selective institutions (26% vs. 12%).
Also, twice as many students in highly selective colleges
graduated from private secondary schools as did students in
less selective institutions (18% vs. 9%). Another interesting observation was that blacks in highly selective white
colleges achieved academic success without having to resort
to a "nothing-but-study" lifestyle; these students also
participated extensively in extracurricular activities. In

fact, students in highly selective colleges participated more
often in extracurricular activities than did students in less
selective colleges. For example, 16% of black students in
highly selective colleges participated in radio station
broadcasting and newspaper activities, versus only 8% at less
selective colleges. Part of the reason is that a greater
proportion of students in highly selective colleges lived on
campus than did black students in less selective colleges
(70% vs. 48%).

Black Students in White Colleges
Located in Different Regions

The 1970s have not produced identical patterns of experience for black students in white colleges in all regions
of the country; there is considerable variation from one region to another. For example, we found in 1973, 1975, and
1977 that black students' dissatisfaction with their college
experience was greater in the West than in other regions and
lowest in the South.

Several factors produced the high rates of black student
dissatisfaction in the West. In 1975, the West was an exception to the reduction in black students being admitted under
special programs: 60 percent of the black students entering
white colleges in this region did so under special admissions
programs. In 1977, four out of ten black students in the
West still entered white colleges under special admissions
programs. By contrast, the South consistently had the fewest
special admissions students in 1973, 1975, and 1977.

The West also had far fewer black students living on
campus than did other regions. Studies have documented the
impact of residential versus nonresidential living on students' evaluations of their college experiences. The greater
satisfaction with the college environment associated with
being a resident rather than a commuter has been reported by
many other investigators (Astin, 1977; Baird, 1969; Chickering
and McCormick, 1973). More black students in the South were
living in interracial dormitories (over 60 percent in all
three years) than did any other region of the country.
Lastly, we found that the West was the only region in which
50 percent or more of the black students in all three surveys
reported that they were victims of racial discrimination at
white colleges. The South ranked third or fourth in all
three years on this measure.

Educational Aspirations of
Black College Students

Because there is much concern about the representation
of black students at the graduate and professional level, we
obtained data on the post-college plans of black students
in white colleges. We found that having attended a high
school that had excellent secondary academic training was
more strongly related (and positively so) to students' plans
to attend graduate schools on a full-time basis after college
graduation than any other variable. In addition, black
students who were planning to attend graduate school were
less likely to be attending a college in the same geographic
region as their high school and were twice as likely to be
graduates of private secondary schools. These students were
almost twice as likely to have a GPA of "B-" or better than
black students who were not planning to attend graduate
school immediately (59% vs. 32%).

The characteristics of the colleges which black students
attended were even better indicators of students' plans to
attend college than were student and secondary institutional
characteristics. Fifty-eight percent of the black students
in highly selective institutions planned to attend graduate
school on a full-time basis versus 42 percent of the students
in less selective colleges. In addition, blacks in private
colleges more frequently indicated plans to enter graduate
school than did blacks in public colleges. In the 1977 survey, only two of the thirteen colleges which had 55 percent
or more black students planning to attend graduate school
on a full-time basis were public.

Conclusion

Our survey indicates some interesting trends regarding
the academic experiences of black students in white colleges.
One very obvious trend is that the quality, type, and
regional location of the predominantly white colleges which
black students attend differentiate their academic, social,
and racial experiences in these institutions. Black students'
experiences in predominantly white colleges cannot be fully
understood without taking these college characteristics into
consideration along with the academic and social background
of the students themselves. In considering all these factors,
our findings suggest that many black students have positive
experiences in white colleges, particularly in the private
and more select colleges. It is important that this general
conclusion and the specific findings discussed in this chapter be replicated by other studies of black students on white
campuses and comparative samples involving black and white

students. ABC plans to conduct some of these studies during the 1980s[5]

A second conclusion that can be drawn from this study is that predominantly white colleges, like the remainder of mainstream American society, have made only beginning efforts toward the decade-old challenge of the Kerner Commission. If these institutions and higher education in general do not complete their mission of moving toward a more integrated and equitable society, it will not be the fault of black students. Clearly, this generation of black students does not appear to want two societies any more than previous generations wanted slavery or Jim Crow. In fact, one reason the current integration of colleges has occurred so rapidly is that a substantial number of black students and their parents desire the same types of academic opportunities available to whites.

Appendix

Stage III Colleges and Universities (1977):

Abilene Christian College
California State University (Chico State)
Carleton College
Central Connecticut State College
Connecticut College
David Lipscomb College
Drew University
Drexel University
Duke University
Eastern Michigan University
Georgia State University
Gettysburg College
Hillsdale College
Mankato State University
Metropolitan State College
Northeastern University
Northern Illinois University
Oberlin College
Occidental College
Ohio State University
Oregon State University

Stage III Colleges and Universities (1977) Continued:

Rockhurst College
State University of New York (Cortland)
Tennessee Technological University
Texas A & I University
University of Arkansas (Fayetteville)
University of California (Berkeley)
University of Chicago
University of Kansas
University of Maryland
University of Massachusetts (Amherst)
University of Nebraska (Lincoln)
University of Notre Dame
University of Pittsburgh
University of Rochester
University of Southwestern Louisiana
University of Virginia
University of Washington
University of Wisconsin
Virginia Commonwealth University

References

Astin, A.W.
    1972   "College dropouts: A national profile."
           ACE Research Reports 7 Washington: ACE.

    1977   Four Critical Years. San Francisco: Jossey-Bass

Astin, H.W., A.W. Astin, A.S. Bisconte and H.H. Frankel
    1972   Higher Education and the Disadvantaged Student
           Washington: Human Service Press.

Baird, L.L.
    1969 "The effects of college residence groups on
           students' self-concepts, goals and achievements."
           Personnel and Guidance Journal 47:1015-1021.

Bayer, A.E.
    1972 "The black college freshman: characteristics and
           recent trends." ACE Research Reports 7.
           Washington: ACE.

Brazziel, W.F.
    1974   Quality Education for All Americans: An Assess-
           ment of Gains of Black Americans with Proposals
           for Program Development in American Schools and
           College for the Next Quarter Century.
           Washington: Howard University Press.

References Continued

Cass, J. and M. Birnbaum
    1969   Comparative Guide to American Colleges: 1970-
            1971. Princeton, N.J.: CEEB.

Chickering, A.W. and J. McCormick
    1973   "Personality development and the college
            experience." Research in Higher Education.
            1:43-70.

Epps, E.G.
    1972   Black Students in White Schools.
            Worthington, Ohio: C.A. Jones Publishing Co.

Peterson, M.W., R.T. Blackburn, Z.E. Gamson, C.H. Arce,
R.W. Davenport and J.R. Mingle
    1978   Black Students on White Campuses: The Impacts
            of Increased Black Enrollments. Ann Arbor,
            Michigan: Institute for Social Research,
            The University of Michigan.

Sedlacek, W.E. Strader, M.A. and G.C. Brooks, Jr.
    1974   A National Comparison of Universities Successful
            and Unsuccessful in Enrolling Blacks Over a Five
            Year Period. College Park, Md.: Cultural Study
            Center, University of Maryland.
            Research Report 3-74.

Spurlock, L.A.
    1974   Minorities in White Colleges. Washington:
            American Council on Education.

Footnotes

1. In the original survey, 979 face-to-face interviews were conducted, lasting approximately forty-five minutes, at forty colleges and universities across the United States during the 1972-73 academic year. There were 785 black students and 194 faculty members and administrators interviewed. A stratified random sampling technique has been used in each of the survey years to select institutions and the respondents.

2. Support for this research was from the Ford Foundation, the Rockefeller Brothers Fund, and the National Institute of Education.

3. Of the forty institutions in the 1977 survey sample, 60% were public and 40% were private.

4. James Cass and Max Bienbaum's (1969) typology of selectivity was presently employed in ranking institutions.

5. Astin (1977) begun in 1979 to conduct some national studies. In addition, Peterson et.al. (1979) and Sedlacek et.al. (1974) plan to continue their studies on blacks and minorities in predominantly white institutions.

11

Black and White Students
in Maryland Community Colleges

JAMES D. TSCHECHTELIN

Introduction

In its report, the National Advisory Commission on Civil Disorders (1968) concluded that racism in the United
States kept blacks in inferior schools, barred them from fair
employment, and created a sense of hopelessness and despair.
One change that has taken place in higher education since
1968 has been the number of students enrolled in the community colleges. The proportion of college students enrolled
nationally at the community college level has risen from 24
percent in 1968 to 35 percent in 1975 (NCES, 1977). Black
students have been more heavily involved in this growth than
whites. In 1976, 45 percent of black college students were
in community colleges, versus 37 percent of the white college
students (Thomas, 1980). Among the basic types of institutions in the United States, community colleges enroll a
higher proportion of blacks (11.8 percent) than four-year
colleges (9.8 percent), graduate schools (6.1 percent) or
professional schools (4.8 percent). Thus, black community
college enrollment more closely approximates the percentage
of "college age" blacks in the population, 12.5 percent.
Since community colleges have figured so prominently in the
increased enrollment of black students, more information is
needed about their status and achievements. This chapter
describes black and white students, their goals and achievements in one state with an extensive community college
system. Policy implications for the federal government,
education agencies, and institutions are explored.

Maryland Higher Education

Structure and Mission. Higher education in Maryland is
organized in a tripartite structure, with community colleges,

state universities and colleges. The university and the
state college segments have separate governing boards appointed by the Governor. Community colleges are locally controlled, each having a board of trustees. Coordination is
exercised by the State Board for Higher Education over all
institutions, and by the State Board for Community Colleges
for its segment. Twenty percent of all public board members are black and 14 percent of the community college board
members are black.

The mission of the University of Maryland is to provide
teaching, research, and service, with emphasis on upperclass
instruction and advanced research. The primary mission of
the state universities and colleges is to provide high quality baccalaureate and masters education, and the secondary
mission is to engage in limited research and service. The
major mission of the community colleges is to provide high
quality transfer and career programs, continuing education
and community service at low tuition in response to local
educational needs.

Enrollment and Tuition. In the Fall of 1978, Maryland
had 49 colleges and universities, 26 public and 23 private.
The public institutions enrolled 186,689 students in 17
community colleges, 8 state universities and colleges, and
one multi-campus university. In a state where 21 percent of
the population is black, the public institutions enrolled
19 percent black students and the community colleges enrolled 19 percent blacks. Of the 26 public institutions,
4 are predominantly black and 22 are predominantly white.
Slightly over half of the black students are enrolled in the
predominantly white institutions. Among the community colleges, one is predominantly black, and it enrolls 39 percent
of the black community college students. With a few exceptions, community colleges enroll black students in proportion to their numbers in the college's service area, defined
as a county or several contiguous counties. In 1978, 23 of
24 counties, representing 99 percent of the population,
were served by a community college. Willingham (1970) defined a free-access college, in part, as one located within
45 minutes from the students' homes. The criterion is met
for nearly every citizen of Maryland.

In Fall, 1978, tuition at the University of Maryland
and the state universities and colleges for a full-time
student was about $800 annually. At the community colleges,
it was about $500. Willingham's (1970) definition of a
free-access college also required a tuition less than $400
in the 1968-1969 academic year. Allowing for nearly 100
percent inflation in the last ten years, all of Maryland's

public institutions meet the financial criterion.

Programs. The University of Maryland offers a wide
range of programs including the doctorate, and first professional degrees in law and medicine. The state universities and colleges offer programs up to the Master's level.
Community colleges are comprehensive institutions, offering
transfer, occupational, and community service programs. A
statewide transfer agreement allows students to move to
four-year colleges with minimal loss of credits. The community colleges offer programs in 119 occupational areas.
While the number of programs offered varies by college, most
offer such programs as secretarial science, law enforcement,
data processing, nursing, and business management. Awards
for occupational programs include a certificate for 12-45
credits, and the Associate in Arts degree for 60 credits.
Fifteen high-cost, low-enrollment occupational programs are
offered on a regional basis, with students able to attend
from other counties at in-county rates.

Remedial programs are available to some extent at the
University of Maryland, to a greater extent at the state
colleges, and extensively in the community colleges. In
the community colleges, credit and non-credit courses are
offered primarily in English and Mathematics. Using diagnostic tests or high school grades, students are counseled
into the appropriate courses. Some courses meet in the traditional mode, while others are open laboratories. Most
programs deal primarily with cognitive skill development,
and not with affective development, such as self-concept.
One problem is that placement into remedial courses is done
more readily with full-time students; part-time students
are not required to submit transcripts or test scores, and
such students constitute the majority of the community college student body.

Student Characteristics

Black and white students differ considerably on many
demographic characteristics in Maryland community colleges.
There are more females among black students (61 percent vs.
56 percent among whites) and more of the black students
attend community colleges on a full-time basis (37 percent
vs. 31 percent). The greater full-time attendance among
blacks may be explained by increased receipt of financial
aid, which often requires full-time attendance. However,
the critical point is that the majority of community college students attend part-time, a very different character-
istic from their counterparts in the four-year institutions.

Approximately equal numbers of students are in transfer
programs as are in occupational programs, and blacks and
whites are in transfer programs in about the same proportion. In the occupational programs, black students enroll
slightly more often in business and commerce programs. Mingle (1978) also found that blacks were overrepresented in
business and management disciplines nationally. Black
students tend to carry more credits per semester than whites
(8.5 vs. 7.7), a predictable result since more black students attend full-time. While the median age of black students at 24.5 is one year higher than white students, the
distribution is different. Blacks are more concentrated in
the 20-29 year interval; whites are more frequent than
blacks among students aged 40 and above. A similar proportion of black and white students are from out-of-state, a-
bout two percent.

Information about the abilities of incoming students
is incomplete because not all colleges require standardized
tests for admission, and the colleges that do require them
generally collect results only for full-time students. However, scores from the Scholastic Aptitude Test and the American College Testing Program are available for a sample of
Maryland community college students. The ACT composite for
enrolled freshmen was 16.4, the SAT-Verbal was 378 and the
SAT-Math was 411. Using data from the CEEB Student Data
Questionnaire, the median family income of black students in
1976 was $12,400 while the median income of white families
was $17,600. In fiscal year 1978, 52 percent of black stu-
dents received an average Basic Educational Opportunity
Grant of $604, while 6 percent of the white students re-
ceived an average BEOG of $617. During the same year, five
percent of the black students received an average National
Direct Student Loan of $360, while one percent of the white
students received an average NDSL loan of $404.

Within three and one-half years after entry, black students typically complete 27 credits, compared with 33 credits for whites. The fewer credits completed and a higher
credit load per semester suggests that blacks attend for a
somewhat shorter period. At the end of 3 1/2 years, 14 percent of the entering students are still enrolled in the college, and about 15 percent have received an Associate degree, 12 percent of the entering blacks and 16 percent of
the whites.

Student Goals and Goal Achievement

Information about the goals and goal achievement of
community college students was obtained from a survey that

was mailed in Spring 1978 to all persons who were first-time
students in Maryland community colleges in Fall, 1974.[1]
Previous studies of community college students indicated
the need to survey students several years after entry, because so many students attend part-time. A standard survey
was mailed by each college to a total of 23,199 students.
Forty-three percent of the students receiving the survey responded.

Student Goals. Information about the academic goals of
the students is given in Table 1. Although a majority of
the students sought a certificate or Associate degree, a
high percentage of the students came to the community college for courses of interest, apart from a degree. Such a
phenomenon is quite different from that of the four-year
colleges and universities, where it is assumed that nearly
all students come at least with the intention of completing
a degree program. There are significant racial differences
in academic goals, with black students being more interested
in a degree or certificate than whites.

Personal goal reflects the functional concern of the
student, "What do I want to do with my community college
education?" Transfer is the most frequent personal goal
for whites (34 percent), but only 22 percent of blacks seek
transfer. Career-related goals are more important to the
black students, with 43 percent seeking to prepare for a
new career or to upgrade skills in a current job. The comparable figure for whites is 29 percent, and only half as
many whites are attending to update skills in their current
job. Such a career orientation may serve black students
well in the future, as manpower projections show substantial
growth in opportunities for persons with technical skills,
and much more restricted openings for persons with advanced
degrees. A recent study of the economic impacts of community college attendance showed that a Maryland community
college student will earn 25 percent more than a high school
graduate (Linthicum, 1978). About one-third of the students
of both races attend for personal growth reasons, and not
to prepare specifically for transfer or employment.

Goal Achievement. Table 1 also shows student goal
achievement among blacks and whites in Maryland community
colleges. Twenty-three percent of the black students that
held a degree-goal received an Associate degree. The comparable figure for white students was 37 percent, a statisti-

Table 1

Goals and Goal Achievement Among Black and White Students
in Maryland Community Colleges

1974 Entrants

	Percentages Among Blacks	Percentages Among Whites
	(N=782)	(N=6,247)
Academic Goal		
Courses of interest	26%	36%
Certificate	10	6
Associate in Arts	64	58
Personal Goal		
Exploration of New Career or Academic Area	15	14
Preparation for New Career	21	17
Transfer	22	34
Update Skills in Current Job	22	12
Interest and Self-enrichment	17	19
Other	3	3
Degree Goal and Received Degree	23	37
Career Goal and Was Employed Full-time	76	75
Transfer Goal and Transferred	53	71

All racial differences significant at .001 except career goal achievement.

cally significant difference. It should be noted here that
degree goal achievement was used in this study rather than
simple degree status because so many students attend only
for courses. Table 1 also shows that for black and white
students who attend community colleges to prepare for a new
job or to upgrade their skills, about three-fourth of both
groups are successful. About 60 percent of all former
community college students are employed full-time and 20
percent are employed part-time. About half of the students
are employed in the county of their community college, and
over 90 percent work in Maryland and the District of Columbia.

Among students who entered community colleges with hopes
of transferring to a four-year college, 53 percent of the
blacks and 71 percent of the whites were successful in transferring, a statistically significant difference. About one-
third of all entering students transfer. Most of the students transfer to public institutions in Maryland, 25 percent
to state colleges and 30 percent to the University of Maryland. Blacks are more likely to attend one of the state
colleges than whites (38 percent vs. 26 percent for whites).

Reasons for Lower Goal Achievement. Why do black students have less degree and transfer goal achievement than
whites?[2,3] Results from our analysis indicated that black
students are academically less prepared than whites upon
enrolling in Maryland community colleges. The high school
grade point average of blacks is 2.03, compared to 2.55 for
whites. First-time black students comprise 30 percent of
the students in remedial English courses but only 10 percent

of the introductory college-level English courses (Linthicum
1979). Linthicum (1979) examined the effectiveness of remedial programs by comparing first-time students who took
remedial English courses with students who enrolled directly
in college-level English. She found that forty-one percent
of the students who began in remedial English stayed at the
college for four semesters, versus 53 percent of the students who began in college-level English. The latter group
also completed a higher percentage of their hours attempted
(90 percent vs. 76 percent) and earned higher cumulative
grade point averages (2.66 vs. 1.94, based on a 4.0 system).
Linthicum (1979) concluded that students in remedial programs were reasonably successful in their community college
work, but there was a need for competent diagnostic testing
of all students (full and part-time), more faculty development, and programs that go beyond cognitive skills to personal factors such as self-concept and attitudes about
learning.

   Reasons for Discontinuing. Table 2 shows the various
reasons why blacks and whites leave Maryland community colleges and how they rate their experiences in these colleges.
Here we see significant racial differences in reasons for
leaving among non-graduates. The primary reason that blacks
and whites leave is because they achieved their educational
goal. While predictably fewer black students leave to
transfer to four-year college, nearly twice as many blacks
leave because of a scheduling conflict between their job and
their studies. In addition, six times as many blacks stated
that they discontinued their studies because their financial
aid was not sufficient to meet their needs. This observation emphasizes the need for strong state and federal financial aid programs to ensure equal educational opportunity
for blacks and other disadvantaged students. Since blacks
experience less degree and transfer goal achievement, we
examined whether blacks evaluated their program and college
differently than whites. Table 2 shows that this is not the
case; black students tended to rate their program and their
college as favorably as white students. About 80 percent
of the blacks stated that they would recommend their program
of study to a friend, and about 86 percent indicated that
they would recommend their college.

   In Four Critical Years, Astin (1977) noted that for the
eighteen-year-old going directly from high school to college,
the public community college does not represent an "equal
educational opportunity" compared with other types of institutions. The chances of persisting to a baccalaureate degree are considerably lower among community college students.

Table 2

Reasons for Leaving and College Evaluation
Among Blacks and Whites
In Maryland Community Colleges

1974 Entrants

Variable (Sample Size)	Percentage Among Blacks (782)	Percentage Among Whites (6,247)
Primary Reason for Leaving[a] Among Nongraduates		
[b]Achieved Educational Goal	27%	29%
Transferred	9	17
Scheduling Conflict	19	10
Personal-Marriage	11	10
Accepted Job	7	8
Program Not Available	3	7
Changed Goal	4	4
Unsure of Major	3	4
Dissatisfied with Teaching	2	2

[a]Racial differences in reasons for leaving significant at .001;
differences on evaluation questions not significant.

[b]Educational goals include the academic and personal goals listed in Table 1.

160

Table 2 Continued

Reasons for Leaving and College Evaluation
Among Blacks and Whites
In Maryland Community Colleges

1974 Entrants

Variables	Percentage Among Blacks	Percentage Among Whites
(Sample Size)	(782)	(6,247)
Low Grades	1	1
Courses Too Difficult	1	1
Aid Not Available	2	1
Aid Not Sufficient	6	1
College Was Too Expensive	1	1
Would you Recommend This Program of Study To a Friend?		
Yes	80	78
No	6	8
Uncertain	14	14
Would You Recommend This College To a Friend?		
Yes	86	90
No	4	3
Uncertain	9	7

Astin's conclusion is based upon assumptions about the de-
sirability of most students getting bachelors degrees and
the similarity of students at community and four-year colleges. The Maryland study found that only 22 percent of the
first-time entrants were 18-19 years old and desired to
transfer to a four-year college (25 percent of the whites
and only 8 percent of the blacks). While Astin's (1977)
finding may be applicable to some community colleges, his
analysis does not include the majority of U.S. community
college students. The point with reference to Astin's
(1977) finding and the observation from the Maryland study
is that many community college students may not want a
baccalaureate degree. For example, a student's personal
goal may be to take three courses in accounting at a community college to increase his/her job skills. Upon completing
these courses, that student has achieved his/her goal. Thus
he is not a dropout, but a drop-in, who enrolled for the
purposes of completing a short-term goal.

Conclusion

In the last ten years, an increasing proportion of students have enrolled in community colleges, and blacks have
come to community colleges in even greater numbers than
whites and other minorities. Therefore, in concluding this
chapter, it is important to address some critical policy
issues that must be seriously assessed to assist black students in achieving greater equality of educational opportunity in community colleges. These issues are as follows:

Distorted Perception of the Community College. There
is an urgent need for persons in state and federal agencies
and in educational institutions to see community colleges
through clearer lenses. Having been educated in a four-year
college, many policy-makers assume that a community college
is half of a four-year experience. Policy makers must look
at the reality of community colleges, and how students are
using them. The language used by policy-makers reflects
their thinking, and prevents competent and sensitive planning and decision-making. For example, the Student Data
Questionnaire of the CEEB asks about educational aspirations, but allows no provision for simply courses of interests. Many students do enter community colleges to take
a few selected courses, but that option is not available to
the student respondent, who either leaves this questionnaire
item blank or bends his or her intention into a category
that really does not describe the facts. Many individuals
are surprised and dismayed to learn that 15 percent of
community college students graduate with an Associate

degree. Persons (even among community college faculty) are
surprised and are dismayed because they believe that the
graduation rate "should" be so much higher, when viewed
through four-year lenses.

Mission of the Community College. When policy-makers
see more clearly how community colleges are being used by
students, a more rapid development of a new and more relevant mission for these institutions will be possible. The
new mission is already being approached in many states.
There is an increasing trend for education and work to be
less separate and for persons to move in and out of educational institutions periodically throughout their lives.
Community colleges have become a part of the trend with
noncredit courses, weekend schedules, televised courses and
contractual arrangements with business and industry. This
continuing education mission may be more valuable to blacks
than whites because blacks are more often than whites employed on a full time basis and enrolled in job-related
courses.

Research and Dissemination. There must be more research about the role and experiences of blacks in community colleges, and more awareness of the research that already exists. Specifically, statewide follow-up studies of
entering students are needed to find out more about goals
and correlates of black success in community colleges.
Additional federal funds must be made available to conduct
such research. Another subject for additional research is
remedial education and its impact upon course attrition
grades, and the graduation of black and white students in
community colleges. Perhaps even more important than additional research is the need for better dissemination of the
results of current studies on community colleges. Educational researchers have a tendency to address primarily
other researchers, journals, the ERIC system, and professional meetings. However, their results must be disseminated to educational and political policy makers and to the
broader educational community.

Student Financial Aid. Our analysis indicated that
six times as many blacks as whites left community college
because of inadequate financial aid. Thus there is a strong
need for continuation and expansion of state and federal
student financial aid. A comprehensive program of student
financial aid will not only help black students gain access
and achieve greater college persistence; it will help to
ensure that students' choices about which college to attend
will be made on the basis of their goals and abilities,

rather than their socioeconomic status. The fact that so
many community college students attend part-time raises
a special problem in relation to financial aid. Because of
eligibility guidelines and processing formulae of the federal government, 64 percent of the community college students
nationally receive less than eight percent of the federal
aid dollars (Hamilton, 1979). A student must take 12 credits to qualify for federal assistance. If a student takes
between 6 or 11 credits, he or she is eligible for only
half the amount. Carrying fewer than six credits disquali-
fies a student for any type of federal aid. Because most
federal policy-makers view part-time students as less than
serious about their academic work, millions of persons among
the working poor are denied student financial assistance.

Remedial Education and the Open Door. In embracing the
open-door concept, most community colleges have tried to
eliminate as many barriers as possible to community college
entrance. In many places, a student can walk off the street
on the last day of registration, apply, register, and enroll
in the same day. The openness of the community college
doors has been as asset; however, one unintended consequence
of the open door policy has been in some instances a poor
match between the students' academic skills and personal
goals and the offerings of the college that he/she enters.
High school transcripts, aptitude tests, and placement inventories may discourage some potential community college
students. However, they may be necessary to provide adequate
counseling to incoming students. Some commentors have noted
that community college students are not adequately served
by the revolving door policy. Therefore certain entry requirements may be necessary to adequately place and provide
academic instructions to incoming students.

Changes in Society. Black success in the community
college is linked with the broader success of blacks in U.S.
society. In comparison with whites in the United States,
blacks generally earn a fraction of the wages, work in lower
status jobs, have inferior health care, and live in less adequate housing. Based on these facts, it would be naive
to assume that community colleges should provide all the
support needed to erase vestiges of discrimination. To the
contrary, the broader society and all of its educational,
occupational and social institutions must work towards eliminating discrimination and providing greater equality of
educational and job opportunity for blacks and other minorities.

References

Astin, A.
   1977   Four Critical Years. San Francisco: Jossey-Bass.

Chickering, A.
   1974   Commuting Versus Resident Students.
          San Francisco: Jossey-Bass.

College Entrance Examination Board
   1975   College Bound Seniors, 1974-1975. Princeton, N.J.:
          College Entrance Examination Board.

Hamilton, B.E.
   1978   "Adult part-time students and the higher
          education act." Change May-June : 37-45.

Linthicum, D.S.
   1978   The Economic Impacts of Maryland Community
          Colleges. Annapolis, Maryland: State Board for
          Community Colleges.

Linthicum, D.S.
   1979   A Statewide Assessment of Developmental/Remedial
          Education at Maryland Community Colleges.
          Annapolis, Maryland: State Board for
          Community Colleges.

Mingle, J.R.
   1978   Black Enrollment in Higher Education: Trends in
          the Nation and the South. Atlanta, Georgia:
          Southern Regional Education Board.

National Advisory Commission on Civil Disorders
   1968   Report of the National Advisory Commission on
          Civil Disorders. Washington, D.C.:

National Center for Education Statistics
   1977   Projections of Education Statistics to 1985-1986
          Washington, D.C.: National Center for Education
          Statistics.

Thomas, G.E.
   1980   "Race and sex group equity in higher education:
          institutional and major field enrollment statuses."
          American Educational Review Journal, 17 (June).

Willingham, W.W.
   1970   Free-Access Higher Education. New York:
          College Entrance Examination Board.

Footnotes

1. Appreciation is extended to the follow-up study coordinators in each community college.

2. In an attempt to isolate the reasons why black students have less degree and transfer goal achievement than whites, the one predominantly black school in the sample was eliminated from the analysis. However, racial differences still persisted between blacks and whites.

3. Studies by Astin (1977) and Chickering (1974) suggest that full-time residential attendance enhances persistence and degree achievement. None of Maryland's community colleges offer housing; therefore Astin's observation was not relevant. However, because full-time students do have a more extensive educational experience than part-time students, we controlled for full-time/part-time attendance (results not presented); however, racial differences in degree and goal achievement were still significant although slightly reduced.

12

The Major Field Choices
and Occupational Career Orientations
of Black and White College Students*

JOMILLS HENRY BRADDOCK II ⸻

Introduction

One of the most important aspects of educational attainment is its role in facilitating entry into the world of work.
Apart from the intrinsic value of obtaining formal education,
most people avidly pursue higher education in search of
extrinsic rewards. That is, most Americans regard education
as an investment, and expect their educational pursuits to
enhance both their job opportunities and future earnings. The
relationship between educational attainment and occupational
mobility has been well documented by social scientists (Blau
& Duncan, 1967; Duncan, Featherman, and Duncan, 1972). One of
the most interesting aspects of this social process concerns
the allocation and recruitment of individuals to particular
careers.

Very little is known about how the process of individual
career choice operates. However, recent studies have noted
the importance of college students' choice of major fields in
determining occupational placement and status outcomes (Thomas,
1979; Gottfredson, 1978a); Wilburn, 1974). Also, Jencks and
Brown (1975) have noted that choice of a college major is as
important in determining status outcomes as the type of college selected, or the level of education attained. Although
these studies demonstrate that occupational attainment is
affected by college major field and pre-college preparation,
they do not inform us as to how students develop their career
orientation. Three types of variables, however, are relevant
in this regard:

1. Role Modeling and Reference Groups - Researchers have
noted the influence of imitation and vicarious socialization
on the allocation of individuals into various occupations.

*This research was supported by the United States National
Institute of Education, Department of Education.

This view holds that individual career choices are often
heavily influenced by extensive and/or intensive exposure
to attractive and visible adult (career) role models
(Wallace, 1976; Sewell, Haller and Ohlendorf, 1970). The
family is thus believed to play a major role in the vocational choice process (Grandy and Stahman, 1974). Research
on whether offspring tend to enter the same occupations as
their parents has generally been limited to father-son relationships and has failed to demonstrate strong associations
(Crites, 1969).

   2. Subcultural Values - Observers, both scientific and
casual, have frequently noted that blacks and whites are
concentrated in different occupations. While these observers
have acknowledged the role of racial discrimination in maintaining multiple-labor markets, some have argued that much
of the difference in black-white employment patterns may be
attributed to differences in values and socialization
between the two groups (L. Gottfredson, 1978b). Vocational
interest inventories often reveal stronger preferences among
blacks for social "people-oriented" occupations (Doughtie,
et.al., 1976; Hager and Elton, 1971; Kimball, Sedlacek,
Brooks, 1973) and recent data for college students show that
black undergraduates more often major in social service and
education and less often in natural science and engineering
than do whites (Bayer and Boruch, 1969; El-Khawas et.al.,
1971).

   3. Personality Types - The recent work of Holland
(1973) and his colleagues has shown that people choose
careers in types of work that are compatible with their
personalities. For example, individuals with high personality needs for working with other people rather than things
or ideas often choose careers in social occupations (e.g.
teaching, social work, nursing). On the other hand, persons
with a strong inclination to work with ideas often select
careers in investigative fields (e.g., science, engineering,
mathematics). Thus, individuals are presumed to choose
work in labor-markets congruent with their psychological
needs.

   While each of these theoretical orientations are useful
to understanding the determinants of career choice, the
personality emphasis of Holland has received more thorough
empirical test and validation and thus will be the focus of
this chapter. Specifically, this chapter will evaluate the
effect of secondary and postsecondary education on the
distribution of black college students among Holland's six
occupational personality types. A number of studies have

examined and documented race and sex differences in occupational aspirations and employment patterns (Brief & Aldag, 1975; Gurin & Gaylord, 1976; L. Gottfredson, 1978c). This chapter extends that research tradition by examining differences in the major field and occupational orientations of black and white college students who were participants in a recent nationwide longitudinal survey of high school seniors. It also considers, briefly, returns for educational attainment and career orientations on occupational attainment for various educational groups.

Holland's Theory of Vocational Choice

Holland's theory of vocational choice (1973) proposes that individuals tend to choose actual occupational environments consistent with their own personal orientations. Existing research also suggests that people tend to select college majors that are consistent with their personal orientations (Holland, 1962, 1968, 1973; Osipow, Ashby & Wall, 1966).

The theory of vocational choice developed by Holland assumes that most individuals in our culture can be characterized as one of six personality types: Realistic, Investigative, Artistic, Social, Enterprising, or Conventional. These personality types are usually identified by their vocational interests. Table 1 describes Holland's occupational types and the various academic majors associated with each type. The personality characteristics associated with the Holland typology have been detailed elsewhere (Holland, 1966, 1973; Campbell & Holland, 1972; Harvey & Whinfield, 1973). However, they may be briefly described as follows: (1) Realistic - masculine, unsociable, aggressive, materialistic, uninsightful; (2) Investigative - curious, introspective, asocial, introverted; (3) Artistic - independent, introspective, feminine, self-expressive; (4) Social - sociable, responsible, feminine, friendly, humanistic; (5) Enterprising - dominant, energetic, sociable, masculine; (6) Conventional - subordinate, desires structured activities, defensive, efficient.

The classification was empirically developed from data on personality, aptitudes, worker traits, and job duties for people in different occupations (Holland, 1962, 1966, 1973). A full description of the types and a description of other major theoretical constructs not discussed here are provided by Holland (1973), Walsh (1973), and Osipow (1973).

Table 1

Description of Holland's Occupational Types

Occupational Environment	Sample Occupations	Sample Major Fields
Realistic		
Fosters technical competencies and achievements, and manipulation of objects, machines, or animals; rewards the display of such values as money, power, and possessions. Encourages people to see the world in simple, tangible, and traditional terms.	Mechanical Engineer Plumber Auto Mechanic Forklift Operator	Vocational Fields: Drafting Electronics
Investigative		
Fosters scientific competencies and achievements, and observation and systematic investigation of phenomena; rewards the display of scientific values. Encourages people to see the world in complex, abstract, independent and original ways.	Physicist Weather Observer Laboratory Assistant	Natural & Physical Sciences: Engineering Physical Sciences Mathematics Biological Sciences
Artistic		
Fosters artistic competencies and achievements, and ambiguous, free or unsystematized work; rewards display of artistic values. Encourages people to see the world in complex, independent, unconventional and flexible ways.	Editor Decorator Garment Designer	Arts & Humanities: Humanities Fine Arts

Table 1 (Cont'd)

Occupational Environment	Sample Occupations	Sample Major Fields
Social Fosters interpersonal competencies and informing, training, curing, or enlightening others; rewards the display of social or humanitarian values. Encourages people to see the world in flexible ways.	Minister Elementary Teacher Physical Therapist Ward Attendant	Social & Behavioral Sciences: Social Sciences Home Economics Health Services
Enterprising Fosters persuasive and leadership competencies or achievements, and the manipulation of others for personal or organizational goals; rewards the display of enterprising values and goals such as money, power, and status. Encourages people to see the world in terms of power, status, responsibility and in stereotyped and simple terms.	Lawyer Contractor Automobile Dealer	Business & Management Business Law Marketing
Conventional Fosters conformity and clerical competencies, and explicit manipulation of data, records, or written material; rewards the display of such values as money, dependability, conformity. Encourages people to see the world in conventional, stereo-typed, constricted, simple, and dependent ways.	Certified Public Accountant Secretary	Documentation & Clerical Fields: Bookeeping Stenography

Source: Linda S. Gottfredson, "The Construct Validity of Holland's Occupational Classification in Terms of Prestige, Census, Dept. of Labor & Other Classification Systems," Technical Report #260 (Sept 1978d) Center for Social Organization of Schools, the Johns Hopkins University, Baltimore, Md. 21218.

171

Data

The data for this analysis are taken from the National Longitudinal Survey of the High School Graduating Class of 1972 (NLS). This large-scale longitudinal survey was designed to provide information on high school students moving into early adulthood and is, perhaps, the best available data for studying the relationship between educational attainment and career patterns. The NLS study is conducted by the National Center for Education Statistics in the Office of the Assistant Secretary for Education, Department of Health, Education and Welfare. In the Spring of 1972, a baseline survey was conducted on a nationally representative random sample of 23,451 high school seniors drawn from 1,318 high schools. The first follow-up survey began in October 1973 and obtained data from 93 percent of the students in the sample, a second follow-up in the Fall of 1974 obtained a 94 percent response rate, and a third follow-up in October 1976 yielded a 92 percent response rate.

The present analysis is based on a randomly chosen twenty percent sub-sample (3,333) of the total white population and the total black sub-sample (3,119). For both groups, college major fields and detailed census occupational codes as reported in the survey instruments are recoded into one of the Holland's six occupational types (See Table 1).

Findings

To provide the clearest and most meaningful description of the significance of the occupational orientations of black college students, we first present data on the actual employment patterns of selected comparable age-sex cohorts of young blacks and whites. Table 2 presents black-white comparisons of the employment distribution of males and females in the American occupational structure. Here we see that among both sexes, a higher percentage of whites than blacks are more highly represented in Investigative and Enterprising occupations. It is quite clear from this Table that there are many differences in the proportion of blacks and whites in different job types. This racial difference in Holland's type of work has been noted in previous studies and the question has been raised whether such differentials in employment patterns are largely attributable to subcultural value differences, differences in orientation to type of work or to racially based constraints imposed through discriminatory practices in the labor force (L. Gottfredson, 1978b).

Table 2

Distribution (Percentages) of Actual
Holland Type Jobs Held
by 14-24 Year-Old Blacks and Whites, by Sex

| Occupational | SEX | | | |
| | Males | | Females | |
Type	Whites	Blacks	Whites	Blacks
Realistic	68	84	27	48
Investigative	6	1	1	--
Artistic	2	1	1	1
Social	5	5	25	20
Enterprising	12	2	10	3
Conventional	7	7	36	28
Total (100%)	100	100	100	100

Source: Gary D. Gottfredson. Using a Psychological Classification of Occupations to Describe Work, Careers,
and Cultural Change. Unpublished Ph.D. disserta-
tion, The Johns Hopkins University, Department of
Psychology, 1976.

Whatever the reason for the racial difference in jobs held, the consequences are highly significant. Even after controlling for social class and educational attainment differences, blacks are significantly underrepresented in "enterprising" careers (e.g., sales and management), while being significantly overrepresented in "social" careers (e.g., education and social services). These racial differences across types of occupations have important consequences for black-white earnings. For example, a white male college graduate in investigative and enterprising work earns on the average from $5000 to $9000 more annually than the college graduates in other types of work. In contrast, the college graduates in the social category earn the lowest mean incomes among the six occupational types (L.Gottfredson, 1978b). Therefore, blacks are less likely to be distributed in those types of occupations that yield high income without advanced educational credentials or in occupations in which one receives an income gain for each additional year of schooling.

Table 3 compares the major fields (classified by Holland occupational types) of black and white college students. These data reveal several interesting patterns. First, there is considerable similarity in the career orientations of the two groups. Among males, for example, the largest difference between the black and white students' career orientations are in the Investigative and Enterprising categories (7 and 9 percentage points, respectively).

These differences are not altogether surprising, since other studies have noted racial differences in these two areas. However, among this sample we find a somewhat stronger career orientation toward Enterprising work among black males rather than white males. This observation differs from L. Gottfredson's 1978a) finding. However, her study was based on actual employment patterns rather than career orientations as indicated here. Many factors, including racial discrimination and class-linked differential opportunities, may inhibit the conversion of black career orientations into actual occupational attainments. For example, black access to enterprising work has in fact been shown to be affected by what Becker (1967) refers to as employer "taste for discrimination" against minorities in sales careers. In addition, the entry of a greater number of blacks in entrepreneurial and business careers has been affected by the lack of available credit, high insurance costs, and monopoly capital (Knowles and Prewitt, 1969). Thus, the discrepancy between black career orientations and actual employment patterns in the realm of enterprising work may

Table 3

Distribution (Percentages) of Major Fields[a]
Among Black and White College Students
according to Holland Type of Work

| Occupational | SEX | | | |
| | Males | | Females | |
Type	Blacks (N=233)	Whites (N=329)	Blacks (N=313)	Whites (N=261b)
Realistic	13	10	0	--
Investigative	13	20	5	8
Artistic	6	8	6	10
Social	29	32	62	54
Enterprising	38	30	20	20
Conventional	1	0	7	8
Total (100%)	100	100	100	100

[a] College major field areas are recoded into Holland
type career orientation, where: (Natural and Physical
Sciences, & Engineering = Investigative), (Arts &
Humanities = Artistic), (Vocational Fields = Realis-
tic), (Health Services, Home Economics, Social &
Behavioral Sciences = Social), (Business, Marketing,
Law = Enterprising), (Accounting, Bookkeeping,
Documentation & Clerical Fields = Conventional).

[b] The present **Ns** reflect the twenty percent random
subsample that was drawn from the total NLS sample
for purposes of this analysis.

Source: National Longitudinal Survey of the High School
Class of 1972.

generally be accounted for by the existence of structural constraints which limit black access.

Other notable differences among males in the investigative category are shown in Table 3. One finding here which shows that white males have a somewhat stronger career orientation towards Investigative work, is consistent with other studies((L.Gottfredson, 1978a, 1978b). It is also consistent with other research showing that black undergraduates less often major in natural science and engineering than do whites (El-Khawas and Biscontin, 1974; Thomas, 1980). Some programs aimed at attracting minority students to the natural sciences and engineering have been recently developed (Richards, Williams, and Holland, 1978; Melnick and Hamilton, 1981).

Though not significant (3 percentage points), the difference in major field Social career orientations between black and white college men shown in Table 3 is noteworthy. As documented in earlier studies of actual employment patterns, black men, significantly more often than white men, are located in Social occupations. Therefore, it is surprising to find slightly more white college males than blacks choosing Social career-oriented fields of study. The small difference here, however, warrants against speculation about why white males are slightly more represented than black males in the Social category. Consistent with other empirical work in this area, our findings as shown in Table 3 reveal no notable differences between black and white college males in career preferences for Realistic, Artistic, or Conventional types of work.

There has been considerably less empirical research on race differences in career orientations among females than males. But some evidence suggests that black and white women are as dissimilar in their career orientations and employment patterns as are black and white men (Brito and Jusenius, 1978). Table 3 shows that more black females (8 percentage points) are in the Social category than their white female counterparts. This is, however, the only notable difference between the two groups. In contrast to their male counterparts, black and white females fail to choose major fields which are traditionally low status male occupations (e.g., Realistic). Instead, they are equally distributed in the Conventional career orientations category, which is typically female and low status.

Table 4 presents comparisons of actual employment patterns among blacks with different educational attainment.

Table 4

Distribution (Percentages) of Black Full-Time Work Force According to
Holland Type, Level of Education, and Sex 1976

Occupational Type	Total Full-Time Employed		Educational Level					
			High School		Vocational School		Some College	
	Male	Female	Male	Female	Male	Female	Male	Female
Realistic	70	16	76	27	73	19	55	12
Investigative	5	4	2	2	11	--	7	--
Artistic	1	1	1	--	--	--	--	1
Social	7	16	4	10	9	13	14	12
Enterprising	8	8	7	6	5	6	8	13
Conventional	9	55	10	55	2	61	16	62
Total (100%)	100	100	100	100	100	100	100	100

Source: National Longitudinal Survey of the High School Class of 1972.

Here we find that having attained at least some college produced significant changes in the distribution of blacks, both males and females, among the six categories of Holland's classification scheme.

Among males who have attained at least some college, there is a sizable drop in their employment in the traditional low status Realistic category. Additionally, their representation in the Social and Investigative categories of work increases more than three-fold, and their involvement in Conventional occupations increases by one-half. Among females there is a significant drop in their involvement with traditional low-status masculine work (Realistic) with the attainment of at least some college. Similarly, there is a doubling of their involvement with Enterprising work with the attainment of at least some post-secondary training.

These findings indicate that the early career patterns of black youth are affected by their educational attainment. Generally, the occupational distribution patterns across levels of education shown in Table 4 indicate greater black participation in high-status, high-reward occupational categories with the attainment of post secondary training, particularly some college. The notable exception to this pattern involves Enterprising types of work for black males. Here we find little variation in the rate of black participation in Enterprising work across levels of educational attainment. This finding, in combination with the results presented in Table 3 showing a strong orientation among black males toward Enterprising work (as indicated by college major field), might lend further support to the "structural constraints" explanation of black underrepresentation in this type of work. However, because our sample consists of a relatively young age-cohort, only four years past high school graduation, such an interpretation here would be speculative at best.

Conclusion

The study has examined the career patterns of black college students, exploring the relationship of educational attainment to occupational differentiation and Holland type career orientation. The findings, indicate that the attainment of higher education is related to increased occupational differentiation among blacks. For example, we found that as blacks obtain higher levels of education, their career orientations shift away from those areas of the occupational structure which have typically been characterized by large numbers of black workers. Employed black men and women

have generally been overrepresented among Realistic and
Conventional types of work, respectively. However, our
findings show the career orientations of black college
students to be quite different in that there is a clear trend
toward occupational orientations which, with few exceptions,
parallel those of their white counterparts. Specifically,
we find that black college students are increasingly adopting
the Enterprising and Investigative career orientations which
may lead to higher rates of return for both the individual
student and black people collectively. These two arenas of
work--Enterprising (businessmen) and Investigative (scientists and engineers)--perhaps more than any others form the
core of the high status-high reward positions within the
American occupational structure.

We must, of course, view these results with guarded
optimism. These data reflect the occupational orientations
and aspirations of the current generation of black college
students, but we must also consider the other side of this
equation, i.e., the structural dynamics of the labor market
itself. Further research is needed to examine the relationship between career orientations and actual employment
patterns as a function of the diverse, racially determined
structural constraints that may be operative in the economy.
Employed blacks, for example, may be underrepresented in
Enterprising occupations, not because of a lesser affinity
for such work, but because of restricted opportunities and
exclusionary processes operating in these areas of employment.
While this chapter has provided some insight into the career
orientations of black college students, a more detailed
examination of the process which operates to transmit the
educational aspirations and career orientations of blacks
and whites into actual occupational attainments is needed.

References

Bayer, A.E. and R.F. Boruch
    1969 "Black and white freshmen entering four-year
          colleges." Educational Record 50:371-386.

Becker, G.
    1967 The Economics of Discrimination. Chicago:
          University of Chicago Press.

Blau, P. and D.D. Duncan
    1967 The American Occupational Structure.
          New York: Wiley.

Brief, A. and R. Aldag
    1975 "Male-female differences in occupational attitudes

References (Continued)

Brief, A. and R. Aldag (cont'd.)
    1975   within minority groups." Journal of Vocational
           Behavior 6:305-314.

Brito, P.K. and C. Jusenius
    1978   "A note on young women's occupational expectations
           for age 35." Vocational Guidance Quarterly 27:
           165-175.

Campbell, D. and J. Holland
    1972   "A merger in vocational interest research:
           applying Holland's theory to Strong's." Journal
           of Vocational Behavior 2:353-376.

Crites, J.O.
    1969   Vocational Psychology. New York: McGraw-Hill.

Doughtie, E., W. Chang, H. Alston, J. Wakefield and L. Yorn
    1976   "Black white differences on the vocational
           preference inventory." Journal of Vocational
           Behavior 8:41-44.

Duncan, O.D., D. Featherman and B. Duncan
    1972   Socioeconomic Background and Achievement:
           New York Seminar Press.

El-Khawas, E., M. Shaycoft, J. Richards and J. Claudy
    1971   Project Talent: Five Years After High School.
           Pittsburg: American Institute for Research and
           University of Pittsburg.

El-Khawas, E. and A.S. Bisconti
    1974   Five and Ten Years After College Entry.
           Washington, D.C.: American Council of Education.

Gottfredson, G.
    1976   Using a Psychological Classification of Occupations
           to Describe Work, Careers, and Social Change. Un-
           published Ph.D. Dissertation, Department of Psycho-
           logy, The Johns Hopkins University: Baltimore,
           Maryland.

Gottfredson, G., J. Holland and L. Gottfredson
    1975   "The relation of vocational aspirations and assess-
           ments to employment reality." Journal of Vocational
           Behavior 7:135-148.

Gottfredson, L.
  1978a "Race and sex differences in occupational aspira-
         tions; their development and consequences for
         occupational segregation." Report No. 254.
         Center for Social Organization of Schools: Johns
         Hopkins University, Baltimore, Maryland.

  1978b "An analytical description of employment according
         to race, sex, prestige, and Holland type work."
         Report No. 249. Center for Social Organization of
         Schools: The Johns Hopkins University, Baltimore,
         Md.

  1978c "Providing black youth more access to enterprising
         work." Vocational Guidance Quarterly 27:114-123.

  1978d The Construct Validity of Holland's Occupational
         Classification in Terms of Prestige Census.
         Department of Labor and other classification sys-
         tems. Report No. 260. Center for Social Organi-
         zations of Schools: The Johns Hopkins University,
         Baltimore, Maryland.

Grandy, T.G. and R.F. Stahman
  1974   "Types of produce types: an examination of person-
         ality development using Holland's theory."
         Journal of Vocational Behavior 5:231-239.

Gurin, P. and C. Gaylord
  1976   "Educational and occupational goals of men and wo-
         men at black colleges." Monthly Labor Review
         99:10-16.

Hager, P. and C. Elton
  1971   "The vocational interests of black males."
         Journal of Vocational Behavior 1:153-158.

Harvey, D. and R. Whinfied
  1973   "Extending Holland's theory to adult women."
         Journal of Vocational Behavior 3:115-127.

Holland, J.L.
  1962   "Some explorations of a theory of vocational
         choice: One- and two-year longitudinal studies."
         Psychological Monographs 76(26): 1:49.

  1966   The Psychology of Vocational Choice: A Theory of
         Personality Types and Model Environments. Waltham,
         Massachusetts: Blaisdell

References Cont'd.)

Holland, J.L. (cont'd.)
   1968   "Explorations of a theory of vocational choice:
          longitudinal study using a sample of typical col-
          lege students." Journal of Applied Psychology
          52 (monograph supplement).

   1973   Making Vocational Choices: A Theory of Careers.
          Englewood Cliffs, New Jersey: Prentice-Hall.

Jencks, C.S. and M.D. Brown
   1975   "Effects of high schools on their students." Har-
          vard Educational Review 45:272-324.

Kimball, R., W. Sedlacek and G. Brooks
   1973   Black and white vocational interests on Holland's
          Self-Directed Search (SDS)." Journal of Negro
          Education 42:1-4.

Knowles, L. and K. Prewitt
   1969   Institutional Racism in America. Englewood
          Cliffs, New Jersey: Prentice-Hall.

Melnick, V.L. and F.D. Hamilton
   1981   "Participation of blacks in the basic sciences:
          an assessment and strategies." Pp. 282-293
          in G. Thomas (ed.), Black Students in Higher
          Education: Conditions and Experiences.
          Westport, Connecticut: Greenwood Press.

Osipow, S.H.
   1973   Theories of Career Development. New York:
          Appleton - Century - Crofts.

Osipow, S.H., J.D. Ashby, and H.W. Wall
   1966   "Personality types and vocational choice: a test
          of Holland theory." Personnel and Guidance Jour-
          al 45:37-42.

Richards, J., G. Williams and J. Holland
   1978   "An evaluation of the 1977 minority introduction
          to engineering summer program." Report No. 270.
          Center for the Social Organization of Schools.
          The Johns Hopkins University: Baltimore, Md.

Sewell, W.H., A.D. Haller and G.W. Ohlendorf
   1970   "The educational and early occupational attainment
          process: replication and revisions." American
          Sociological Review 35:1014-1027.

References (cont'd).

Thomas, G.E.
   1980   Equality of representation of race and sex groups
          in higher education: institutional and program
          enrollment statuses. American Education Research
          Journal. 17 (June).

Wallace, P.A.
   1976   Pathways To Work Unemployment Among Black Teenage
          Females. Massachusetts Institute of Technology.
          Lexington, Mass.: Lexington Books

Walsh, W.B.
   1973   Theories of Person-Environment Interaction:
          Implications for the College Student. Iowa City:
          American College Testing Program.

Wilburn, A.L.
   19741 "Careers in science and engineering for black
          Americans." Science 184:1148-1154.

Section IV
Critical Factors Affecting Black
Higher Educational Access and Survival:
Overview

In 1968, professional schools were assertive in their efforts to increase the number of minorities among their student bodies. Odegaard's (1977) survey showed that 89 of the 100 predominantly white U.S. medical schools indicated that by 1972-73, they were actively engaged in promoting equality of educational opportunity for minorities. As a result, the number of blacks admitted to predominantly white medical schools increased substantially. However, data presented in this volume and by the American Medical Association show that black enrollment in professional schools is now experiencing a "stand still" or a decline.

The cessation of progress in black professional school enrollment has been attributed by some individuals to the effects of the Bakke decision and universities cautious reactions to the decision (Blackwell, 1981). Others have noted that the problem is largely associated with the inadequate secondary and postsecondary school preparation of blacks and their low performance on professional school entry exams. Reitzes (1958) study showed that the mean MCAT test scores of blacks from black college applicants to Meharry and Howard University were lower than the mean scores of all nonblack applicants to medical schools. He attributed these differences to cultural factors and the lack of adequate educational opportunity for blacks. Cobb (1973; 1979) identified the lack of finances and the failure of blacks to obtain adequate pre-socialization into the professions as major barriers to black professional school access.

Problems of retention and prompt promotion also confront blacks in professional schools. Data reported by Odegaard (1977) and the American Bar Association (1979) show that black students have lower retention rates in medicine and law and take a longer time to complete their professional schooling than whites. Carey, Singh and Pillinger (1981), Kolstad (1977), Morris (1979) and Thomas (1980) have also documented the problem of black persistence in comparison to whites at the undergraduate level.

The chapters in this section address the problem of black access and persistence in professional schools and in undergraduate institutions. The first chapter by James Blackwell describes recent trends in black professional school enrollment and attempts to account for these trends within the context of Bakke and the political and social sentiment of society. The next three chapters by Ada Fisher, Ralph Smith and Will Scott approach the problems of black access and persistence in professional and undergraduate institutions from narrative perspectives based on long term observations and experiences. These chapters go beyond mere enrollment statistics and discuss a variety of factors (e.g., psychological, economic, political, institutional) associated with minority access and retention in higher education.

References

American Bar Association
   1979   Annual Survey of Minority Group Students Enrolled in Approved Law Schools. Chicago: American Bar Association.

Blackwell, J.E.
   1981   "The access of black students to medical and law schools: trends and Bakke implications." Pp. 189-202 in G. Thomas (ed.), Black Students in Higher Education: Conditions and Experiences in the 1970s. Westport, Connecticut: Greenwood Press.

Carey, P., B. Singh and B. Pillinger
   1981   "Impact: a summer enrichment program for minority disadvantaged undergraduates at the University of Minnesota." Pp. 294-305 in G. Thomas (ed.), Black Students in Higher Education: Conditions and Experiences in the 1970s. Westport, Connecticut: Greenwood Press.

Cobb, W.M.
   1963   "A New dawn in medicine." Ebony (Sept.).

   1979   "What hath God wrought: notes on some breached walls." Journal of the National Medical Association 71:15-20.

Kolstad, A.
    1977   Attrition from College: The class of 1972 Two and
            One Half Years After High School Graduation.
            Washington, D.C.: Government Printing Office.

Morris, L.
    1979   Elusive Equality: The Status of Black Americans
            in Higher Education. Washington, D.C.: Howard
            University Press.

Odegaard, C.E.
    1977   Minorities in Medicine from Receptive Passivity
            to Positive Action 1966-1876. New York: Josiah
            Macy, Jr. Foundation.

Reitzes, D.C.
    1958   Negros and Medicine. Cambridge, Massachusetts:
            Howard University Press.

Thomas, G.
    1980   The Impact of Schooling and Student Characteristics
            on the Four-Year College Graduation of Race and Sex
            Groups. Baltimore, Maryland: Center for Social
            Organization of Schools. Johns Hopkins University.

13

The Access of Black Students
to Medical and Law Schools:
Trends and *Bakke* Implications

JAMES E. BLACKWELL ⸻⸻⸻⸻⸻⸻⸻⸻⸻⸻⸻⸻⸻

Introduction

This chapter examines the access of black students to
professional schools. The problem of minority access has
concerned higher education policy makers for at least two
decades, but the achievement of greater access has been a
goal of minority groups for more than a century. Specifically, as minority groups demanded equality of access to
graduate and professional schools, individuals and powerful
interest groups from the dominant population subsequently
organized social action and litigation designed to protect
what they perceived to be dominant group entitlements.
Inter-group conflict followed, and progress toward the
elimination of exclusionary practices was halted.

This chapter argues that the decision-makers in professional schools tend to respond to external pressures and perceptions of prevailing national sentiments regarding the
admissions of minorities to these institutions. They are not
likely to initiate new recruitment policies to increase their
current representation of minorities or provide greater financial aid for these students without seriously considering
the social and political implications of organized pressure.
Because prevailing national sentiments regarding rights of
minority groups are conditioned by situations that invariably
impact on the dominant group's control over economic, political and social resources, any perceived threat to that

control will create shifts from positive to negative sentiments, and changes in social policies. Similarly, minority
group pressure for access to professional schools is not
always sustained. It tends to decline when significant
numbers of their members appear to be gaining access and
when it appears that historical policies of either exclusion
or limited access are being vitiated. This situation
supports the proposition that the unequal access of minorities to professional schools is a manifestation of an inequality in the total society rooted in an imbalance of power
which has always favored the dominant group. Increases in
access for minority group students, however limited, are
frequently perceived as an erosion of dominant group entitlements, especially when changing power relations are defined
as real by the dominant group (Blackwell, 1975:1977). The
analysis of data on black student enrollment in professional
schools which is discussed in this chapter depicts a process
of exclusion, retardation, and decline. This contention will
be borne out in an examination of recent trends in medical
and law schools.

The Underrepresentation of Minorities in Professional Schools

According to the U.S. Commission of Civil Rights, the
underrepresentation of minorities in the health fields has
reached a critical state. A recent issue of the Civil
Rights Digest (1977) reports that:

"A severe lack of minority health professionals
exists, particularly among blacks and Native
Americans. Among Afro-Americans, long-standing
patterns of racial discrimination and economic
disadvantage have resulted in the fact that only
2 percent of American physicians are black although
Afro-Americans represent at least 12 percent of the
Nation's population. For reasons of preference and
because of the restrictions imposed by discrimination, black physicians primarily serve black
patients.   .... Thus, while there are some 6,000 black
physicians there are only 26 black physicians per
100,000 black Americans. Among Mexican Americans,
the second largest minority group representing 2.5
percent of the population, there are only 250
practicing physicians. Of every one million Native
Americans and Alaskans, only 72 are professionally
trained physicians."

Minority groups comprise only 4.5 percent of the dentists, 1.7 percent of the optometrists, 3.4 percent of the pharmacists, 4.3 percent of the podiatrists and less than 1 percent of the veterinarians (Bardolph, 1979). In each of these professions, more than 90 percent of all persons practicing in the field are white. With one exception (e.g. pharmacy) more than 90 percent of the professionals working in each of these health fields is a white male. Women comprise only 11.9 percent of the pharmacists in the country. But in nursing, which is still primarily a female dominated field, females constitute 97.3 percent of the registered nurses in the United States (Department of Health, Education and Welfare, 1976).

The 7,500 black lawyers in the United States represent only 1.8 percent of the total number. There are approximately 380,000 white lawyers in the U.S. (Caldwell, 1976). Whereas the ratio of white lawyers to white population is about 1 to 627, that of black lawyers to black population is 1 to 7,000 (Poinsett, 1974). Also, blacks represent only 2.5 percent of the total number of dentists in the country. While there is one white dentist for every 2,500 white persons, there is only one black dentist for every 12,500 black Americans (Blackwell, 1977). Clearly, blacks and other minorities are significantly underrepresented among practicing professionals.

Efforts to Increase Minority Student Presence

Efforts to increase the numerical representation and proportion of black students in professional schools have taken several varied forms. First, a genuine commitment was made by the federal government, by private foundations and by philanthropic organizations to take positive steps toward rectifying past inequities. For a few years that commitment was clear and pervasive, and resulted in creative action. Second, medical and law schools began active recruitment. These institutions established minority recruitment programs which were adequately financed, and developed liaisons between predominantly white and predominantly black undergraduate colleges from which the majority of minority group students were recruited. Third, these schools developed flexible admissions policies and supplemental programs in order to guarantee seats for the disadvantaged students, especially disadvantaged minorities. Several special admissions committees were established to attend to the specific needs of minority medical and law students.
This procedure was very similar to the responses of white

institutions to white students whom admissions officers and
university officials wanted to admit for special reasons.

Medical and law schools also created attractive financial aid packages to compensate for the economic disabilities
that most minority students suffered. As a result, various
support programs for minorities were established. These
programs involved a cross section of groups in both public
and private sectors. Among them were: (1) The U.S. Public
Health Scholarship Program, (2) the Armed Forces Health
Profession Scholarship Program, (3) National Medical Scholarships Program, (4) the Medical Education Guarantee Program,
(5) The Medical Student Opportunity Loan Guarantee Program,
(6) Martin Luther King, Jr. Fellowship Program, and (7) the
Council of Legal Education Opportunities (CLEO). The availability of financial assistance through these programs was a
major factor contributing to the access of minorities to
professional schools.

Project 75 was another important program that was
established to increase the number of blacks in medical
school. The program was specifically designed to increase
the proportion of black students in medicine up to a minimum
of twelve percent of the medical school student body total
by 1975. Project 75 was a joint venture sponsored by the
National Medical Association, American Medical Association
and the Association of American Medical Colleges. The project established counseling and tutorial programs for minority students and an early identification plan which located
junior and senior high school black students with a promising
potential for pursuing medicine. The program also established regional learning centers where minority students
could have contact with role models and practicing members
of the medical profession.

Despite the herculean efforts by sponsors and supporters
of Project 75, the project's goal was not achieved. The
goal was probably not reached because the distance between
a 2.8 percent black student enrollment in 1969-70 and a projected 12 percent enrollment in 1975 was too much to cover
in five years. Also, increases in white student enrollment
during that period, which were not anticipated, depressed the
percent of total black enrollment despite numerical gains
made by blacks.

Minority Professional School Enrollment: 1969-1978

Changes in the enrollment patterns of blacks have
occurred as an integral part of an overall pattern by which

total enrollment in professional schools soared beyond
previous expectations. Consider first the period between
1969 and 1974, the period before the Bakke suit. During this
period, DeFunis had already filed his suit for admission into
the University of Washington's School of Law, and similar
suits were filed in New York and Colorado charging prefer-
ential treatment for Puerto Rican and Chicano students,
respectively. The early efforts to increase minority
presence in professional schools were legally challenged.
Nevertheless, special programs did produce substantial
improvements in minority group presence. For instance,
Table 1 shows that in medical schools, between 1969 and 1974
the total number of first year enrollees increased from
10,422 to 14,763. Total enrollment in all classes in medical
schools increased from 37,690 in 1969-70 to 53,554 in 1974-75.
Black Americans enrolled at Howard and Meharry accounted for
120 of the 440 black American first year enrollees in 1969-70
and 195 of the 1,106 black student first year enrollees in
1974-75. Black students at Howard and Meharry accounted for
496 of the 1,042 blacks enrolled in all medical schools in
1969-70 and for 695 of the 3,355 black students enrolled in
medical colleges by 1974-75. Students at these two institutions represented 0.1 percent of the total enrollment in all
medical schools. Even then, nine of ten seats in first year
classes went to white students.

A similar profile is derived from Table 2 which shows
the total medical school enrollment for the same period,
1969-74-75. The 1,042 black students enrolled in all medical
colleges represented a mere 2.8 percent of 1969-70 enrollment. The proportion of black students climbed to 6.3 percent of total enrollment in 1974-75 (3,555 black students of
a total enrollment 53,554 students). Again, more than nine
of every ten seats in medical schools were occupied by white
students. The figures would not change appreciably if Asian-
Americans were included in these total percentages of minority students.

The enrollment of minority students in ABA-approved law
schools actually began to show dramatic increases following
the articulation of a fair and equal admissions policy in
1964. In that year, the 700 blacks enrolled in law schools
represented two percent of the 65,000 students enrolled.
By 1968-69, there were 2,154 black students enrolled in law
schools, a 300 percent increase (Educational Testing Service,
1976). It is important to note that predominantly black law
schools exist in North Carolina, Louisiana, Texas and in the
District of Columbia. In these states, most of the

Table 1

Selected First Year Minority Enrollment in U.S. Medical Schools, 1969-70 - 1977-78[a]

Year	Black American[b]		American Indian		Mexican American		Puerto Rican		Total Number Enrolled	Minority % of Total
	Number	%	Number	%	Number	%	Number	%		
1969-70	440	4.2	7	0.1	44	0.4	10	0.1	10,422	4.8
1970-71	697	6.1	11	0.1	73	0.6	27	0.2	11,348	7.4
1971-72	882	7.1	25	0.2	118	1.0	40	0.3	12,361	8.4
1972-73	957	7.0	34	0.3	137	1.0	44	0.3	13,677	8.6
1973-74	1,023	7.5	44	0.3	174	1.2	56	0.4	14,134	9.4
1974-75	1,106	7.5	71	0.5	227	1.5	69	0.5	14,763	10.0
1975-76	1,036	6.8	60	0.4	224	1.5	71	0.5	15,295	9.2
1976-77	1,040	6.7	43	0.3	245	1.6	72	0.5	15,613	9.1
1977-78	1,085	6.7	51	0.3	245	1.5	68	0.4	16,136	8.9

Source: Compiled From Data Made Available by the Association of American Medical Colleges

a. These data do not include Oriental (Asian) American student enrollment. Their enrollment in medical schools increased from 1.7 percent of the total in 1972-73 to 2.2 percent of the total first year enrollment in 1977-78. Cuban Americans, Commonwealth of Puerto Ricans and Pacific Islanders are also excluded.

b. Black Americans at Howard and Meharry Medical Colleges accounted for 120 of the 1969-70 enrollees and 195 of the 1974-75 freshmen.

Table 2

Selected Total Minority Enrollment in U.S. Medical Schools, 1969-70 - 1977-78[a]

Year	Black American[b] Number	%	American Indian Number	%	Mexican American Number	%	Puerto Rican Number	%	Total Number Enrolled	Minority % of Total
1969-70	1,042	2.8	18	*[c]	92	0.2	26	*	37,690	3.0
1970-71	1,509	3.8	18	*	140	0.4	48	0.1	40,238	4.5
1971-72	2,055	4.7	42	0.1	251	0.6	76	0.2	43,650	5.6
1972-73	2,582	5.5	69	0.2	361	0.8	90	0.2	47,366	6.7
1973-74	3,045	6.0	97	0.2	496	1.0	123	0.2	50,716	7.4
1974-75	3,355	6.3	159	0.3	638	1.2	172	0.3	53,554	8.1
1975-76	3,466	6.2	172	0.3	699	1.3	197	0.4	55,818	8.1
1976-77	3,517	6.1	186	0.3	780	1.4	232	0.4	57,765	8.2
1977-78	3,587	6.0	201	0.3	831	1.4	261	0.4	60,099	8.1

Source: Compiled from Data Made Available by the Association of American Medical Colleges.

   a. These data do not include Oriental (Asian) American student enrollment. Their enrollment in medical schools increased from 778 or 1.5 percent of the total enrollment in 1972-73 to 1,177 (2% in 1976-77. Since then, the AAMC has aggregated such data under the label "Asian or Pacific Islanders." In 1978, enrollment for this group of students was 1,422 or 2.4 percent of total enrollment. Even when these students, plus Commonwealth Puerto Ricans, Cuban Americans and others are subtracted from the total enrollment white students comprised 86.6 percent of total medical school enrollment in 1977-78.

   b. Black Americans at Howard and Meharry Medical Schools accounted for 496 of the 1969-70 enrollees and 695 of the 1974-75 enrollees.

   c. Calculations not shown (*) are less than 0.1 percent.

black law students are enrolled in the predominantly black
institutions (Morris, 1979). Black students have limited or
almost no access to the law schools located at the traditionally white institutions in these States (American Bar
Association, 1976).

Enrollment data in Tables 1 and 3 show that although
blacks made enrollment gains in medical school and law school
between 1969 and 1974, their enrollment particularly in
medicine tapered off or declined after 1974, which corres-
ponded to the Bakke era. For example, Table 1 shows that in
1974-75, blacks were 7.5 percent of the first year medical
school enrollment. But in 1975-76 they were only 6.8 percent
of the first year class and in 1976-77 only 6.7 percent.
American Indians also experienced a slight enrollment
decrease (although less than blacks) between 1974-75 and
1975-76, while Mexican Americans and Puerto Ricans experienced no change in medical school enrollment during this
period. With reference to blacks, a report by the Association of American Medical Colleges (1978) showed that the
first-year enrollment of white students increased by 2.5
percent between 1977 and 1978 while black first-year enrollment decreased by 1.9 percent.

Table 3 also indicates a decline and leveling off effect
for minorities in law school enrollment during the Bakke era.
In 1976-77, blacks were 5.3 percent of the first year law
school enrollment, but in 1977-78, their enrollment had
dropped to 4.9 percent. Their enrollment remained at 4.9
percent in 1978-79 (American Bar Association, 1976). Table 3
further shows that black first-year law enrollment declined
by 8.6 percent between 1976-77 as compared to 2.7 percent
for all minorities and 0.6 percent for non-minority students.

The recent decline in black law and medical school
enrollment may be due to a number of factors, including the
1974-1975 recession and a decrease in the availability of
financial aid for minority students. However, it is
believed that the manifest and latent fears that professional
schools developed in the wake of Bakke greatly contributed
to the decrease in affirmative action programs and efforts
to recruit black and minority students to professional
schools. Many of the predominantly white institutions
appeared to have adopted a "wait and see" strategy as a
result of Bakke litigation. The Bakke suit may have also
had an effect on black students themselves. Those students
who were interested in applying to professional schools were
probably reluctant to do so for fear of being rejected, even
though their chances of gaining admissions may have been
good.

Table 3

First-Year and Total Enrollment in ABA-Approved Law Schools, 1969-78[a]

	1969-70	1971-72	1972-73	1973-74	1974-75	1975-76	1976-77	1977-78
First Year Enrollment (Percent)								
Total	(---) 29,128	(---) 36,171	(---) 35,131	(---) 37,018	(---) 38,074	(---) 39,038	(---) 39,996	(---) 39,676
Black	(3.8) 1,115	(4.7) 1,716	(5.4) 1,907	(5.2) 1,943	(5.0) 1,910	(5.2) 2,045	(5.3) 2,128	(4.9) 1,945
Minority	(5.3) 1,552	(7.1) 2,567	(8.4) 2,934	(8.4) 3,114	(8.7) 3,308	(8.7) 3,413	(9.2) 3,669	(9.0) 3,571
Non-Minority	(94.7) 27,576	(92.9) 33,604	(91.6) 32,197	(91.6) 33,904	(91.3) 34,776	(91.3) 35,625	(90.8) 36,327	(91.0) 36,105
Total Enrollment (Percent)								
Total	(---) 68,386	(---) 94,468	(---) 101,707	(---) 106,102	(---) 110,713	(---) 116,991	(---) 117,451	(---) 118,557
Black	(3.1) 2,128	(4.0) 3,744	(4.3) 4,423	(4.5) 4,817	(4.5) 4,995	(4.4) 5,127	(4.7) 5,503	(4.5) 5,304
Minority	(4.2) 2,933	(5.9) 5,568	(6.6) 6,730	(7.2) 7,601	(7.5) 8,333	(7.4) 8,703	(8.1) 9,524	(8.1) 9,567
Non-Minority	(95.8) 65,453	(94.1) 88,900	(93.4) 94,977	(92.8) 98,501	(92.5) 102,380	(92.6) 108,288	(91.9) 107,927	(91.9) 108,960

Sources: American Bar Association, A Review of Legal Education in the United States - Fall, 1977.
National Advisory Committee on Black Higher Education and Black Colleges and Universities,
Access of Black Americans to Higher Education: How Open is the Door? (1979)

Bakke Implications and Future Concerns

The long awaited Bakke decision from the U.S. Supreme Court was handed down in June of 1978. In six separate decisions and by two split votes of an identical 5-4 margin, the U.S. Supreme Court upheld the right of Alan Bakke to be admitted to the medical school of the University of California at Davis while striking a blow at rigid quota-like set-aside special admissions programs. But by the same 5-4 margin, the Supreme Court (Regents of the University of California v. Bakke (1978):

1.   supported the use of race and ethnicity in college and professional schools admissions programs;

2.   confirmed the authority of colleges and professional schools to use their discretionary powers in the formulation of admissions policies and in the implementation of admissions procedures (See remarks made by Justice Blackmun).

3.   said that flexible admissions goals may be used but not rigid, arbitrarily fixed quotas;

4.   said that programs which give special advantage to minority students to help remedy past discrimination are constitutional, but admissions programs must be sure that the procedures utilized are not in violation of Title VI of the Civil Rights Act of 1964;

5.   permitted most existing admissions practices and voluntary affirmative action programs in admissions to continue undisturbed;

6.   said that universities and their professional schools should seek a diverse student body (and by implication, that diversity is also encouraged among faculty, staff and administrators at professional schools);

7.   acknowledged the continuing need for "race-conscious" programs as one method of meeting the need for diversity and a compelling State interest which may be so served.

The Bakke decision, as well as the suit itself, generated a national debate concerning graduate and professional schools admissions criteria. Bakke supporters, in general, endorsed the principle of meritocracy in which a strict adherence to performance on objective measures would theoretically be sole determinants of admission. In this regard, such factors as race and exclusion due to historic patterns of discrimination were viewed as irrelevant factors. Opponents to this view recognized the salience of test scores, grade point averages and class rank in admissions decisions, but insisted that subjective factors must also be considered. They argued that subjective factors had always been employed in admissions decisions and to insist that objective factors now be regarded as exclusive criteria was tantamount to even more blatant discrimination against black and other minority group students. This fact may be illustrated in the experiences of blacks in medical schools in the post-Bakke era.

The actual implications of the Bakke decision focus on (1) rejection of rigid quotas in admissions and (2) a reduction in the support for affirmative action in admissions procedures. The decision raises this essential question: will the decline in enrollment of black students and other minorities, which began when the Bakke suit was filed, be reversed through the utilization of affirmative action in admissions to professional schools? A definitive reply cannot be given at this point; however, systematic monitoring of admissions procedures, policies and results is required in order to understand the full impact of the Bakke decision.

In one of the most powerful justifications for the use of race as a factor in selection and admissions, Justice Thurgood Marshall stated:

"It is because of the legacy of unequal treatment
that we must now permit the institutions of this
society to give consideration to race in making
decisions about who will hold the positions of
influence, affluence and prestige in America,
if we are ever to become a fully integrated
society, one in which the color of a person's
skin will not determine the opportunities
available to him or her . . . .
I do not believe that anyone can truly look into
America's past and still find that a remedy for
the effects of the past is impermissible . . . ."
(Regents of the University of California v. Bakke 1978)

Four Associate Justices agreed with Justice Marshall in favoring race as a factor in the admissions process and four Justices abstained. The close 5-4 margin, coupled with what appears to have been the response of professional institutions to the Bakke decision, suggests that the nation has lost its commitment to obtaining equality of opportunity for minorities. Retrenchment of special admissions programs for minorities appears to be in demand at the same time that minorities are trying desperately to overcome the barriers to higher educational access.

A renewed national commitment is clearly required to turn the situation around. This commitment must be accompanied by clearly defined educational policies, procedures and practices. The federal government can no longer vacillate in policy determination and implementation, nor can it afford to bow to the pressures of opponents to equality of opportunity and social justice, because every delay solidifies resistance to change and exacerbates the problem of underrepresentation of black Americans in the professions. If federal action means enforcement of existing laws, then those laws should be enforced. If it means increasing the availability of financial assistance to black students, then that should be done. The increase in allocations to support the Graduate and Professional Opportunity Fellowships Program made by the last session of Congress is a step in the right direction.

Educational reform also demands action on the part of the professional schools and renewed support from the foundations. Selection and admissions procedures and practices need to be clarified and restructured so as to be clearly defensible. This process is already underway at such institutions as the Medical School of the University of California at Davis, the University of Missouri-Kansas City School of Medicine, Rutgers University Law School, and several other professional schools. But increasing the proportion of minorities who are not only entering but graduating and practicing their professions should become a greater priority for higher educational institutions and for U.S. society in general.

More specifically, extensive reforms must be made in our economic structure so that opportunities will be available to minorities for jobs and better incomes which will eliminate the pervasive consequences of economic disabilities. This will also necessitate the implementation of meaningful affirmative action programs in employment and in higher education. Perhaps, this is what Justice Marshall meant by "steps to open those doors."

References

American Bar Association
   1976   Law Schools and Bar Admission Requirements:
          A Review of Legal Education in the U.S.,
          Fall 1975. Chicago: American Bar Association.

Association of American Medical Colleges (AAMC)
   1977   Information for Minority Group Students,
          Medical School Admissions Requirements.
          Washington, D.C.: AAMC

   1978   Results of Fall Survey Conducted by AAMC
          Medical School Enrollments at Record High
          News Release, AAMC (November).

Bardolph, R.
   1979   The Civil Rights Record: Black Americans and
          the Law, 1849-1970. New York: Thomas Y. Crowell.

Blackwell, J. E.
   1975   The Black Community: Diversity and Unity.
          New York: Harper and Row.

   1977   The Participation of Blacks in Graduate and
          Professional Schools: An Assessment.
          Atlanta: Southern Education Foundation.

Caldwell, J.
   1976   ABA Report to the Senate on Council for Legal
          Education Report. (April). Washington, D.C.

Civil Rights Digest
   1977   "Minorities in medicine." Washington, D.C.:
          The U.S. Commission on Civil Rights Report 10:1.

Department of HEW
   1976   Women and Minorities in Health Fields. DHEW
          Pub. No. (HRA) 78-22 p. 10. Washington, D.C.

Educational Testing Service
   1976   1976 Review of Legal Education. Princeton, N.J.:
          Education Testing Service.

Morris, L.
   1979   Elusive Equality: The Status of Black Americans
          in Higher Education. Washington, D.C.:
          Howard University Press.

References Continued

Poinsett, A.
    1977   "The whys behind the black lawyers shortage."
            Ebony:95-102 (November).

Regents of the University of California v. Bakke
No. 76-811 (1978).

14

Black Medical Students:
Too Few for So Large a Task

ADA M. FISHER

Introduction

In a study conducted in the mid 1950s, Reitzes (1958) reported that U.S. society was confronted with a serious shortage of black physicians that not only affected the medical care of blacks but the health of the entire country. Brown (1979) noted that in his 1911 report, Abraham Flexner recommended that only Meharry and Howard be continued of the then existing seven black medical schools. The closing of the remaining five black schools that were not approved for continuation severely limited black opportunity for medical education. In 1910, there was only one black physician for every 2,883 blacks in the United States as compared with one physician to every 684 Americans for the nation as a whole. By 1942, the shortage of black physicians to the black population had increased as there was only 1 black physician for every 3,377 blacks (Brown, 1979). In 1975, the ratio was 1 black physician to 3,800 blacks (Black Enterprise, 1975 (2)) and in 1976, the ratio was 1:5,000 as compared to a ratio of approximately 1:600 in the same year for the general population. Therefore, while the ratio of doctors to patients shows general signs of improvement for the nation as a whole, the situation is clearly reversed in terms of the number of black physicians available to the black population.

In 1950 blacks constituted 10 percent of the total population and black physicians constituted only 2.2 percent of all physicians. Reitzes (1958) concluded that although there was a continuous increase in absolute numbers of black physicians in the 1950s, no progress had been made toward improving the numbers of black physicians in relation to the increasing demand for them. Findings by Blackwell (1981) and Odegaard (1977) indicate that Reitzes' (1958) observation in the fifties applies to the current status of black physicians

in the 70s. The proportion of black physicians in 1970, was
still 2.2 percent, far below the proportion of blacks in the
U.S. population (11%) in 1970 (Odegaard, 1977. It is predicted that by 1985, there will not be a physician shortage
in this country for the population in general. This prediction is supported by the Department of Health and Human
Services 1980 report which indicated that the supply of U.S.
physicians could exceed their demand by nearly 50,000 in 10
years (Raleigh News and Observer, April 14, 1980). This report, however, like most recent predictions, fails to include the dramatic shortage of black physicians. The current
black shortage will become even more severe in the near
future as the intake and training of blacks in medical
school continued to deescalate (Brown, 1979; Blackwell,
1981).

   An increase in the number of black physicians can be
achieved only by increasing and retaining the number of
black students enrolled in medical schools. Some of this
increase must take place at the predominantly black medical
schools (Howard and Meharry) which continue to enroll and
graduate a high proportion of black medical students
(Institute for the Study of Educational Policy, 1976). However, it is even more important that the predominantly white
medical schools assume a major role in this task. In 1974,
there were 112 predominantly white medical schools in the
country. It was only in this year that these institutions
exceeded the two predominantly black medical schools
(Howard and Meharry) in the number of black physicians
graduated in a given year (Gray, 1977). In addition, 83
percent of the more than 6,000 black physicians in this
country have received their education from Howard and Meharry
(Nelson, Bird and Rodgers, 1971).

Black medical students in predominantly white programs
have higher rates of attrition than whites and most other
minorities (Johnson, Smith and Tarnoff, 1975). More blacks
than whites spent an extra year in predominantly white medical schools as a result of course difficulties during their
freshman year.

This chapter addresses the problems of black student
access and retention in predominantly white medical schools.
Much of the discussion is based on interviews and informal
discussions that the author has had with over one hundred
black students in these institutions around the country.

The Decision to Go and Actually Going to Medical School

For many young black students, medicine is a dream or a
goal with little basis in reality. At no time is this more
clear than on graduation day from medical school when one
meets the fathers, mothers, and other relatives of white
students who are in medicine. The majority of black students
who choose medicine as a career will be first generation
physicians and will have had few role models to observe and
emulate. Very few black students have a firsthand view of
what it is like to be a doctor, much less a black doctor
where double standards and "racism" are a reality.

Getting in. In 1978, only one percent of 200,000
eligible black college students applied to medical school
(Journal of the American Medical Association, 1978b). The
exact percent of these applicants admitted is unknown, but
it is estimated that only 36% were admitted, with the
average applicant applying to approximately 9.2 schools
(Journal of the American Medical Association, 1978b). There
are many "games" that white students use to get into medical
school that black students cannot or do not use. The "buy
your way in" approach is one such game. In one medical
school, families and friends of 77 of the 91 entering white
students in 1973 pledged an average of $50,000 per student
to that institution (Rafalik, 1976). Nesmith (1976) has
documented similar "buying" strategies employed by white
students in the medical school admissions process. The
average white medical student comes from a family with an
annual income of $21,333; only half of these students require
institutional aid (Watkins, 1975; Petty, 1976). In contrast,
approximately 80 percent of the black medical students come
from families that earn less than $10,000 annually and most
of them require financial aid (Watkins, 1975; Petty, 1976).

Other routes of access that white medical school applicants use which black medical students often do not or cannot use include: (1) prearranged jobs with influential
medical school faculty at institutions that they would like
to attend; (2) using relatives in the medical professions;
(3) "twisting the arms" of medical alumni and "standing on
their heads" when necessary (Melleck, 1976).

Additional factors which limit the access of black and
minority students to medical school are academically based.
For example, poor undergraduate counseling often results in
black students having taken the wrong courses to get into
medical school. Other students who have taken the appropriate courses often do not have the grade point average
(GPA) required to enter some medical schools. However, many
medical schools are currently confronted with too many
applicants who have high grade point averages due to grade
inflation. As a result, most of these schools have developed their own formulas for determining which students are
admitted. These formulas consider the applicant's school
in evaluating his/her GPA. For example, an "A" at one school
may be equivalent to a "C" at a more prestigious institution.
The student's weighted GPA is then considered along with his/
her Medical College Admission Test (MCAT) score, letters
of recommendations, and his/her interview ratings. Based
on these criteria, an overall score is assigned to all applicants. If an applicant's score is sufficiently high, he/she
is admitted, if not he/she is rejected. Many white students
realize how important their MCAT scores are for medical
school entry. As a result they enroll in MCAT drill sessions
or prep courses to increase their test score performance.
These courses sometimes cost in excess of 250 dollars; hence
economically disadvantaged students cannot participate in
these pre-test preparation activities.

Rightly or wrongly, MCAT performance has traditionally
counted and continues to count substantially in the medical
school entry process; and test score performance is clearly
lower for black than for white students (Odegaard, 1977).
However, a new test component has been recently added to the
MCAT which is expected to be less culturally biased. The
new aspect of the test, which was developed by the Medical
College Admission Assessment Program was initially administered in the Spring of 1977. The cognitive section is
designed to identify desirable qualities in physicians such
as compassion, sensitivity, awareness, and an appreciation
for people. Both the academic and cognitive components of
the test will be given equal weight in computing student

test scores. As with all tests, if one can improve MCAT
scores with prep courses (and there is evidence to suggest
that one can) there is little reason to think that the new
test will be immune to this ploy.

Staying in and Remaining Sane. In past years it was
common to hear professors tell incoming medical students to
look to their left and then to their right, because at the
end of the year, one of them would not be there. Today, the
average white student who enters medical school will graduate
on schedule; their attrition rate is only 2 percent of the
total enrollment (Journal of the American Medical Association, 1978b.) But as previously noted and as shown in
Table 1, black students have a lower retention experience
than white medical students and other minorities. Racial
disparities regarding the promotion of black medical students
from the first to the second year also show that blacks are
less likely to be promoted than whites (Johnson et.al.,
1975). In all schools combined, 12.9 percent of the black
students had to repeat the first academic year and 6.3
percent had to repeat other years; only 1.6 percent of the
whites had to repeat the first year and 0.7 percent had to
repeat other years (Journal of the American Medical Association, 1978b). These figures are down from 1975, when 14% of
minority medical students had to repeat their first year
(Journal of the American Medical Association, 1978b). These
figures do not take into consideration the number of individual courses and exams through the year that minority students may repeat. They do not reflect constantly changing
academic requirements. They also do not account for
"special students" -- students allowed to take medical school
courses who aren't formally admitted; hence aren't counted
for purposes of data gathering. Nor do they reveal the
mental stress, social isolation, anxiety, and embarrassment
that minority students are subjected to as a result of their
failures.

In the process of acquiring a medical education, some
black students become their own worst enemies. Having no
relevant role models, many of these students develop false
and often misleading preceptions of what it takes for a
black person to matriculate successfully in medical school.
For example, some blacks think that they can emulate the
informal values and conduct of white students. But, although
white male students may be able to wear jeans and long hair
and go unnoticed, the same code of conduct when adopted by
blacks is often viewed as unprofessional. Also, black
students cannot readily afford to display negative atti-

Table 1

Students Admitted 1972-73 Through 1974-75
and Still in Medical School or Graduated, June 1975

	Admitted 1972-73 Number	Retained June 1975 Number	%	Admitted 1973-74 Number	Retained June 1975 Number	%	Admitted 1974-75 Number	Retained June 1975 Number	%
Black American	838	727	87	908	790	87	934	886	95
American Indian	30	27	90	37	31	84	63	62	98
Mexican Indian	140	134	96	167	157	94	203	198	97
Mainland Puerto Rican	37	35	95	48	47	98	60	59	98
All other Students	12,045	11,751	98	12,393	12,066	97	12,892	12,750	99

Source: AMA data, Journal of the American Medical Association 234 (December 1975): 1339,
    Table 14. Copyright 1975, American Medical Association

tudes and hostility toward most professors in white institutions even if they have a valid reason for doing so.
Politeness and reserved behavior by blacks are more often
welcomed by whites than aggressive behavior. Cutting
classes is also a luxury which black students cannot afford,
particularly because their absence in predominantly white
classes is so obvious. All of these factors can and often
do affect the grades and other evaluations that black students receive from white faculty. In addition, black students can inhibit their own success in white medical
schools. Frequently, their pride or else their deflated
egos keep them from spontaneous and meaningful interaction
with their white peers and with faculty members. They are
also reluctant to ask questions or seek assistance from
whites for fear of being labeled inferior or stupid.

The normative climate of the medical school and minority students' perceptions and misperceptions of the environment produce psychological pressure and ambivalence for
blacks over and above that experienced by the typical incoming medical student. These pressures are all a part of
the medical school game, but blacks enter the game without
previous experience and exposure, and, as a result, they
do not play the game as well as whites.

The Challenge Confronting Those Who Survive

Many black students think that once they survive medical
school, their problems are over. In reality, their problems
have just begun. By the third or fourth year, all students
must decide what kind of doctor they want to be. For most
students, this crucial decision comes at the time when they
are exerting all of their efforts to try to stay in school.
Foresight and curriculum planning are required to allow
time for evaluating and visiting prospective residency
training programs. Also, having adequate funds to interview at programs, which most black students lack, is an
important prerequisite for being selected to a good position.

Another problem which all black physicians must confront
is whether the National Interns and Residents Matching Program will exclude most of them from choice (many predominantly white) training programs. The matching process is
administered by a computer without any human efforts to
ensure that programs meet affirmative action guidelines. It
is therefore quite possible that white institutions can
legitimately fail to consider black residents in the matching process. During 1977, the states of Arizona, Hawaii,
Minnesota and Washington had only one black resident placed

in their state at the first year post-graduate training
level; thirteen states (Arkansas, Iowa, Kentucky, Nebraska,
New Hampshire, New Mexico, North Dakota, Oklahoma, South
Dakota, Utah, Vermont, and West Virginia), which had training
programs had no black residents at the first year level
(Journal of the American Medical Association, 1978). Black
students who wish to practice medicine must therefore face
the strong possibility of being denied access to major job
sites and even if they get the job, there is the all too
possible reality that they may be the only black in any position of influence there. In addition, black students can
expect to be salaried and government employees (as many black
physicians are) as long as they rely substantially on financial aid for their medical school training (Gray, 1977).
Those who do practice will find it necessary to locate their
practices in areas where discrimination is not likely to be
great.

Though for many white physicians medicine is a land of
opportunity, black physicians will have more restricted
opportunities as indicated by statistics showing that "more
than 85% of black residents were in training in internal
medicine, family practice, obstetrics/gynecology, and
pediatrics" Journal of the American Medical Association
(1978a). "Racist" referral patterns within the profession
may limit the numbers of patients referred by white doctors
to black doctors. At the same time, black doctors may have
problems of access to "good" specialists or follow-up for
their patients referrals. Ideally, one could believe the
myth of equal access to health care. However, it is imperative that the medical community and general public understand that the only entry the majority of black patients
have into the health care system, outside of clinics, is
the black physician (Gray, 1977). This can be further
appreciated given the realization that the black physician
will most likely continue to follow a pattern of all-black
practices as are 75% of those currently established (Gray,
1977; Watkins, 1975).

Conclusion

No matter how one manipulates statistics, there are
still too few black doctors for the population they serve.
The demand for black doctors is even more crucial when we
consider the fact that the black doctor is the only access
that the majority of black patients have to health care
outside of public health clinics. Some of the crucial
elements regarding black student access to, and success in,
medicine which must be addressed are as follows:

1. Role Models must be provided for black students.
This can be best achieved by increasing the current number
of black physicians to adequately reflect the black population; recruiting more black faculty to predominantly white
medical schools without pulling away those necessary for the
sustenance of the predominantly black medical schools; and
providing black physicians with a greater opportunity to
be more visible and influential within the administrative
and leadership capacities within medical associations, health
care planning committees, health care boards, governmental
health affairs, etc.

2. Greater Family and School Support must be given to
black students who are interested in pursuing medical careers. Minority youth need to be involved very early in work
experiences at hospitals, doctor's offices, nursing homes,
health clinics, and similar settings that will expose these
youngsters to the medical field and the rewarding experiences
of black doctors. Also, greater school support and better
counseling services for the health professions need to be
offered to students at the secondary and post-secondary level.

3. Financial Aid in the health professions for minority students must be continued at the federal level to encourage a greater number of these students to pursue medicine. Information concerning these programs must be better
disseminated in black churches and black community organizations as well as in local high schools and post-secondary
institutions. It is also important that more grant and
fellowship awards, as opposed to loans, be offered to these
students so that their financial burdens in future years will
be reduced and their ability to make rewarding contributions
without substantial personal economic sacrifice reduced.

4. Active Recruitment of minority students must be
broadened. The predominantly white medical schools need to
establish an ongoing relationship with predominantly black
colleges and high schools where black students are largely
represented. The interaction between these insitutions
should be aimed at identifying potential medical school candidates and assuring that these students are taking the
necessary courses for medical school entry. This might be
combined with summer enrichment programs or exposure opportunities such as those offered at Harvard, Howard, Meharry,
Tulane, and the University of Wisconsin.

5. Medical School Commitment to the needs of black and
minority peoples should be demonstrated in admissions policies, hiring practices, and health care delivery. The civil

rights laws must be enforced by schools, training programs,
hospitals, and health care workers to ensure minority access
to equal opportunities in the field. Internal retention efforts must be made to deal with the problems of educating
students, fairly assessing their progress, and removing hidden barriers to academic success. Schools should make known
to students their admittance status, their course and curriculum requirements, procedures for advancement and continuation, appeals procedures, criteria for grading (with papers
being graded blindly), graduation requirements, and licensing requirements if any.

   6. Future Establishment of Premedical Programs at Predominantly Black Institutions is needed. A group of black
medical professionals included this specific need among
recommendations for encouraging a greater number of black
students to enter medicine (Curtis, 1965). These programs
should continue to enhance the teaching and research skills
of the faculty at black institutions who would participate
in the premedical programs. Black insitutions of higher
education should be used as feeder institutions to prepare
promising minority students for careers in medicine. In
addition, the institutions should be weighted more favorably
in the admissions formulas used by many medical schools
(see "Getting In" section of this paper).

   7. National Acceptance of black people as professionals
must occur if black physicians and black people are to successfully utilize the health care system. The cause of
"white backlash" and cries of "reverse discrimination" must
be tempered by schools and officials pointing out the statistical realities--minorities are grossly underrepresented
in the professions and do have the capabilities to successfully and competently deliver health care.

   Some of these recommendations have been implemented to
some extent (Blackwell, 1981). For example, the Josiah
Macy, Jr. Foundation established a Post-Baccalaureate Premedical Fellowship Program to help blacks improve their preparation for admissions to medical school (Odegaard, 1977).
Other major efforts by private foundations and the federal
government have been identified by Melnick and Hamilton
(1981). Also a two-year medical program has recently been
established at Morehouse College which is intended to serve,
among other things, as a feeder institution to Emory University in Atlanta, Georgia.

All of these efforts are commendable and will hopefully increase the chances of minorities to obtain greater access and success in medicine. However, it is important that present programs be evaluated and that successful programs be developed on a broader, long-term basis. In addition, a greater political commitment to expanding the black professional class must be demonstrated by the many local and federal politicans who have not lived up to their promises in exchange for the black vote. Black alumni of predominantly white and black medical schools must give their respective schools the truth about their treatment and must openly encourage the expansion of minority opportunities in medicine. They must take a greater role in admissions procedures, financial support for minority students, and provide realistic experiences through preceptorships, internships, and other means of clinical and basic science teaching. Lastly and most importantly, the goal of increasing black physicians lies in the willingness of blacks themselves to be spokespersons for this important cause and to challenge the system to promote greater equality of opportunity for blacks and other minorities in medicine and in the professions in general. We must not ignore the rights of women and other ethnic minorities, but let us not forget that we are the most visible and easily distinguishable minority whose need for representation in health care is critical. If we cannot safeguard our health, our lives and personal welfare will be constantly threatened.

References

Blackwell, J.
1981   "Access of black students to medical and law schools: trends and Bakke implications," Pp.189-202 in G. Thomas (ed.), Black Students in Higher Education: Conditions and Experiences in the 1970s. Westport, Connecticut: Greenwood Press.

Brown, E. Richard
1979   Rockefeller Medicine Men: Medicine and Capitalism in America. Berkeley, California: University of California Press.

Curtis, J.L.
1965   "A plan to promote professional careers for Negros." Journal of the National Medical Associations 7:168-172.

Gary, L.C.
1977   "The geographic and functional distribution of black physicians: some research and policy considera-

tions." American Journal of Public Health
67:519-526.

Institute for the Study of Ecucational Policy
1976   Equal Education Opportunity for Blacks in Higher
Education: An Assessment.   Washington, D.C.:
Howard University Press.

Johnson, D.G., V.C. Smith and S.L. Tarnoff
1975   "Recruitment and progress of minority medical
school entrants 1970-73." Journal of Medical
Education 50:713-755.

Johnson, G.
1974   "The black patient: A catalogue of Abuses."
Medical Dimensions 6:19-21.

Journal of the American Medical Association
1975   "Students admitted 1972-73 through 1974-75 and
students still in medical school or graduated,
June, 1975." Table 14 (p. 1339).

1978a   "Undergraduate medical education," 78th Annual
Report: Medical Education in the United States,
1977-1978. December 22/29 240:2822-2824.

1978b   "Graduate medical education in the United States,"
78th Annual Report: Medical Education in the
United States, 1977-1978. December 22/29
240:2841-2844.

Melleck, N.
1976   "The other dean's list: the back door to Davis."
The New Physicians 25:33-35.

Melnick, V.L. and F.D. Hamilton
1981   "Participation of blacks in the basic sciences:
Assessment and federal program intervention,"
Pp. 282-293 in G. Thomas (ed.), Black Students in
Higher Education: Conditions and Experiences in
the 1970s. Westport, Connecticut: Greenwood
Press.

Nelson,B.W., R.A. Bird and G. Rodgers
1971   "Educational pathways analysis of the study of
minority representation in medical school"
Journal of Medical Education 46:745-748.

Nesmith, J.
1976   "The Philadelphia story: how to buy friends and

influence admissions." The New Physicians
25:30-32.

Petty, R.
   1976   "Money becoming an admissions criterion."
            AMA Newsletter 2/16:1.

Odegaard, C.E.
   1977   Minorities in Medicine From Receptive Passivity to
            Positive Action 1966-76. New York: The Josiah
            Macy Jr. Foundation.

Rafalik, D.
   1976   "Getting in, games people play," The New
            Physicians 25:29-31.

Reitzes, D.C.
   1958   Negroes and Medicine. Cambridge, Mass: Harvard
            University Press.

Watkins, R.
            "On becoming a black doctor." Black Enterprise
            5:20-25.

15

Black Law Students
and the Law School Experience:
Issues of Access and Survival

RALPH R. SMITH

Introduction

During the 1974 annual meeting of the Association of
American Law Schools, about forty black law professors met
with other minority law professors in San Francisco to
discuss the status of minorities in legal education. Among
the many matters clamoring for priority was a disturbing
trend in the enrollment figures. The number of black applicants seemed to be declining. Black first year enrollment had reached a plateau far below that number which would
offer hope for parity in the foreseeable future. (See
Table 1). Moreover, blacks seemed to be victimized by a
disproportionately high attrition rate (See Table 2). A
few black professors began an informal inquiry into these
matters. This chapter discusses some of the findings and
conclusions of this investigation. While most of the
issues relate to the law school milieu, some of the factors
discussed can be generalized to the experience of minorities
in predominantly white graduate and medical schools.

Access Barriers

Without some major new initiative that would offer
additional incentives for students to choose law as a profession, there is no reason to expect that a larger segment
of the eligible student population will do so. This is
especially true given increasing inflation and dismal reports regarding the job market for lawyers and for professionals in general. These factors are even more crucial for
blacks and other minorities who are unlikely to have the
money and other advantages that middle class whites have to
invest in a law school education.

In addition, it is becoming more difficult for all

Table 1

First Year Law School Enrollment, 1969-1979

Year	Black American	Mexican American	Puerto Rican	Other Hispano American	Asian or Pacific Islander	American Indian or Alaskan Native	Total 1st Year Minority	Total 1st Year National	% First Year Minority to National
1969-70	1115	245	29	35	–	44	1468	29,128	5.0%
1971-72	1716	403	49	74	254	71	2567	36,171	7.0%
1972-73	1907	480	73	96	298	79	2933	35,131	8.34%
1973-74	1943	539	96	94	327	109	3108	37,018	8.39%
1974-75	1910	559	117	182	429	110	3307	38,074	8.68%
1975-76	2045	484	113	217	436	118	3413	39,038	8.74%
1976-77	2128	542	119	225	484	133	3631	39,996	9.07%
1977-78	1945	529	134	316	509	137	3570	39,676	8.99%
1978-79	2021	551	190	334	557	145	3798	N/A	N/A

Source: Annual Survey of Minority Group Students Enrolled in Approved Law Schools. American Bar Association, 1979.

Table 2

Gross Attrition Rates of Minority Students in ABA-Approved Law Schools, 1969-1977

1969-1970	1st year	2nd year	% decrease 1st year to 2nd year	3rd year	% decrease 1st year to 3rd year
Black	1,115	N/A	N/A	761	31.74%
Mexican American	245	N/A	N/A	170	30.61%
Puerto Rican	29	N/A	N/A	18	37.93%
Asian	N/A	N/A	N/A	72	N/A
1971-1972					
Black	1,716	1,324	22.84%	1,207	29.66%
Mexican American	403	337	16.37%	271	32.75%
Puerto Rican	49	40	18.36%	25	48.97%
Asian	254	218	14.17%	202	20.47%
1972-1973					
Black	1,907	1,443	24.33%	1,329	30.30%
Mexican American	408	386	5.39%	329	19.36%
Puerto Rican	73	47	35.61%	56	23.28%
Asian	298	297	0.33%	288	3.35%

Table 2 Continued

	1st year	2nd year	% decrease 1st year to 2nd year	3rd year	% decrease 1st year to 3rd year
1973-1974					
Black	1,943	1,587	18.32%	1,452	25.27%
Mexican American	539	447	17.06%	381	29.31%
Puerto Rican	96	87	9.37%	96	0.00%
Asian	327	322	1.52%	287	12.23%
1974-1975					
Black	1,910	1,511	20.89%	1,488	22.09%
Mexican American	559	421	24.68%	446	20.21%
Puerto Rican	117	121	-3.41%	100	14.52%
Asian	429	343	20.04%	378	11.88%
1975-1976					
Black	2,045	1,654	19.11%	1,508	26.25%
Mexican American	484	435	10.12%	388	19.83%
Puerto Rican	113	94	16.81%	100	11.50%
Asian	436	439	-0.68%	423	2.98%
1976-1977					
Black	2,128	1,648	22.55%	1,572	26.12%
Mexican American	542	459	15.31%	445	17.89%
Puerto Rican	119	95	20.16%	111	6.72%
Asian	484	409	15.49%	398	17.76%

Source: Annual Survey of Minority Group Students Enrolled in Approved Law Schools. American Bar Association, 1979.

219

students, regardless of race, to secure admission to the
nations's law schools. In just over a decade, law school
enrollment nearly doubled. Yet, many law schools still
receive between ten and twenty applications for each seat in
the first year class. As in any situation where the demand
for a resource outweighs the supply, the suppliers are able
to increase their price for the commodity in demand. In law
schools, that price increase is manifested in increased
selectivity. In short, law schools are currently demanding
better credentials from their applicants than they did a
decade ago.

The increasing reliance on the LSAT presents a major
barrier to black students. Blacks are consistently outperformed by whites on this test. (White, 1979; Schrader
and Pitcher, 1973.) As more and more law schools curtail
and abandon their minority admissions programs in wake of
Bakke, the exclusionary impact of this disparate performance
will become an increasingly obvious problem.

The poor quality of counseling that black students
receive on legal studies is another factor affecting black
access to law school. Many undergraduate institutions
are not equipped to provide students with adequate law school
counseling. Pre-law advisers are often unable and in some
instances unwilling, to give black students adequate information about available law opportunities.

Interestingly enough, none of the reasons noted thus
far appear to have as great an impact on potential black law
school applicants as their own genuine concern for their
academic and emotional survival. The message that potential
applicants get from the anecdotal reports of their immediate
predecessors is that law school entry is almost impossible
and that for those blacks who do get in, there is a high
probability that they will fail. In addition, these students
are told that black students who do not flunk out maintain
marginal academic existence and that this marginal performance makes it difficult to pass the bar examination and
obtain a decent law job. Although only a part of this is
true, the point is that black students' perception that each
step in the law school process is a direct threat to their
survival is a formidable access barrier.

The extensive financial investment required for a law
school career poses an additional barrier for black students.
Rather than the doorway to economic security, some black
students view the beginning of legal education as the path
to financial ruin. Tuition has increased dramatically over

the past decade (See Table 3). Today, the normal three-year process can cost a student in excess of thirty thousand dollars. Black students often enter law school with little in the way of financial resources and much in the way of previous outstanding loans. Consequently, it is not un-common for these students to leave law school with loan obligations in excess of $20,000 to be repaid with interest during the initial stages of their professional career.

The financial obligation is particularly onerous to those students who practice law in the lower paid public service sector. This financial burden also affects the em-ployment opportunities available to blacks. Therefore black students lack the flexibility and mobility that white pro-spective lawyers enjoy. In many respects, black law students are being required to mortgage their future to acquire a legal education. Even so, many of these students must still work one or more jobs during the academic year. In doing so, they significantly increase their chance of becoming aca-demic failures.

Retention Barriers

Black law students are outperformed by their white counterparts. As a result, they drop out of law school at a higher rate than whites. Even where black students do persist, they are not evenly distributed across the law school grading curve. The most salient example is illus-trated by the membership rolls of law reviews at the major law schools which are based on high grade point averages. Only a mere handful of blacks have managed to be selected to participate in this educationally important prestigious and career-boosting experience. This is not surprising. Regard-less of personal legal skills, law review membership is generally, conditioned on demonstrated excellence in the taking of first year exams.

The traditional law school exam is supposed to test the student's ability to identify, analyze and develop issues by requiring the application of general principles to a specific fact situation. However, at each step along the way, the student is assigning values with reference to the cues he has been given or has deduced from the instructor. The student knows intuitively that his grade will in large measure de-pend upon the degree of congruence between the value and treatment he accords the issues and the value and treatment which is accorded by the professor. This process assures that students on the same cultural wavelength as the profes-sor have a definite advantage. These students are more

Table 3

Tuition and Fee Increases at the Nation's Elite Law Schools

Law School	68-69	78-79	Percent Increase
University of California (Berkeley)*	$1516.50	$2705	78%
University of Chicago	$2100	$4935	135%
Columbia University	$1904	$5032	164%
Harvard University	$1845	$4200	127%
University of Michigan*	$1760	$4073.84	131%
University of Pennsylvania	$2150	$5073.00	136%
Stanford University	$1920	$5331.00	178%
Yale University	$2150	$4900.00	128%

*Public Institution; nonresident costs.

Source: Law Schools and Bar Admission Requirements, A Review of Legal Education in the United States, Fall 1968-Fall 1977. Published by American Bar Association.

likely to be white than black.

The law school environment often fails to facilitate
learning. Many blacks view the highly competitive legal
environment as hostile and alienating. Interacting in the
classroom on a daily basis, most black students must confront
what W.E.B. DuBois (1899) described as the "duality of being
black" in America. As law students, blacks must be able to
discuss even slavery in dispassionate terms and legalese. In
addition, they must approach the study of law with the same
single-mindedness as their white counterparts, despite the
fact that their historical, cultural, and social experiences clearly warrant against such an approach. In many
schools, black law students are also forced, individually
and as a group, to assume the role of quasi-administrators,
and to undertake time-consuming duties in the recruitment and
admissions of other students. One black student expressed
this sentiment to several law school deans:

> "It is apparent to me that the local Black Amer-
> ican Law Students Association (BALSA) chapter,
> within the (region), is playing an invaluable
> administrative role at your institution. The
> very students whom you have admitted often with
> an expectation of "difficulty" (if not failure)
> are now, in addition to their studies and, for
> many jobs, serving as tutors, recruiters, coun-
> selors, ...etc. Though not required to, these
> students are fulfilling needs not adequately
> being served by the institution. I believe it
> is time that every law school which professes
> an interest in increasing its black enrollment,
> evidence this interest by providing institu-
> tionalized services that would remove the pre-
> sent 'burden' from the black students" ...
> (Smith, 1978).

Given the certainty of being outperformed by whites,
perceived alienation from the law school environment, and a
lack of adequate support and assistance from law schools, it
should not be surprising that many of the black students who
do get past the admission process are emotionally crippled
by the law school experience. The offices of many minority
law faculty are frequently visited by minority students
whose self-concepts have been undermined and shattered by
the law school experience.

The Final Hurdle

The few blacks who do survive the law school experience
must face still another obstacle--the passing of the bar.

Before a law graduate can practice law, almost every juris-
diction in the country requires that he/she pass an intensive
two- to three-day examination. The statistics on black law
graduates are disheartening. In state after state, blacks
are far less successful in passing the bar examination than
whites. This is particularly so on the first try. Thus,
after having survived the hurdles of law schools, black
students still find themselves confronted with a greater
probability of being defeated by the bar than whites.

Conclusion

The access and retention problems of black law students
are being confronted on several levels. BALSA has initiated
regional and national activities which aid in counteracting
some of the isolation black students feel at their respective
schools. BALSA provides black students otherwise unavailable
opportunities to develop their administrative, leadership,
and legal skills. The best example of this is the
Frederick Douglas Moot Court Competition which allows dozens
of law students from across the country to research, write,
and argue legal issues of genuine concern to the black
community.

Black law faculty are continuing and expanding their
efforts to assist black and other minority students by
serving as counselors, role models and sources of support.
They are also moving more aggressively to end the "revolving
door" policy within their own ranks. Over 60 percent of all
minority law faculty are presently untenured. The awareness
of their own vulnerability has served to sensitize black
faculty even more to the plight of minority law students.

From outside the academic community, the National Conference of Black Lawyers (NCBL) has also moved to assist black
students by reconvening its National Commission of Inquiry
which will again investigate allegations of discriminatory
practices in the nation's law schools.

The academic, emotional, and economic survival of today's black law student is important in order to promote the
still infant process of achieving a critical minority mass in
a most important profession. Minority lawyers are indispen-
sable to the legitimacy of the legal system. If America is
to maintain any sense of pluralism, it must assure its minorities a professional cadre. More specifically, it must provide them with equal access to the courts, to the legisla-
ture, and to other levers of power and influence in U.S.
society. Only black lawyers can fill that role. Legal education must make the institutional changes which are neces-

sary to allow black students to negotiate the tortuous trip
from a hopeful applicant to a successful professional.

References

DuBois, W.E.B.
    1899   Philadelphia Negro: A Social Study. Philadelphia:
            University of Pennsylvania.

Schrader, B. and E. Pitcher
    1973   "Predicting law school grades for black American
            law students." Reports of Law School Admission
            Council Sponsored Research: 1970-1974. Law
            School Admission Council.

Smith, R.
    1978   "Bakke's case vs. the case for affirmative action."
            New York University Education Quarterly 4:1-8.

White, D.
    1979   "Culturally biased testing and predictive
            invalidity: putting them on the record." 14
            Harvard Civil Rights - Civil Liberties Law
            Review 89:21-29.

16

Critical Factors for the Survival
of First Generation College Blacks

WILL B. SCOTT ──────────────────────────────

The importance of values, attitudes, and behaviors of
black first generation college students has been badly mis-
understood and poorly interpreted. Despite their good faith
intentions, many teachers, administrators, and researchers
involved with black college students lack the relevant experience, perspectives, and role-taking ability to adequately understand and respond to the educational needs and aspirations of first generation blacks. These experiences and an
adequate understanding and acceptance of these students is
paramount if members of the higher educational community are
to become more effective in the delivery of services to
black undergraduates. This chapter identifies factors that
are essential to the survival of first generation college
blacks. The discussion is primarily based on the author's
long-term and systematic interaction with black undergraduates in a teaching, counseling, administrative, and multi-
supportive capacity.

There are distinct social characteristics shared by
many black students. The first of these is a behavioral
pattern which on the surface appears to be expressive of
anti-intellectual values, inasmuch as such behavior of
black students frequently leads to early dismissal from
college and/or failure to fulfill well established academic
expectations operating in the college environment. For
example, students in sociology, whose major areas of study
are social structure and social process, often exhibit formal and informal behavior which demonstrates little or no
understanding of group and/or collective behavior. Also,
psychology majors who have strong beliefs about individuals
express these beliefs in terms of "God's will," fate, and

other non-scientific ways; and many black political science
majors often demonstrate interpersonal behavior with almost
no recognition of the importance of power, prestige, influence, negotiation, and arbitration.

Also present among first generation college blacks are
a few students whose behavior is quite consistent with the
norms and expectations operating in the college environment.
It is this group of black students that provides a meaningful point of reference for the larger group of black undergraduates. The smaller group of blacks do not differ from
the larger group in terms of innate intelligence, nor in
terms of demonstrated motivation or ability. Instead, the
major differences are: (1) interpersonal skills appropriate
for the academic environment; (2) internalization and trans-
lation of educational beliefs and values into appropriate
behavioral expressions; (3) participation in and development
of functional peer and reference groups that are consistent
with future personal, academic and professional expectations;
and (4) possession of a clear understanding of one's self
as a responsible person.

For the typical middle-class student these four attributes are generally developed and learned within the immediate family during adolescent and childhood socialization.
However, this is not the case for most first generation
black college students. Instead, an interested teacher,
relative, and/or friend often serves as a role model or
source of support for most first generation blacks. The
influence and support of these role models often result in
highly motivated students.

The learning and refinement of interpersonal skills
for first generation black college students can be incorporated into college curricula and academic and professionally
related activities through the collective efforts of faculty
who are willing to serve as role models for these students.
Some interested faculty have initiated these activities by
regularly inviting black students to their homes, meeting
and interacting with these students' relatives and friends,
taking students to various local, regional, and national
professional meetings and introducing these students to other
appropriate role models. These series of structured formal
and informal activities can, and often do lead to the modi-
fication of dysfunctional values and attitudes that first
generation blacks bring with them to the college environment.
The process of resocialization for these students is quite
comparable to the "normal" experiences of middle class black
and white college students whose family prestige and influ-

ence insure them the mix of formal and informal activities just described.

Unfortunately, first and second generation black students are often characterized and treated by faculty and college administrators in terms of their past socialization rather than their potential for new learning and resocialization. For example, it is often claimed that black undergraduates do not have the ability to communicate effectively in terms of reading comprehension, writing and speaking skills. This purported problem is often defined in cognitive terms (i.e., a failure to learn). The solutions to the "perceived" problems are traditional remedial approaches that have little or no impact on achieving the desired set of cognitive skills. However, when the "problem" of inadequate cognitive skills is alternatively defined as a lack of interpersonal skills and a lack of exposure, more productive solutions can be achieved. For example, more than ninety percent of the sociology and social service student majors in one public historically black institution in which I taught were from rural areas of the state and attended public secondary country schools or schools that were in small school districts. As freshmen students, these students displayed the range of reading comprehension, writing and communication that were typical of their prior environment and educational training. A positive approach to these students entails: (1) recognition and conceptualization of the cognitive and affective socialization factors which account for the kinds and levels of communication skills that these students possess; and (2) implementation of a series of corrective activities designed to develop the interpersonal skills of these students.

The matter of recognition and conceptualization of students' interpersonal skills should be made during initial advisory conferences. During these sessions, students' responses regarding choice of major, place of birth, father's/ mother's occupations, level of education of parents and siblings, future career plans, and use of leisure time provide excellent clues to weaknesses and strengths in students' prior socialization. In listening to students' responses during conferences, what one often finds is that these students: (1) demonstrate acceptable ability to comprehend, read and respond verbally; (2) demonstrate acceptable ability to comprehend, read and respond verbally but need assistance with communication skills to achieve greater precision; or (3) do not demonstrate appropriate communication skills. In addition, a careful and unbiased observer will often find that these students' native intelligence ranges between

"average" to above "average"; and that their native intelligence has been limited, without exception, by race, sex and
class factors. More importantly, one finds that the behavior of these students, which was appropriate for successful survival in their previous environment has been learned
and is therefore subject to change to meet the norms and
expectations operating in the college environment.

The copious outpouring of frustration and negativism regarding the deficiencies of first generation college blacks
is often the result of middle class faculty failure to understand the prior socialization and background of these students. The obvious is seldom apparent to these faculty.
For example, it ought to be quite evident that if first
generation blacks are socialized to attend college for
purposes of getting a "good job" after four years of college,
it will require considerable resocialization to motivate and
prepare these students for graduate and professional study.
If black college students are socialized to achieve short-
term success in their homes, and local communities, it
should be obvious that these students will need to learn
how their previously successful behavior is capable of being
modified for continued success on college campuses. If
black college students have had little or no direct involvement with their chosen profession and relevant professional
role models prior to college entry, it should be obvious
that there is crucial and immediate ongoing need for these
students to be socialized into the professions by relevant
professionals.

Many faculty frequently bemoan a perceived lack of am-
bition and motivation by black undergraduate students.
They insist that black undergraduate students currently
have more and greater "opportunities" than ever before to
enter college, study and perform well, and continue graduate
education, with more than adequate supports along the way.
I find this assessment of the "opportunities" available to
black students essentially incorrect and misleading. An
"opportunity" is not a singular, unrelated event; it is a
combination of favorable circumstances--almost always with
an element of chance. To state that black students do not
take advantage of their opportunities may be saying little
more than black students do not engage in sufficient risk
taking; or that some black students view their "opportunities" as extremely limited.

I have frequently obtained funds for the purpose of
providing black undergraduates with opportunities to travel
and meet outstanding black scholars and professionals. The

initial incentive (especially for freshmen and sophomores)
for student participation in this activity is an opportunity
to travel and to "get away" from the campus. However, subsequent exposure of these students to and interaction with
black and white professionals in formal and informal settings
proved to be an effective means of sensitizing first generation blacks to opportunities for personal development and
achievement. Without this exposure, college graduation
for most of these students means preparation for a job in
a racist and select society not responsive to blacks.

In the absence of college educated parents and grand-
parents, and college educated adults in the neighborhood,
as well as an understanding of career opportunities and the
importance of major field choice, the pursuit of a professional career also must be taught formally and informally to
first generation college blacks. Less than one percent of
all of the black students that I have taught and advised
had prior knowledge of the importance of professional
affiliations and experience in utilizing professional organizations for meeting peers, financial aid and entry to
graduate and professional school, future employment, becoming familiar with issues and trends in the professions, and
becoming a part of ongoing informational networks.

Very early in the educational process, first generation
black undergraduates need to understand that there are only
three "real" jobs necessary for self-survival and the
maintenance of society: the production and distribution of
food, clothing, and shelter. All other jobs are "invented"
in that they are the result of political decisions and/or
personal preferences of the dominant group. Black students'
understanding of these basic facts is necessary to sensitize
them to the importance of active political participation
within and outside of higher education for obtaining subsequent educational and career options.

All college students should understand the nature of the
political process. However, this knowledge is particularly
crucial for first generation blacks whose social and economic background has barred them from the mainstream social,
economic and political benefits of U.S. society. The
recognition and acceptance of the influence of the political
process also forces black students to re-examine the widely
held belief that black and other minority recipients of a
"good education" will subsequently enjoy the "good life."
All too often, black and minority graduates encounter constraints to social and career mobility that are the result
of public and private organizations that exert considerable

influence on career access and maintenance.

Black undergraduates must also recognize early in their
educational careers the importance of informal, social and
professional networks (e.g., "old boy networks" or "little
groups of friends"). These networks exist at all levels of
education and in all formal organizations. The professionals in these groups not only have prestige, but also power
and influence with reference to educational, employment and
other formal organizations. Somewhat similar to the informal networks in formal groups are the peer networks and
friendship groups which students form themselves. These
groups are also very influential on the educational and
career aspirations and attainment of college students.
Among most first generation blacks, the primary motivation
for group formation and friendship selection appears to be
based on who is "nice" or "friendly" rather than on who is
"scholarly" and/or "highly productive". It is only after
repeated reinforcement and experiences that these students
grasp the importance of selectively integrating career,
peer, and family networks into a comprehensive mutual
support group that is capable of providing the personal,
academic and professional reinforcement required for satisfactory engagement in career development and mobility.

A final requirement for the successful survival of
first generation college blacks and all black students is
the development and/or strengthening of a black perspective
useful for appropriate definition of self, and for enhanced
learning. As long as there are any forms of racism, and
especially as long as racist ideologies are expressed
overtly or covertly in textbooks and other educational
media, first generation blacks need appropriate identification and analyses of these ideologies. Where the contributions of black scholars and researchers are omitted,
they must be identified; when research findings are distorted by cultural and/or ethnic bias, these distortions must
be clarified; where real racial differences are noted between blacks and others, these differences should be clearly
interpreted as differences, not as "problems". When this
interpretive and clarification process does not occur, the
educational process of black students is negatively affected, as is the development of educational objectivity.
Therefore, a comprehensive approach must be employed by
faculty to aid black undergraduates in maintaining and further developing a black cultural perspective. The major
objective of this approach should be to help students identify and understand biological, psychological, and social
differences and similarities between themselves and the

dominant culture. It is only through this multiple and comprehensive approach that first generation college blacks, who constitute a major part of America's future hope and productivity, will be able to contribute effectively and simultaneously to their culture and the dominant culture.

Section V
Programs and Strategies for Increasing Black Access and Retention: Overview _____

Section V of the volume addresses the question: What is being done to increase the access and retention of blacks at all levels of higher education? The future status of blacks and other minorities in higher education will largely depend on the extent to which the Federal government and the public and private sector make this issue a greater priority and generate more effective programs and strategies to increase the quality and level of higher education for minorities.

The papers in this section describe and evaluate various programs and strategies designed to increase the access and retention of minorities in higher education. The first chapter by James Richards, Gerald Williams and John Holland evaluates the effectiveness of a summer engineering program (Minority Introduction to Engineering) implemented at a number of colleges and universities to encourage minority high school students to select engineering as a career. The second chapter by Randolph Bromery suggests methods for increasing the access and retention of minorities in engineering and describes a program that has incorporated these strategies. The next chapter by Herman Young proposes an "affective" approach for increasing the access and retention of minorities in the basic sciences. The fourth chapter by Robert Geertsma discusses a tutorial program at the University of Rochester School of Medicine that was designed to help black students overcome initial academic problems.

The fifth chapter by Vijaya Melnick and Franklin Hamilton focuses on structural intervention and describes federal and foundation efforts designed to increase the participation of minorities in the basic sciences. In chapter 22, Philip Carey, Baldave Singh and Barbara Pillinger describe a summer enrichment program at the University of

Minnesota that was instituted to increase the access and
retention of minority undergraduates. In Chapter 23,
Paul Mohr and James Sears report on a recent matriculation
program between a predominantly white two-year college
and a predominantly black four-year college in Virginia
which was developed to facilitate desegregation and to increase the access of blacks to a four-year college. In the
final chapter, Frank Brown proposes a number of strategies
for increasing the access and retention of minorities at all
levels of higher education.

17

An Evaluation of the 1977 Minority Introduction to Engineering Summer Program*

JAMES M. RICHARDS, JR., GERALD D. WILLIAMS, and JOHN L. HOLLAND

INTRODUCTION

In recent years, increasing concern has been expressed about the relatively small number of minority group members in the United States who pursue professional and technical careers. Consequently, numerous efforts have been made to attract students from minority groups to curricula that would prepare them for such careers. For example, Talent Search, has attempted to attract minority students to college as well as to professional and technical curricula. Other efforts have involved specific attempts to attract minority students to specific curricula and careers. This chapter describes one such specific effort, the Minority Introduction to Engineering (MITE) program of the Engineers Council for Professional Development, which has the specific goal of increasing the number of minority students studying engineering.

The MITE program brings selected minority group members to the campuses of engineering colleges during the summer between their junior and senior years in high school.

*This evaluation was conducted under a contract between the Engineers Council for Professional Development and the Johns Hopkins University, and was supported, in part, by a grant from the Exxon Corporation to the Council. The work was performed at the Johns Hopkins University Center for Social Organization of Schools, supported in part as a research and development center by the National Institute of Education, Department of Education.

(The Engineers Council for Professional Development also
sponsors other interventions which attempt to reach students
at younger ages.) In programs lasting one to three weeks,
participants are exposed to a variety of activities designed
to familiarize them both with engineering and with college
life. These programs usually involve some combination of
classroom instruction, "show and tell" presentation in
which practicing engineers demonstrate interesting apparati,
visits to firms employing substantial numbers of engineers
and "hands on" experience with such devices as computers.
Programs vary in the extent to which the classroom instruction is designed to simulate the experience participants
would have in college; that is, some programs have required
assignments that are graded by the instructors while other
programs do not.

This chapter summarizes an evaluation of the 41 different programs (i.e., for groups of minority student participants) operated by the 30 institutions listed in Table 1
during the summer of 1977.[1] As nearly as we can determine,
these programs served a total of 1,271 different participants. Because a few students attended more than one
program this number is somwehat uncertain.

The data collection provides a nearly classic example of
the difficulties and limitations of evaluations of this kind
of intervention. The basic plan called for pre- and post-MITE
questionnaires, with the pre-MITE questionnaire administered
to all applicants. In addition, one program agreed to conduct a "true experiment" in which participants were chosen
randomly from a pool of applicants meeting a few minimum
requirements. The basic procedure for collecting pre-MITE
data was to provide questionnaires to MITE Program Directors
with the hope that these questionnaires would be completed by
all applicants. For various reasons, only a few programs were
able to administer the questionnaire to applicants, and some
programs were even unable to administer the questionnaire to
participants. In those programs that did administer the
questionnaire, the most typical procedure appeared to have
been to distribute the questionnaires to participants on the
first day of MITE. This procedure yielded a total of 996
useable pre-MITE questionnaires from participants. Only 104
useable pre-MITE forms were obtained from applicants who were
not accepted for participation; these data were further
limited to a small number of institutions.

Table 1

Institutions Operating MITE Programs
in Summer of 1977

University of Alaska
University of Arkansas
University of California, Irvine
University of California, Los Angeles
Clarkson College of Technology
Georgia Institute of Technology
University of Houston
Howard University
University of Illinois
Lafayette College
Lehigh University
University of Maryland
Massachusetts Institute of Technology
University of Massachusetts
University of New Mexico
New Mexico State University
North Carolina State University
University of Notre Dame
University of Oklahoma
Prairie View A. and M. University
Purdue University
Rochester Institute of Technology
Tulane University
U.S. Air Force Academy
U.S. Coast Guard Academy
U.S. Military Academy
U.S. Naval Academy
Vanderbilt University
Villanova University
University of Washington

The post-MITE data were collected by mailing question-naires to participants regardless of whether or not they had completed the pre-MITE questionnaire. To maximize response rate, two separate mailings were made to participants. Consequently, the post-MITE data were obtained four to six months after the end of the MITE experience. These procedures yielded 620 useable post-MITE questionnaires from participants, of which 540 came from participants who had completed the pre-MITE questionnaire. The response rate was especially low in the "true experiment" program; so low that separate analyses of this program were not possible. Post-MITE data were collected from unaccepted applicants through a single mailing of the follow-up form. Only 78 useable questionnaires were obtained. Finally, the Engineers Council provided information about the number and length of programs operated by MITE institutions.

FINDINGS

An obvious question about MITE would involve the number of various minority group students participating in MITE. Relevant data are presented in Table 2.[2] The modal MITE participant is a 17-year-old Black male. The second largest group consists of participants with one form or another of Spanish heritage, and the third largest group consists of Native Americans.

Students participate in MITE after their junior year in high school. It obviously would not be possible for students to take all of the math courses required by engineering colleges in their last year in high school. Therefore, one would expect participants to be chosen on the basis of their math background, to have relatively strong academic backgrounds in general and to come from relatively privileged family backgrounds. These expectations are confirmed by the data in Tables 3 and 4. The strong academic background is clearly evident in the number of science and math courses they have taken and the grades they have received. Their test scores also are high compared to other reported scores for minority groups (although they might still be somewhat low compared to non-minority applicants for engineering). It is also clear that participants come from very privileged family backgrounds compared to the representative sample of minority group students in general in the National

Table 2

Distribution of 1977 MITE Participants by
Ethnic Category, Age, and Sex

	Males (N=733) %	Females (N=538) %	Total (N=1271) %
Ethnic Category			
Black	69.5	79.0	73.6
Latino	20.3	13.2	17.3
American Indian	4.6	4.7	4.6
Oriental American	2.9	1.1	2.1
Other	2.7	2.0	2.4
Total	100.0	100.0	100.0

	Males (N=547)	Females (N=442)	Total (N=989)
Age			
16 or Under	12.8	12.9	12.8
17	71.0	77.9	74.1
18	14.6	9.0	12.1
19 or Over	1.6	0.2	1.0
Total	100.0	100.0	100.0

239

Table 3

Academic Backgrounds of 1977 MITE Participants by Sex

Variable	Males		Females	
	$\overline{X}$	SD	$\overline{X}$	SD
Grade Point Average	(N=541)		(N=440)	
Overall GPA	3.46	0.48	3.58	0.45
Math GPA	3.40	0.61	3.45	0.59
Science GPA	3.41	0.61	3.50	0.54
Number of Courses Taken in:	(N=551)		(N=445)	
Math	2.93	1.03	2.78	0.97
Science	2.13	0.85	2.15	0.82
Aptitude Test Scores	(N=283)		(N=213)	
PSAT Math	52.51	9.43	49.85	8.47
PSAT Verbal	44.73	9.96	44.85	9.96
SAT Math	542.60	86.47	505.43	80.98
SAT Verbal	463.41	95.15	473.72	93.33

Table 4

Comparison of Parents' Education and Family
Income of MITE Participants with National Longitudinal Study Sample

Ethnic/Racial Category	Father B.S. Degree or More		Mother B.S. Degree or More		Family Income Over $15,000	
	MITE (N=867) %	NLS (N=21,783) %	MITE (N=922) %	NLS (N=21,877) %	MITE (N=597) %	NLS (N=16,549) %
Black	33.6	5.1	35.0	5.3	47.0	6.1
Latino	29.4	5.2	12.1	2.9	30.4	8.6
American Indian	29.2	7.9	17.3	5.4	29.4	17.0
Oriental American	35.3	15.3	5.9	10.1	58.7	24.7

Longitudinal Study of the High School Class of 1972 (Peng, Stafford and Talbert, 1977). Indeed, non-minority students from such backgrounds would be regarded as at least above average in socio-economic status. Given the purposes and emphases of most MITE programs, these characteristics of participants appear appropriate. It should be clearly recognized, however, that MITE is <u>not,</u> to any major extent, a program for salvaging high school dropouts and non-achievers.

The institutions that offered MITE programs in the summer of 1977 were very diverse; they were widely dispersed across the United States, and included public and private institutions as well as predominantly white and traditionally black institutions. A large body of research and theory (Astin, 1965; Astin & Holland,1961; Holland, 1973; Hoyt, 1968; Richards, Seligman & Jones, 1970) suggests that such diversity usually is accompanied by a similar diversity in educational program, student body characteristics, and so forth. Therefore, it appeared important to explore the homogeneity vs. diversity among the MITE programs operated by these institutions.

Table 5 summarizes data for the number and length of MITE programs operated by participating institutions in 1977. The number of separate programs, or groups of participants, varied from 1 to 3, and the length of these programs varied from 1 to 3 weeks (a week, however, might be either 5 or 7 days long). The modal MITE program lasted two weeks and was the only program offered by its host institution. These results indicate rather narrow variations in program characteristics.

On the other hand, Table 6 summarizes the variation in group characteristics among the participants in programs at various MITE institutions. These results indicate a high degree of diversity in the composition of participating groups. For example, the highest group on each PSAT score exceeded the lowest group by about one and one half standard deviations; the highest group on number of science courses had taken more than twice as many such courses as the lowest group; the highest group on family income claimed an income more than $13,000 higher than the lowest group; and the ratio of highest to lowest group on the percent of participants saying that the chances are "Very Good" that they will study engineering was about 5 to 1.

Diversity of this magnitude could strongly affect the experiences that participants have in various MITE programs and the impact of those experiences, but unfortunately too many institutions were missing from the present data to

Table 5

Number of Programs by Institution and Distribution of Programs by Length

Number of Programs Offered by Institution	Institutions N	Offering Percent
1	21	70.0
2	7	23.3
3	2	6.7

Program Length in Weeks	Programs N	Percent
1	14	34.1
2	24	58.6
3	3	7.3

Table 6

Variation in Characteristics of the Group
of Participants for MITE Institutions

	No. of Institutions	Score of Institution with Lowest Score	Score of Institution with Highest Score	Average Score for all Institutions
Percent of Participants Who Are:				
Male	25	37.5	72.4	57.1
Black	24	0.0	100.0	63.8
Latino	24	0.0	94.7	17.8
Indian	24	0.0	100.0	10.2
Oriental	24	0.0	50.0	4.7
Other	24	0.0	19.0	3.6
Average High School GPA				
Math	20	2.90	3.69	3.33
Science	20	2.88	3.80	3.36
Total	20	2.99	3.75	3.43
Average Test Score:				
PSAT - Math	13	42.64	56.61	49.78
PSAT - Verbal	13	36.75	53.08	43.71
Average No. of Courses in:				
Math	20	1.71	3.59	2.86
Science	20	1.20	2.83	2.11

Table 6 Continued

	No. of Institutions	Score of Institution with Lowest Score	Score of Institution with Highest Score	Average Score for all Institutions
% of Participants Who Say Chances are "Very Good" They will:				
Go to College	20	71.4	100.0	92.9
Graduate from College	20	52.4	100.0	88.0
Study Engineering	20	13.0	68.4	45.9
Average Number of Persons Encouraged Participant to:				
Go to College	15	3.88	5.77	4.82
Study Engineering	15	1.13	2.85	2.05
Median Family Income	15	$8,999	$22,499	$13,849
Average Score On:				
College Potential	20	3.83	6.93	5.63
Engineering Potential	20	3.63	6.76	5.65

Note: For each variable, only institutions with scores for 5 or more participants are included.

permit a meaningful examination of these issues. In future
evaluation of interventions, however, investigators should
remember that such diversity can exist among ostensibly
similar programs. At the same time, it should be emphasized
that the only point of the present analysis is the degree of
diversity, and no implications are intended about how MITE
participants should be chosen.

The primary goal of the MITE program is to increase the
number of minority engineers. Consequently, the most important criterion for evaluating MITE is whether or not the proportion of participants planning to study engineering increased. Data pertaining to this criterion are presented in
Table 7. Two comparisons are shown for those participants
who responded to both the pre- and post-MITE questionnaires.
The first set of results, which compares pre- and post-MITE
answers to free response questions about preferred field of
study, are limited by the fact that a substantial proportion
of participants responded to the pre-MITE question in terms
of the field they wanted to study in college. The second
set of participant results compares responses to two post-
MITE questions about intent to study engineering before and
after MITE. Similar data are shown for the small number of
non-accepted applicants who provided post-MITE data.

Both sets of data indicate a substantial increase in the
proportion of participants choosing engineering as a field
of study, and the two post-MITE estimates for each sex of
the proportion choosing engineering are in close agreement.
On the other hand, the limited data for non-accepted applicants suggests some decrease in plans to study engineering
(other data suggested non-acceptees had substantially weaker
academic backgrounds). Overall, these results suggest, that
MITE is attaining its basic purpose of increasing the number
of minority students planning to study engineering. In
interpreting these data, it should be remembered the post-
MITE data were collected four to six months after the MITE
experience. Therefore, the influence of any "hello-goodbye"
effect" (that is, a tendancy for participants to choose
engineering on their last day in MITE without any lasting
commitment to the field) should have dissipated.

More detailed breakdowns were performed to determine
the fields from which MITE attracted recruits to engineering. Results are shown in Table 8. To some extent, MITE
attracts participants from nearly all fields. In terms of
absolute numbers, however, the major course of recruits to
engineering (both male and female) is the group of participants previously interested in mathematics and the physical

Table 7

Choice of Engineering as Field
of Study Before and After MITE

	Participants		Applicants (non-participants)
	Males (N=223)	Females (N=181)	
Preferred Field of Study Was Engineering:			
a. Before MITE	38.5%	20.4%	
b. After MITE	85.7%	56.9%	
Chi Square	87.93**	48.01**	
	(N=333)	(N=287)	
Answered "Yes" to Post-MITE Question:			
a. Were you planning to study engineering in college before you participated in MITE?	63.7%	41.1%	
b. Are you now planning to study engineering in college?	83.8%	57.5%	
Chi Square	32.04**	18.18**	

Applicants Who Were Not Accepted

	Applicants (non-participants) (N=78)
Answered "Yes" to Post-MITE Question:	
a. Were you planning to study engineering in college before you applied for MITE?	75.6%
b. Are you now planning to study engineering in college?	64.1%
Chi Square	3.04

* p < .05, ** p < .01

247

Table 8

Pre-MITE Fields of Study and Post-MITE
Choice of Engineering for Participants

Field	Males			Females		
	Choosing Field Before MITE N	Choosing Engineering After MITE N	Percent Choosing Engineering After MITE	Choosing Field Before MITE N	Choosing Engineering After MITE N	Percent Choosing Engineering After MITE
Arts & Architecture	7	4	57.1	14	6	42.9
Biological Sciences	7	2	28.6	6	3	50.0
Business	-	-	-	8	2	25.0
Engineering	86	82	95.3	37	34	91.9
Mathematics and Physical Science	75	65	86.7	57	34	59.6
Professional	13	10	76.9	24	9	37.5
Social Sciences	4	1	25.0	5	1	20.0
Education	-	-	-	3	0	0.0
Other Fields	31	27	87.1	27	14	51.9

sciences, or, in other words, the group of students who
appear most appropriate to attract to engineering. There is
little indication the MITE is <u>inappropriately</u> attracting,
"would-be physicians" to engineering. If we assume the
worst and call participants who chose either the biological
sciences or professional fields "would-be physicians," MITE
attracted only 12 male (5.4% of all males) and 12 female
(6.6% of all females) "would-be physicians" to engineering.
The results further indicate that an even lower proportion
of the total groups were would-be lawyers, businesspersons,
and so on who were attracted to engineering. Therefore,
there is little basis for criticizing MITE on the grounds
that it is attracting promising candidates from other, equally suitable fields.

In addition to increasing the number of minority persons
studying engineering, the MITE program has a number of more
general goals such as giving participants a clear idea of
what engineering is like, familiarizing them with college,
and increasing their confidence in their ability to cope
with college. Because participants themselves are the best
source of information about how well these goals have been
attained, it seemed that the best way to assess attainment
of these goals would be to ask participants directly.
Accordingly, a series of evaluation items was constructed,
each of which asked participants to indicate their degree
of agreement with a statement relevant to these goals on a
four-point scale containing the categories: "strongly disagree," "disagree," "agree," and "strongly agree."

Table 9 shows the percent of participants responding
"agree" or "strongly agree" to each statement. These results indicate that the participants' own evaluation of MITE
is overwhelmingly favorable. In interpreting this pattern,
it is again important to remember that the influence of any
"hello-goodbye" effect should have dissipated. Therefore,
these results provide rather impressive evidence that nearly
all participants had a positive experience in MITE and that
nearly all participants viewed MITE as having achieved much
of its broader purpose.

Conclusion

In terms of the narrow goal of increasing minority group
participation in engineering, the results from our evaluation
seem to indicate that the MITE program is a success. A more
interesting question is how success with respect to such narrow goals relates to the more general goal of attaining social justice in the United States. Obviously, opinions about

Table 9

Percent of MITE Participants Responding "Agree" or
"Strongly Agree" to Various Evaluation Items [a]

| | Percent Agree | |
Attitude Item	Males (N=331)	Females (N=287)
I have a clear idea of what I have to do to go to college.	96.4	93.7
It would be very difficult for a student like me to get good grades in college.	5.1	5.3
I am confident that my current career choice is right for me.	95.5	88.2
I am not good enough at math & science to be an engineer.	4.6	14.9
I have a clear idea of what it is like to be an engineer.	84.0	78.7
I believe that minority groups & women are not welcome in engineering.	2.4	3.2
Attending the MITE program raised my hopes of attending college & having a professional career.	88.8	88.6
I wish I had not participated in MITE.	0.0	0.0
I learned a lot about engineers and engineering from the MITE program.	97.6	98.6
The MITE experience frequently was unpleasant.	4.2	2.4
I learned some things about myself from the MITE experience.	96.0	95.1
The MITE experience made me realize that engineering's not for me.	4.5	18.3
Participating in MITE made college professors, deans, and admission officers seem more real, human, even likeable.	91.7	92.2
I would recommend the MITE program to a friend.	100.0	99.3

[a] Includes all participants who completed post-MITE
questionnaires.

this question differ widely. Our own opinion, however, is
that a large number of specific, limited efforts such as
MITE are likely to be as important in achieving social
justice as is a more general effort to achieve an overall
reform of society.

References

Astin, A.W.
      1965   Who Goes Where to College. Chicago, Ill.:
             Science Research Associates.

Astin, A.W. and J.L. Holland
      1961   "The environmental assessment technique: a way
             to measure college environments." Journal of
             Educational Psychology 52:308-316.

Holland, J.L.
      1973   Making Vocational Choices: A Theory of Careers.
             Englewood Cliffs, New Jersey: Prentice-Hall

Hoyt, D.P.
      1968   "Description and prediction of diversity among
             four-year colleges." Measurement and Evaluation
             in Guidance 1:16-26.

Peng, S.S., E.E. Stafford and R.J. Talbert
      1977   National Longitudinal Study of the High School
             Class of 1972: Review and Annotation of Study
             Reports. Research Triangle Park, N.C.: Center
             for Educational Research and Evaluation,
             Research Triangle Institute.

Richards, J.M., Jr., R. Seligman and P.K. Jones
      1970   "Faculty and curriculum as measures of college
             environment." Journal of Educational Psychology
             Col: 324-332.

Richards, J.M., G.D. Williams and J.L. Holland
      1978   An Evaluation of the 1977 Minority Introduction
             to Engineering Program. Report No. 270.
             Baltimore, Md. Center for the Social Organiza-
             tion of Schools, the Johns Hopkins University

Footnotes

1.   A more complete report of this evaluation (Richards, Williams & Holland, 1978) can be obtained from the Center for Social Organization of Schools.

2.   These and all other analyses are based on student self reports about their characteristics, the characteristics of their parents, etc.

18

An Example of Student Retention
for Minority Engineering Programs*

RANDOLPH W BROMERY

A truly viable program aimed at the selection, retention, and graduation of minority students in schools of
engineering must begin as early as primary school. If we
are not successful in changing science education in the
primary and middle schools, we can never hope to develop
literacy in the areas of natural resources and environmental
matters among minority students. We need a continuing
program of awareness in the elementary and secondary schools
describing various personally and professionally rewarding
options in the natural sciences and mathematics. Minority
students in an average urban school setting are never made
aware of their potential for science or engineering careers.
This is due in part to a lack of role models and individually
tailored career counseling and guidance.

Minority students need an identifiable place in a
college or university with both financial assistance and
academic support services. In addition to continuing the
program of individual career counseling, many minority
students need adequate financial assistance and a strong
academic support program, which includes both a tutorial
remedial component and a peer counseling component. They
also need consideration and awareness of job possibilities
early and throughout their academic careers. Minority students even more than non-minority students need an early
visual sighting of job possibilities before graduation. This
will help students to seriously consider alternate professional objectives and to increase their motivation in over-

---

* A version of this paper was published in Proceedings of a
Workshop for Program Directors in Engineering Education for
Minorities published (1976) by the National Academy of
Sciences, Washington, D.C.

coming academic difficulties. Early identification and counseling should be accomplished for those who demonstrate a strong graduate school potential.

A program of this design was developed and established for minority students (Black, Puerto Rican, Cape Verdeen, and Indian) at the University of Massachusetts. The results after eleven years indicated a far better than average minority retention and graduation level at the University. This program was distinct in that it was planned, developed, and operated by the black faculty members at the University of Massachusetts. In addition, these same faculty members obtained the federal, state, and foundation support for the program. The organization, known as the Committee For The Collegiate Education of Black Students, was a private foundation incorporated under Massachusetts General Law.

Massachusetts now has a Puerto Rican population that approximates the Black population in the State. It also has a third group of minority students of which only about 1 or 2 percent ever go to college. They are the citizens of Portuguese extraction who live along the South Shore of which very few of the young people went to college. Our program was extended to try to induce some of these young people to consider college careers.

In 1967, eight black faculty members at the University of Massachusetts at Amherst spoke to the Ford Foundation and asked if they could secure funding for an experimental educational program for admitting and supporting minority students at the University. We carefully selected a class of 128 students to start our program. The 128 students that we selected were personally interviewed by one of the black faculty members in their homes. We interviewed their families, friends, ministers, and we also went to the schools and interviewed school counselors and teachers.

We found that, in general, the least amount of useful information for selecting students was obtained from records maintained by high school counselors. For example, 32 of our student participants were black women, all from the same school, in Springfield, Massachusetts. One high school counselor had written the following on the application form of each of these women: "This student does not indicate a potential for doing college work." Twenty-eight of these students graduated in the normal four year period!

In general, we found that only in rare instances did the high school counselors provide us with information that

was useful in helping select and counsel these students. We
also discovered in the selection process, that regardless of
the quality of a person's school, the student's class standing correlated better with academic success than anything
else we could document. We also found that motivation was
an important factor among students who were at the top of
the class. After personally interviewing each student, we
requested letters of recommendation from neighbors and
friends. We also asked the student applicants to write letters outlining in their own words why they wanted to attend
college.

The adjustment that minority students were required to
make in a large residential predominantly white university
was an additional problem that confronted the staff. At the
beginning of the program in 1968, we had nearly 18,000 students on campus. Of these, about 12,000 lived on campus.
We knew from experience that even when academically prepared
students are brought from a large suburban high school onto
a large residential campus, they sometimes have difficulty
adjusting.

A special three day summer counseling program for
minority students was held on the Amherst campus to help
facilitate the adjustment of minority students to campus
life. In addition to the routine testing and course selection, students were placed in selected dormitories and were
aided in becoming familiar with their class schedules. The
staff wanted to avoid the confusion that usually accompanies
new students arriving on a large campus for the first time.
The beginning is a critical time for most minority students.
They can be turned off rapidly because of relatively simple
things like not being able to find classrooms, dining facilities, or selecting an appropriate roommate. Consequently,
the three day summer orientation session was spent trying to
work out critical logistic problems for the students.

The program had three major components - a well engin-
eered tutorial program, a broad based social counseling program, and a carefully designed remedial program. The tutorial program was designed to assess whether each student would
do better in a group tutorial or an individual tutorial setting. In some of the courses, we found that a student would
do well in a group tutorial and in other courses they needed
individual tutoring. The tutorial program was patterned
after similar arrangements that most of the fraternities and
sororities have used at colleges and universities for a
century or more. We developed a fairly complete file on each
professor including a documented history of that professor's

examinations and what the professor expected in students'
approaches to answers. We then tutored students appropriately. In addition, we placed program staff persons in class
classrooms so they could teach students proper ways to take
notes, and also demonstrate to students a correlation between the individual professor's lecture materials and the
course materials covered in the examinations. Our tutorial
was not simply geared to "Botany 101" but specifically
geared to "Botany 101 taught by Professor Jones". We found
this approach to be of considerable help to the students.
Although we were sincerely hoping that our students would
learn Botany, we were primarily interested in the students
passing the course. The objective was to illustrate that
"program" students sitting in with the "regularly admitted
students" could survive and succeed.

The second component of the program was counseling.
Counseling groups were divided into two major sub-units. One
was more relaxed and consisted of informal social counseling
conducted by other students living in the dormitories. The
individual adjustment problems with the residence halls were
addressed by these counselors. This component also included
peer group counseling on drugs and sex. In addition, we had
a financial counseling service to teach students how to budget their financial aid stipends and "how not to run out of
money two weeks before the end of the month". Included in
our counseling programs were factors that might sound strange
in an educational program but which we nevertheless found to
be very important to the students. We also counseled students on their personal habits such as facial make-up, hair-
styling, and how to dress on a limited budget.

The third component of the program was the remedial
program. This is where we believed our program differed
most from all other programs. The minority student programs
at the other local schools (e.g., Smith, Mt. Holyoke, and
Amherst Colleges) all had one thing in common: a very comprehensive summer bridge program. Our remedial program was
constantly geared up and ready to go, however, we did not
attempt to remedy the students academic deficiencies until
the student recognized the problem and requested assistance.
Our remedial program did not simply tell a student, "You
can't write so you go into the remedial program". We would
help the students themselves find that they needed help even
if it took until midterm before they became aware they were
failing English Composition or Mathematics. We found that it
was more efficient and beneficial to remediate students after
they requested assistance. We had remedial programs in
English Composition, Reading, Writing, and Math Skills.

We also developed several auxilliary programs which
taught students study habits and how to use the library.
There were many students on the campus who graduated at the
end of four years and never knew the proper way to find a
book in the library. It was impressive to hear that our students were showing the "regularly admitted students" how to
find books in the library. Finding a book in our campus
library can present exceptional logistical problems. We have
a library which is described in the Guiness Book of Records
as the tallest library in the world.

There was another aspect of the program which made it
similar to a fraternity or sorority. Once you were admitted
into the program, you stayed in the program. If you were
successful and no longer needed tutorial or remedial assistance, you were then, required to help other students in the
program who needed help. It was like a "four year hitch" in
the military--once you signed on the dotted line, you were
in for the term. By the end of our second year of the program, program students were recruiting new students for the
program. We sent the students to Springfield, Pittsfield,
and Boston.

In Massachusetts it is relatively easy to recruit
minority students, because nearly 95 percent of the minority
persons in the state are concentrated in Boston and Springfield. The Black and Puerto Rican communities are well
delineated and offer an easy geographical problem when recruiting these students. For several years, recruitment for
the program was performed by the students. The students
would talk frankly to potential recruits about the difficult
moments they had experienced and the demands of the
program.

The program channeled students through four years of
college and saw to it that students successfully graduated
with some useful knowledge. The program also required a
serious approach and effort from each student. Among the
inalienable rights of students at colleges and universities
is the right to fail. The program students enjoyed this
same student right of failure. There are too many programs
where students have been enrolled for four or more years and
never graduate. A university, however, fails in its obligation if it never fails the student who should fail. We
took this position because the program had a long waiting
list, and others could make better use of space, effort, and
finances available at that time.

Since, the original class of 128 students in 1968,

nearly 1,900 students have entered the program. To date, we
have graduated nearly 65% of these students. This rate of
success can be appreciated when considering the SAT score
profile of these students. We encourage students to take
their SAT exams in high school. Our experience with the
program suggest that in general SAT scores are meaningful at
the low and high ends. In the middle range, we found that
there was little correlation between the college level academic achievement or grade point average and the SAT scores.
In 1968 the University SAT norm was 550 average Verbal SAT
score and a 570 average Math SAT score in a freshman class
numbering 3,600 students. During the first year of our program (1968), our students had Verbal SAT scores averaging
387 and Math SAT scores averaging 409. At the end of four
years in June 1972, approximately half of our first year students graduated with a 2.6 grade point average out of a 4.0
grade point system. At the end of 10 semesters, or by June
1973, nearly 65% of that first class of students were graduated.

The program also offered students career counseling.
We began counseling students in high school. Among the many
career options we counseled were the varied opportunities
in the natural sciences and mathematics which many minority
students had never considered. One of these careers was my
own profession in geophysics and geology. If one thinks that
recruiting minority students into chemistry, engineering and
mathematics is difficult, then one should try and counsel a
minority student into geological or geophysical careers.

When I came out of high school, I had never heard the
words geology or geophysics. I stumbled into my profession
by accident. When I was an undergraduate student at the
University of Michigan I needed a science elective. I heard
through the "student grapevine" that there was a course in
historical geology which was considered a pushover. It was
conducted in a lecture hall. The lights were turned off and
50 minutes of color slides were shown. It was scheduled at
8 o'clock in the morning, so half the class slept. I took
this easy course in historical geology and to my surprise,
when the lights went out, the professor showed a fantastic
slide collection and delivered a superb and informative
lecture. I was wide awake and being counseled into a geological profession by accident. Currently, we try not to
have students elect career options by accident. We start
at the high school level. Furthermore, we are convinced
that in the sciences and mathematics, one must start talking
to minority students at the 4th and 5th grade level.

Another factor in our program that might have played a
role in our high retention rate was the method of funding for
the program. The program at the University of Massachusetts
was different from similar programs in that the original
black faculty members went to a private foundation for support. Foundation members decided that funds would be
awarded to the black faculty organization instead of directly
to the University. For this reason we became incorporated as
a private foundation and student and program support funds
came directly to our private foundation. We opened a corporate bank account and paid the university to provide service to the program.

In 1968, there were nearly 1,100 faculty members and
only 8 Black faculty; however, we had an annual average
(for over four years) of one quarter of a million dollars in
the bank in the name of our corporation--The Committee For
The Collegiate Education of Black Students, Inc. Actually,
the special student program at the University of Massachusetts at Amherst brought in over 3 million dollars in
federal, state, and foundation funds in five years. The program underwent the normal academic scrutiny. The Faculty
Senate at the University debated the structure and academic
components of the program, and subsequently voted to support
the program. Because the program had credibility and independence, many black and Puerto Rican students not enrolled in the program wanted to enroll in the program. It
meant something to these students to belong to a cohesive
group.

Since 1968, we (the black faculty) decided that in
addition to developing and conducting the undergraduate student program described earlier, we would recruit minority
graduate students, faculty members, and professional and non-
professional staff members. We also decided to expand the
program to include more Puerto Rican, Indian American and
White students who did not normally have access to the
University because of financial and academic reasons.

In 1968, there were 35 black students among the 15,000
students, and one Puerto Rican student. We could not find
one American Indian despite the fact that there are quite a
few Indian Americans living in New England, particularly in
the Commonwealth of Massachusetts. On Cape Cod, there is a
relatively large Indian population, very few of whom if any,
were going to the University. Also in 1968, there were 8
black faculty members and about 3 or 4 black graduate students. In 1979, the total minority population at the
University was nearly 1,500 undergraduate students, approxi-

mately 500 minority graduate students, and nearly 110 minority faculty members of which nearly 60 were black faculty members. In addition, there were more than 200 minority persons in non-teaching professional and non-professional staff positions at the University in 1979.

The University is still recruiting minority students with average SAT scores ranging between 370 and 400, and still continues to graduate more than half of the students with better than 2.5 grade point averages. Throughout our program, we did everything possible to avoid making the students involved in the program feel as if they were part of an experiment. We think that this was one of the important factors which made for the success of the program. Hopefully, graduates of the program will analyze most of the data from the program. It is also hoped that upon dissemination, the information from our pilot effort will aid other colleges and universities in developing similar programs to increase the number of minorities in engineering, math, and the natural sciences. We have been successful in having the University include the minority student program as a solid and integral part of the institution. In addition, the Committee for the Collegiate Education of Black Students, Inc. has dropped it's corporate status and the organization now serves completely within the structure of the University. The University provides the total funding for support of the program as part of the institutional budget submitted to the Commonwealth of Massachusetts. It has been funded this way for the past four years and we fully expect that it will continue into the future.

19

Retaining Blacks in Science:
An Affective Model

HERMAN A. YOUNG

Introduction

Concern for the low number of blacks in the natural
sciences has generated many programs designed to increase
black and minority awareness of opportunities in scientific
careers. The rationale for these efforts is clear. Blacks
and other minorities cannot achieve full representation
within the dominant society unless they participate in the
scientific and technological decision-making process, which
is at the heart of this country's power base. In addition,
the dominant society needs the untapped resources of minority
groups to strengthen its own manpower pool.

The task of increasing minority participation in science
is not small and will take several generations. Even if
the number of minority scientists and engineers were doubled
by the 1980s, black participation would increase only from
1 to 2 percent of the total scientific pool. Major changes
will have to occur in the organizational structure, curriculum, teaching, and counseling techniques of existing
scientific support programs in order to establish a group of
minority scientists of Nobel Laureate calibre.

Current programs primarily address access and entry into
scientific programs (along with occasional follow-up counseling), and are inadequate to retain blacks in these fields.
The discrepancy between the number of blacks admitted to
scientific and professional schools and the number graduating
is alarming. Science educators have not yet attended to the
revisions necessary to build a support structure for blacks
in science. Successful models have been designed and tested,
but they have not been applied to scientific programs and
extended beyond the first year of college.

Research in developmental education has proven that supportive services do work (Rouche and Snow, 1977). The success of underprepared or disadvantaged students is greatly enhanced by a well planned program that addresses both cognitive and affective needs. Successful programs should combine most of the following components:

1. <u>Remedial or instructional programs which begin at students' current level</u>, as opposed to where they are expected to be for their grade in school.

2. <u>Mastery learning objectives.</u> Rather than lowering standards, clear definitions of standards should be identified and alternative modes of instruction should be provided to help students achieve definite goals.

3. <u>Modes of instruction that accommodate differences in learning styles.</u> Science educators should do more to incorporate the black cultural frame of reference into the science curriculum.

4. <u>A positive psychological climate.</u> This includes extensive program involvement that produces strong rapport and a high level of confidence between students and scientific professionals.

5. <u>The development of formal and informal mechanisms that help minority students create a stronger sense of focus or control.</u> This would involve helping minority students realize that they can be the masters of their own fate, that there is a relationship between behavior and the scientific personality.

6. <u>The development of a comprehensive and cohesive program structure</u> in which instructors, counselors and other associated professionals work as a team to serve a common group of students. This approach is different from the popular existing approach which allows underprepared students to take courses randomly within an institution.

These six key elements have not been consistently applied in science. Developmental programs in most colleges have been limited to reading, writing, and mathematics, with little involvement of science professors. Moreover, counselors and other support personnel are unfamiliar with the unique cognitive and affective factors related to the mastery of a scientific curriculum. Also many scientists lack the adequate skills necessary to counsel students, particularly minority students. Current support service programs still

favor preparation of students for the humanities and
social sciences. This chapter reviews some basic psychological determinants that are necessary to pursue science.
It also suggests some practical steps that institutions can
take to foster minority student retention and success in
science.

Effects of Psychological Factors on Career Choices

Because of the heavy demand of its content and methods,
science tends to ignore the affective domain. Anne Roe's
research (1952), however, established the importance of
personality factors in motivating people to pursue careers
in science. Some common traits of outstanding scientists,
according to Roe, are: love for knowledge for its own sake
(a principle held in common no doubt with other scholars),
a strong need to master or control one's own environment,
and creativity. In addition, Roe found among scientists
a preference to work with things rather than people and
a tendency to be loners.

Nay and Crocker (1970), in their inventory of affective
attributes of scientists, list the following factors:

1. Interest: understanding natural phenomena, and
contributing to knowledge and human welfare.

2. Operational Adjustments: dedication or commitment,
experimental requirements, initiative and resourcefulness,
and relations with peers.

3. Intellectual Adjustments: scientific integrity and
critical requirements.

4. Appreciation: an understanding of the history of
science, the relationship between science and society, and
the nature of science.

5. Values and/or Beliefs: philosophical, ethical, and
social perspectives which underlie a person's desire to
become a scientist. Those persons with curiosity and persistence will also be attracted to science (Nay and Crocker,
1970).

Looking at these factors in light of the typical black
environment, it is no wonder that few blacks become scientists. It is difficult for young persons to develop independence and a sense of mastery of their own environment
(hence an internal locus of control) when their psychic
energies are consumed by the problems of daily survival.

The lack of role models of successful black scientists,
the lack of perceived rewards for careers in science, poor
schooling, and the lack of reinforcement for science within
the black community have all been cited as key problems.

Moreover, these obvious concerns are compounded by
major social values that mitigate assertive behavior by
blacks. The Protestant work ethic, one of the basic tenets
of the dominant society has had contradictory implications
for blacks. Hard work, achievement, and assertion may not
bring the same rewards for blacks as for whites. Lives of
famous black scientists bear this out. Even successful
blacks still note that their behavior must remain low-key,
subtle, and definitely not aggressive. For blacks, the
need for self-approval (which requires both assertion and
achievement) is often imcompatible with the fulfillment of
social acceptance.

The Science Curriculum

The current science curriculum and the traditional
approach to teaching science compound the social and psychological problems faced by minority students. The scientific
curriculum is rigorous, sequential, objective, highly
congitive, and apparently divorced from the affective domain.
The human factor, which produces biased judgment, is sup-
posedly minimized within science. But the belief in the
total objectively of science is an exaggeration, if not a
myth, for the work of science is inevitably influenced by
the people behind it. The scientific method itself implies
certain ethical values. Human priorities influence the
selection of research topics, areas of emphasis, synthesis
of data, and the applications of scientific discoveries.
Nevertheless, the discipline of science continues to be
oriented toward the cognitive domain. There is such a vast
amount of knowledge and skills to be acquired that little
time remains for humanistic interpretations and applications.

The absence of positive affect in science teaching
deters blacks from science (and probably many other students).
Although generalizations have many exceptions, research
has verified what most blacks already know and believe
about distinct differences in priorities, perceptual frame-
works, and communication styles between the black and dominant cultures. Black culture generally places stronger
emphasis on the affective domain. There is a sense of
pride in the black community in being people-oriented and
sensitive to feelings. Blacks often evaluate the affect of a
situation before making a decision on the cognitive content.

Thus, black students are more likely to size up the
"vibrations" they receive from a teacher or authority
figure before deciding to believe what that person has to
say (Kochman, 1971).

This can also be explained in terms of a field dependence versus field independence orientation, a gestalt
versus an analytical orientation (Ramirez and Costaneda,
1974). Regardless of the terminology, the black cultural
frame of reference sets different values and priorities in
accepting and evaluating experiences. The mode of communication within the black culture, which is oral-aural,
reinforces the affective domain; wheras the prestige mode
of communication in the dominant culture, which is visual-
mental, reinforces the cognitive framework. Thus, learning
styles and motivational factors vary between blacks and
whites as well as among blacks and whites.

For many blacks, then, the subject of science and its
traditional method of teaching is coldly unattractive. The
traditional content and teaching, which has little room for
personal reinforcement and direct application to one's
personal development, is contrary to what blacks hold most
dear. For college age youth, in general, the psychological
press toward affective concerns and its contrast to traditional science teaching could not come together at a worst
time. Black college youth, as well as many whites, are
undergoing crucial changes in the development of their own
identities. Many are coming to understand, analyze, and
articulate the problems of racism and discrimination while
trying to formulate their role in a different, if not
hostile, society. Counselors attest to the fact that black
youth often take two or three years in their college careers
to "get themselves together," to resolve many basic human
questions, and to set realistic personal and career goals.
For these students the science curriculum provides little
support and reinforcement.

The science curriculum requires that one has already
worked through personal crises prior to its undertaking,
inasmuch as the rigor of its content and skills allows no
time for pre-occupation with personal problems. On the
other hand, the disciplines of the humanities and social
sciences address the issues of a person's role in life,
search for meaning, analysis of social problems, and individual struggles, and thus are more congruent with black
students' personal development. That is, students can work
through personal issues with the help of the curriculum, not
in spite of it. It is our contention that unless affect is

incorporated into the science curriculum, little change will
occur in black participation in science. Despite the very
attractive economic and career rewards that a science degree
may bring, blacks must receive personal satisfaction from
the process of pursuing science and cannot postpone grati-
fication until their degrees are earned. Helping students
develop a love for scientific curriculum and providing support for their individual development must be major goals in
any supportive program to involve blacks in science.

Retention Strategies

Colleges can improve their retention of minorities in
science if they make it a priority to use available information on black students' needs and develop comprehensive
support services programs. Because the performance of
historically black colleges in producing black scientist
has been exemplary (over 75 percent of current black science
doctorates received their undergraduate training from these
institutions), predominantly white colleges would do well to
visit black campuses, study their advising systems, talk to
black scientists who teach black students, and thus ascertain
elements in the hidden agenda which help students persevere
in science. In planning a network of support, scientists
should consider planning and organizational components, the
provision of adequate role models, and the actual achievement
of affective goals and varied approaches to instruction.
The importance of each of these components is described in
the remainder of this chapter.

Planning an Organizational Structure

Supportive programs to retain blacks in science must be
led by capable administrators or faculty members who have the
political clout and expertise to build a coherent, tightly
organized program which addresses both cognitive and affective needs. A supportive services plan which simply adds
a counselor and a few tutors to the science division or
school will not succeed because such a program is on the
periphery of the academic arena. A core of committed faculty who work as a team with a counselor and other support
personnel (such as lab assistants and tutors) is needed to
build the kind of program that will affect both the institution and the students.

Faculty must be willing to work with students whose
values and attitudes differ from their own. They must be
willing to use a variety of instructional methods, to begin
instruction at the students' current level (in contrast to

where they should be), and to develop a program of study
which helps the students both in and outside of class. In
addition, they must be able to appreciate the individuality
of each student, to maintain high expectations that students
will succeed, and to recognize all efforts that students
make. Faculty members must also be secure individuals
themselves, willing to undergo additional professional
development to improve their communication skills increase
their awareness of black culture, increase their knowledge
of innovations, and adapt their curriculum to minority
students' learning styles and frames of reference. They
must be able to share failures and frustrations as well as
successes, and they must be willing to share these experiences with each other.

Obviously, given the demands on most university faculty
to do research and publish, finding a core of faculty willing
to make minority retention in science their major professional focus is not easy. However, if the college administration recognizes this as a valuable activity comparable
to other research efforts, and if the program provides
adequate rewards to faculty for such activity, then recruiting faculty will become less difficult. In fact, reduced
teaching loads, opportunities to publish results or innovative techniques, travel to professional development seminars,
and the challenge of altering the course of science are
positive features which should be built into such a program
to support the faculty.

This kind of program structure, in which a team of
faculty collectively work with a group of students, has
already been identified as the most successful approach in
developmental programs (Rouche and Snow, 1977). However,
there is a common belief that a separate and distinct program of study for disadvantaged students, or "tracking"
system, will make the student feel stigmatized and isolated
from the mainstream of the college. We believe that this
fear has little basis in reality, and is a fear expressed by
faculty and educators, not students. In a large institution
that is unresponsive to the needs of minority students, a
special core of classes creates a more personalized environment in which students are more closely involved with each
other and with the faculty. As long as the program receives
adequate institutional support, and as long as the services
and classes are of high quality, then students and faculty
can develop a keen sense of pride in being associated with
the program. Helping bright students attain a higher standard of excellence in science (as opposed to the remediation
of past deficiencies) should be the purpose of such a program.

Developing Role Models

Role modeling is perhaps one of the oldest proven methods for teaching behaviors, attitudes, and aspirations. By establishing a close relationship with scientists, the student can identify with both the scientist and the career. The student can see that the successful scientist, too, is a human being and can relate to others; therefore, the idea of attaining similar goals is brought within the realm of possibility. For students who place high priority on the affective domain, such personal contact is imperative.

The need for a proportionate share of black faculty to serve as role models at predominantly white campuses in the sciences is obvious. However, the small pool of black scientists at white colleges and universities limits this possibility. Interested faculty should exert more pressure on these institutions to hire more black faculty. Also, the provision of fellowships to blacks currently holding bachelor's or master's degrees in science at white institutions with opportunities for future employment at the institution is one way to increase the number of black Ph.D's in science. White faculty can also provide successful role modeling for black students through personal involvement with students, recognition of accomplishments of black students, and providing for student interaction with scientists in the community. To accomplish this, white faculty may need professional assistance to improve their interpersonal skills in general and to increase their awareness of black culture in particular.

Any supportive services program for science must allow for one-to-one interaction between faculty and student. Although programs may hire counselors who are effective in helping a student work through personal and academic problems, the key to role modeling is in the hands of faculty. Involvement in science, an appreciation of the intrinsic rewards of knowledge and achievement, and a sense of dedication and perseverence come primarily from student involvement with the faculty. A faculty person's affective style is as crucial as his or her cognitive expertise. Because the rewards of the higher education system are primarily based on cognitive factors (e.g. intellectual expertise, research, publications, and continuing education), many scholars have ignored their affective development regarding communication skills, ability to show concern in a way that reinforces the student, and concern for helping students develop professional attitudes and conduct. When students see a caring "human being" who is financially, profession-

ally, and personally successful, they are more apt to be
motivated to follow in the same direction.

In addition to displaying personal qualities that students want to emulate, science instructors should highlight
the past and present contributions of blacks in science and
technology through the curriculum. Special units regarding
these contributions may be appropriate at specific times; at
other times, casual mentioning of such contributions helps
to remind students of what other blacks have done. Also,
arranging for successful black scientists within industry and
other agencies to visit classes would also expand the network
of minority role models and expose black students to the
diverse career options available to blacks in the sciences.

Working Toward Affective Goals and Varied Approaches to Instruction

Affective reinforcements will increase as faculty become more involved with their students. However, a counselor
can facilitate the development of a positive psychological
climate by helping faculty identify affective goals, by
maintaining awareness of students' needs and values, and by
designing additional experiences for the academic and
personal growth of minority students. The development of
study groups, special forums, group counseling sessions,
and science organizations can also strengthen peer relations
among minority students who are interested in science and can
help them more adequately use available resources.

The close student-teacher interaction, peer reinforcement, role modeling and other factors discussed here are not
likely to occur in the typical large introductory science
courses. In these courses, recent innovations such as
computer assisted instruction, audio-tutorial and personalized learning are useful. However, teachers should not
limit themselves to these innovative techniques. The
reason is that students can get just as "turned off" by
being stuck in a learning carrel and plugged into an audio-
slide cassette program as they can while sitting in a large
lecture class. It is important to remember that a variety of
techniques and methods are often necessary to teach the
same concept. But for all methods, priority must be given
to the dynamics of human interaction.

Throughout the science curriculum, emphasis must be
placed on acquiring cognitive skills as well as content.
Some research has shown that most disadvantaged students lack
the cognitive skills necessary to master scientific infor-

mation (Korn, 1978). However, these cognitive skills are not
to be confused with cognitive ability and a student's potential to learn scientific materials. All persons and programs
assisting minority and disadvantaged students should keep
this in mind.

Experiential learning can be an effective tool for
reinforcing cognitive skills and for involving students
personally in science. Many engineering schools and some
black colleges have led the way in providing students with
relevant job experiences as early as their freshman year.
These experiences enable students to realistically evaluate
the pay-offs and challenges of a career in science. In
addition, these opportunities enable science teachers
to introduce more practical teaching methods in classroom
and laboratory instruction. Science presented in an
abstract or theoretical context often has little appeal to
black students who lack the experience to relate to scientific theory. A research project in the area of the student's interests (such as making a radio) which would
actually engage the student could be one way to bridge the
gap between the concrete and the abstract. As the student
experiences difficulties, the instructor can explain the
theory which solves the problem and then progress toward the
theoretical concept behind the entire project. Such an
approach offers a viable way to demonstrate the relevance of
theory and also provides students with a concrete product
for their efforts. In short, scientists may do well to
apply the inductive method to the teaching of science.

Conclusion

Only through a plan which encompasses one's total
experiences within the institution can the important social,
personal, and intellectual reinforcements be brought to bear
on the needs of students. Having researched trends among
black scientists (Young and Young, 1974) and having been
involved in successful supportive services programs, we submit that given a genuine commitment from faculty and administrators, and given adequate resources and careful planning,
colleges can take specific steps to overcome the barriers
many black and minority students encounter in science. We
also contend that minority students can be helped to overcome social and psychological barriers to learning science
and that these students can develop a real liking for
science. In addition, we believe that science can be taught
in a more exciting and humanistic manner whereby bright,
disadvantaged students can acquire the cognitive skills necessary to master science and successfully pursue it as a
meaningful career.

References

Kochman, T.
   1971   "Cross cultural communication: contrasting
           perspectives, conflicting sensibilities."
           The Florida FL Reporter   Spring-Fall: 3-16.

Korn, E.
   1978   "Improving reasoning skills in non-major biology
           classes." Community College Frontiers
           Summer: 36-40.

Nay, M.A. and R.K. Crocker
   1970   "Science teaching and the affective attributes
           of scientists." Science Education 54:59-67.

Ramirez III, M. and A. Costaneda
   1974   Cultural Democracy, Bicognitive Development and
           Education. New York: Academic Press.

Roe, A.
   1952   The Making of a Scientist. New York: Dodd Mead Co.

Rouche, J. and J. Snow
   1977   Overcoming Learning Problems: A Guide to Develop-
           mental Education in College. San Francisco:
           Jossey-Bass.

Young H. and B.H. Young
   1974   Scientists in the Black Perspective. Louisville,
           Kentucky. The Lincoln Foundation.

20

A Special Tutorial
for Minority Medical Students:
An Account of a Year's Experience*

ROBERT H. GEERTSMA

Introduction

Recent reports concerning tutorial programs for minority students (Margolis and Marshal, 1974; Marshal, 1973; Nelson, 1970; Nelson and Gilbert, 1971) have been primarily concerned with academic outcomes and have not dealt with the experience of program participants nor with the interaction process between tutors and minority students. This chapter describes a year's experience with special tutorial activities designed for five minority medical students who were enrolled at the University of Rochester's School of Medicine. These students were referred for a year's tutoring at the University to improve their problem-solving skills and to assist them in retaking the basic science courses that they had failed. It is hoped that this personal account of the tutor-student experiences involving the small group at Rochester will be useful for those who pursue similar undertakings. More importantly, the author hopes that this narrative will provide a better understanding of the interaction between minority medical students and the majority white medical school environment.

Development of Tutorial Activities

Five black first-and second-year medical students at the University of Rochester in 1972-73 failed biochemistry,

*The original version of this paper was published in the Journal of Medical Education, 52 (May, 1977) pp. 396-403. Permission was granted by the author and by the Editorial Board of the Journal of Medical Education to publish the present version of the paper in this volume.

physiology, and microbiology, and were asked to repeat those
subjects the next school year. In general, it was felt that
these students were not successful in solving problems using
the basic science material they had studied. These were not
the first students to have failed nor to have difficulty
with problem-solving. However, this was the first time that
such a tutorial group was made up exclusively of minority
students. No nonminority students had been required to
repeat courses that year, and another seven minority students
who were members of the same classes experienced no difficulty.

At the time the minority students were asked by the
school to repeat courses, considerable tension existed on two
issues between minority students and a small number of first-
and second-year faculty members. The first issue involved
the propostion that minority students are intellectually
inferior; the second was that faculty evaluations are biased
against minority students. The students knew that the first
belief was false but were concerned that some of their instructors thought that it was true; some instructors were
concerned that students did not believe the second issue was
false. In this context, four students were assigned to the
special tutorial concurrently with their retaking of the
failed courses. The fifth student who failed was not assigned to the tutorial, but he asked to be allowed to join
and was permitted to do so. The charge of the special tutorial was to train the students to apply basic science material in solving problems, because problem-solving is given
great weight in the school's basic science courses.

Initial Plan and Focus of Activities

The special tutorial staff of three instructors began
working with the five students at the outset of the 1973-74
school year. For several months the group met for four
90-minute sessions each week. The general plan of the tutorial was to analyze the problem-solving strengths and weaknesses of each student, present him with results of this
analysis, and expose him to a series of exercises designed to
remedy his weaknesses. The remedial exercises took up most
of the year's time and paralleled the progression of the
courses that students were taking, thus making possible the
use of course instructors for tutorial sessions and the use
of course examinations to assess progress. The evaluation of
each student's problem-solving skills began with formal tests
which yielded an initial formulation. This formulation was
then amplified and modified by observations of performance
in the tutorial.

The initial focus of the tutorial activities was on cognitive difficulties. Diagnoses began with the administration of tests of study habits, critical thinking, personality, mathematics, and reading comprehension. The results of these tests, supplemented by observations in the tutorial sessions, permitted the initial formulation of each student's learning and problem-solving skills. Evidence of what may have produced the previous year's difficulties was suggested but incomplete. In general, the students had trouble using basic science material to solve problems, identifying what was being asked in a problem, and framing written answers to problems. The testing also gave evidence of high levels of motivation, resilient personalities, and strong intellectual skills. The students were proficient at absorbing and memorizing a great amount of material, and their premedical preparation in terms of courses taken and areas studied was adequate. The picture of the students' difficulties and strengths which emerged was provocative because it suggested that such problems should have been readily corrected when they first became apparent, as had been the case with many past students. The instructors of the courses which the minority students had failed promptly recognized and responded to these students' difficulties (as they had with several other students), but their response, which was on an individual basis, was not effective.

As the special year-long tutorial progressed, it became apparent that the students were very uncomfortable. Although no protests were voiced, the staff began to receive second- and third-hand reports of what the students were thinking; they usually had feelings of grossly unfair treatment. These reports often came through the unit's secretary, who was black and who provided an invaluable communication channel to the students. When the testing was completed, reports came back that the students thought that the tests were intended to document their inadequacies and that they were insulted by the simplicity of some of the tests. In the tutorial sessions the students were polite but showed no positive feeling. They asked whether the staff felt uncomfortable with them as a group. Clearly, the students felt devalued and were not sure that they could trust the school. Their lack of trust, their diminished self-esteem, and their viewing of the reasons for their difficulties as completely outside themselves precluded any progress with the tutorial. Something was needed to save the tutorial and the students.

Aspects of Intervention

The Affective Sphere: An implicit assumption in the initial planning for the special tutorial was that the

emotional climate would not significantly interfere with
learning. It became immediately apparent , however, that
this assumption was false. Consequently, the staff decided
to try to communicate more forcefully its positive regard
and liking for the students. Although interactions with the
students provided most of the opportunities for projecting
or reinforcing the staff's view of the students as worthy
and capable, some restructuring of the tutorial was also
necessary. For example, because many of the messages from
the black students could be interpreted as expressing the
desire to be seen as competent rather than deficient, it
seemed important to make clear to the students that the
tutorial had a positive function. This was done by explicit-
ly stating that the goal of the tutorial was to make the
students expert problem-solvers and to give them skills
beyond those developed in the regular curriculum, skills
that would be valuable to them throughout their medical
careers.

The staff members also carefully avoided communicating
negatively to black students. The students over the past
year had suffered much erosion of their self-esteem and
found it difficult to acknowledge that their performance had
been substandard even through their test responses in
several of the previous year's courses were demonstrably
poor. If the students were to increase their effectiveness
in problem-solving, it was necessary that they recognize and
accept their weaknesses and then work on those specific
points. Realistic self-evaluation was crucial.

The original plan was to present each student with an
analysis of his problem-solving strengths and weaknesses and
the skills basic to it. But it was thought that an external
opinion of the students' weaknesses would be difficult for
the students to accept. The crucial problems in working with
self-evaluation were not in the cognitive area, but in the
students' feelings about such evaluation, about the evalua-
tors, and about themselves and their environment.

For these reasons, the evaluation sessions were post-
poned until the students developed sufficient trust in the
staff to accept their assistance comfortably. In addition,
the evaluative conclusions were presented to the students
as an initial assessment that they should think about and test
against further information that would be generated as the
tutorial went on. Most of the attempts occurred within the
activities of the tutorial which dealt with the business of
problem-solving. As the year progressed, the students became
more familiar with the staff and at least provisionally

began to trust them. Feedback was received that the students were happy to have their entire relationship to the school mediated through the tutorial. They requested that the tutorial continue into subsequent years. However, they were told that the tutorial could last only for the current year.

The Learning Environment

A more complete appreciation of particular risks faced by minority students can be gained by extrapolating from the typical medical student's interaction with the environment. The account that follows integrates personal observations, reports, and reflections regarding the medical school experiences of minority and nonminority students. Insight into minority students' problems was largely gained from the tutorial students themselves.

Typical first-year medical students, after the triumph of having been accepted into medical school, find themselves on the lowest rung of the school's hierarchical ladder. The entering students' basic emotional need is to resolve the uncertainty they have about their achievements. Can they make it in this school? Will they meet their own expectations (to excel, usually) and those of their instructors? As an unproven quantity in an unfamiliar environment, the students are highly concerned with their academic performance. However, it is very difficult for them to prove themselves. First, they are not assigned to work on doing what doctors do, but are immersed in classroom academic work; then they find that they are unremittingly assigned more work than it seems possible to accomplish. They feel that their classmates are extremely bright and apparently can work interminably. Instructors are distant and terribly busy. It is difficult to do well on examinations, and the return of each examination paper is usually an occasion for further work. Under these conditions the first year medical students are not clear about how the school is treating them or how well they are doing. Because the students' desire to prove themselves in medical school is not easily nor quickly accomplished, most students experience considerable anxiety and frustration. The students who can best endure such emotional deprivation and uncertainty are those whose previous experience has given them a strong sense of self-worth and trust in their environment. Students who are weak in these qualities will be less sure of themselves, more dependent on external evidence that they are doing well, and more upset by evidence of not doing well.

Under conditions of restricted extrinsic rewards, typical medical students must rely on intrinsic rewards. As a result, a variety of previously insignificant signs become very important cues for students. These cues include positive evaluation by classmates and virtually any attention from a faculty member (e.g. being given the opportunity to participate in some clinical or research activity, or getting a favorable discussion group or laboratory assignment). For some students, contact with instructors becomes extraordinarily valued because the instructor's behavior may be taken as evidence of how the student is doing. However, instructors are often unaware of the importance their incidental behavior may have to students, especially as it signals or can be taken to mean liking and respect or disdain and disapproval. They may even feel that friendliness has nothing to do with teaching and learning.

What then is the status of typical minority students entering a middle-class white professional school? How will they interpret the variety of student and teacher norms operating in this environment? How do members of the medical school environment respond to them? To begin with, typical minority medical school enrollees are likely to feel that they are in an alien environment. As a result, they may question whether the school, its faculty, and its students welcome their presence. Furthermore, they may be uncertain as to how their appearance, personality, mannerisms, and attempts to be friendly will be received by their white peers and teachers. These uncertainties may add difficulty to minority students' adaptation to their new environment. In addition, various perceptions and uncertainties regarding the minority entrant may also be operating on behalf of many of the white students and instructors themselves. Therefore, breaking the communication barrier, which will permit a testing of expectations and uncertainties, is one of the first tasks that minority medical students and members of their environment must confront.

Instructor-Student Interaction

The staff, during the tutorial, came to appreciate the crucial effect of instructor-student relationships on students' feelings and performance. For example, a basic science instructor came into a tutorial session to work with students on problems that had been given out several days previously. At the beginning of the session one student was asked to go to the blackboard and write out his answer to the first problem. As the student was writing this answer, the instructor said, "Do you really mean that?" The student stopped writing and reconsidered, and this brought another question. The student abandoned his prepared answer and tried to respond to the questions. However, the questions came more rapidly, along with directions about what to write, and soon the student was writing down what he was told. After the session the student said that his confidence had been crushed and that something like that always happened in tutorial sessions.

Discussion with the students resulted in a different method of interaction. The subject matter expert first explained a problem for which the students had already written out an answer, after which each student asked whatever questions he wished and also indicated how he had responded to the problem. This approach, which was agreeable to the subject matter experts, worked very smoothly. Apparently, it permitted students to interact with the instructor without either party feeling pressured to produce correct answers, which before had proved damaging to the students' self esteem.

Consider a second example. An instructor responds to a minority student's question but after a few words directs his remarks to another student. To the instructor this is a casual and spontaneous event. However, the minority student feels anxious and angry because he has been slighted. Instructors have not usually been asked to be aware of such events and may even regard the feelings of students as outside their sphere of concern. However, because these interpersonal aspects of the environment can influence learning, especially in the less secure student, their neglect may entail serious and undesirable consequences.

The Element of Trust

Controversies occur when a substantial basis of trust does not exist between students and their instructors, and their productive resolution depends on a rebuilding of that trust. For example, after comparing the grading of different answers to the same examination questions, the tutorial students requested that graders not be told whose answers they were marking; that students be given back all test papers with information on how each answer was marked; and that the full-credit (and varieties of less credit) answers to all examination questions, including essay questions, be decided upon before giving the examination. Faculty members responded variously to these suggestions, but were concerned that the students did not trust them. The faculty knew (and the students did not know) that a student who performed poorly on a test had his answers closely reexamined

for all possible credit. Thus, a more mechanical scoring
procedure might well work to the relative disadvantage of
a weak performer. As a result, both students and faculty were
caught in a lack of trust. This Gordian knot dissolved
when, through the special tutorial, the students and their
instructors developed trust in each other. Before that
trust was established, there was no adequate solution to
the problem.

Tutorial Session Formats

Structure was given to the tutorial activities by the
various types of sessions employed. At the outset, several
strategies of problem-solving were discussed, and many
(not medically related) problems were given to illustrate
common procedural errors and to help students identify
their weaknesses. Tutors also stressed communication skills
in the initial sessions. Students were instructed to use
a five-step general model for organizing answers to questions
and problems. Later in the year students were asked to
make verbal responses to problems, tape recording them for
later analysis. This was designed to help students express
themselves cogently in a conversational context, such as
a clinical instructional setting. The most frequent and
continuing type of session involved basic science instructors conducting sessions on material from the courses the
students were taking. As has been noted, the sessions
were problem oriented, with students writing out answers
before the problems were discussed so that each committed
himself to a response that he could then evaluate. In the
first several months of the tutorial, the staff went over
students' answers before they were presented to the basic
science instructors so that answer formats could be considered independently of content. Subsequently, a tutorial
staff member continued to participate in these sessions in
order to reinforce the earlier material on problem-solving
and organization of communications. Finally, practice
examinations were regularly given as a prelude to course
examinations and the results were evaluated and passed back
to the students for discussion. These examinations were
supplemented by sample answers of varying quality so that
students might develop more realistic standards for judging
their own work.

Conclusion

The special set of tutorial activities designed for the five black medical students at the University of Rochester achieved some of its important aims. For example, great improvements were noted in these students' examination performance, and all students were promoted to the next year of the curriculum. The handling of the issues of trust and self-esteem also appeared to be crucial. In considering student learning difficulties, faculty members focused on cognitive factors such as background preparation, reading, and communication skills. On the other hand, in considering the same difficulties, students emphasized affective factors such as issues of trust, liking, and bias. The special tutorial showed that intervention was necessary in both areas.

Based on the results of our small scale activities, the following assumptions and recommendations were formulated:

1. Affective factors are likely to impede academic performance in the adjustment period of the first part of the first year of medical school. First-year students, and particularly students for whom the adjustment can be seen to be difficult, must be helped to establish firm bases for self-esteem and trust in the environment. The communication of liking and positive regard by faculty is a necessary component of this effort.

2. Failure or near-failure in a course may damage a medical student's self-esteem seriously enough to interfere with subsequent learning performance. Therefore, a faculty adviser or tutor should provide help to such a student if, in addition to interest in the student, he is oriented toward affective concerns and has the appropriate sensitivities and interpersonal skills to deal effectively with them.

3. Relationships with instructors, advisers, or tutors should be arranged to provide all students with positive reinforcement. Such relationships would constitute a base for providing remedial work, if necessary, and for encouraging student growth. Again, faculty with appropriate sensitivities are required.

4. Medical education units, which are now found in many schools, should train faculty to relate better to students both in classroom and one-to-one interactions. The ability to deal skillfully with affective issues and

concerns is an interpersonal skill which can be strengthened through instruction.

5.   Students with lowered self-esteem and academic problems must be helped to objectively evaluate their problems, after which meaningful intervention can take place. An instructor whom the student trusts is in the best position to give the student realistic information that can be tolerated and used productively.

References

Margolis, S. and D.L. Marshal
     1974   "A comprehensive retention program for disadvantaged students." Journal of the American Medical Association 228:861-865.

Marshal, C.L.
     1973   "Minority students for medicine and hazards of high school." Journal of Medical Education 48:134-140.

Nelson, B.W.
     1970   "Expanding educational opportunities and hazards of high school." Journal of Medical Education 45:731-736.

Nelson, B.W. and M. Gilbert
     1971   "Education pathway analysis for the study of minority representation in medical school." Journal of Medical Education 46:745-749.

21

Participation of Blacks in the Basic Sciences: An Assessment

VIJAYA L. MELNICK AND FRANKLIN D. HAMILTON

It is imperative that the United States utilize its resources to effect the maximum development of potential in all of its citizenry. The paucity of blacks in the natural and physical sciences points to the severe underutilization of human resources that this country can draw upon for the development of its society. Twenty-five years after the Supreme Court declaration in the <u>Brown v. Board of Education Topeka</u> (1954) in which the court stated "... we conclude that in the field of public education the doctrine of separate but equal has no place," the education of blacks in the sciences remains separate and very much unequal to whites. For example, among the 87,000 scientists and engineers in 1974 only 1.6% were black (Vetter, Babco and McIntire, 1978) (See Table 1). Among doctoral scientists and engineers, less than 0.9% were black (National Science Foundation, 1975). Of approximately 375,000 physicians in this country, only 1.8% (6,800) are black; and of 150,000 dentists, less than 2% are black (Melnick, 1977).

The present enrollment of black students in science and engineering graduate programs is also low. Thus, current training efforts will not lead to a significant increase in the number of minorities in science careers in the near future. In spite of the significant gains in total black enrollment in higher education in the seventies, black students still account for 5.4% of the total first professional degree enrollment and 6.0% of the total graduate enrollment (Mingle, 1978). Graduate enrollment in the life and physical sciences is near 2%, in the health sciences 5%, and 1.4% in engineering (National Science Foundation, 1975). In 1976, black students comprised 6.8% of the total student population in 124 United States medical schools (Bleich, 1977). An analysis of data for the number of minority biomedical scientists shows a decrease from 5.1% in 1973 to 4.2% in 1976

Table 1[a]

Blacks as a Percent of Various Science Populations, By Fields

	Year(s)	Physical Sciences	Math Sciences	Computer Sciences	Envir. Sciences	Life Sciences	Psycho- logy	Social Sciences	Engi- neering
Bachelor's Degrees	1976	2.9	4.9	5.8	-	4.1	6.3	8.5	2.9
Master's Degrees	1976	2.4	3.1	2.1	-	3.1	5.2	5.4	1.3
Ph.D's Degrees	1973-76	1.1	1.2	-	1.6	1.8	2.6	2.6	1.0
Labor Force (All Degrees)	1974	1.9	3.3	1.6	-	2.2	1.6	10.0	0.8
Ph.D. Labor Force	1975	1.0	0.8	0.9	0.3	1.2	1.2	1.5	0.3
Recent BS Grads Empl.	1977	2.1	3.4	6.6	2.5	1.9	4.1	6.9	1.5
Recent MS Grads Empl.	1977	3.8	4.2	2.1	-	1.0	2.3	1.3	1.7
Federal Employed	1976	5.3	14.0	15.3	-	4.8	2.1	12.6	3.2

Source:
[a] Vetter, 1978   Professional Women and Minorities: A Manpower Data Resource Service.
Washington, D.C.: Scientific Manpower Commission.

(National Research Council and National Academy of Sciences, 1977). This decrease has occurred in spite of an increase in the number of doctorates awarded to minorities over the same time span. These figures suggest that the percentage of minority students in biomedical training programs has also begun to decrease, perhaps reflecting the conservative trend that has developed in this country.

A number of federal agencies and private foundations have responded to the underrepresentation of minorities in the sciences by establishing a series of special programs (See Appendix I and also Malcolm, Cownie and Brown, 1976). These programs can be a major resource for increasing the access of minority students to science and engineering careers. This chapter describes some of the federally and privately sponsored programs available to minorities who have an interest in science. We also suggest additional areas that need to be considered in designing programs to increase minority participation in the sciences.

DHEW-National Institutes of Health (NIH) Programs

Two major programs for minorities in science sponsored by NIH are the Minority Biomedical Science Program (MBS) and the Minority Access to Research Careers (MARC) Program. In 1972, NIH's Division of Research Resources initiated the MBS program. This program was designed to strengthen institutional research and research training capabilities in colleges, universities, and health professional schools that enroll significant numbers of minority students. MBS has recently expanded to include two-year colleges and American Indian Tribal Councils that perform substantial governmental functions.

Funds provided by the MBS program are used for release time as well as financial support for students who collaborate on these projects. From a modest budget of $2 million in Fiscal Year 1972 in which 38 awards were made, the program had increased to a budget of $11.6 million in Fiscal Year 1977. For the 1978 fiscal year, the budget for the MBS program was supplemented by Intra-Agency Cooperative Agreements with other Institutes of NIH. A total of 14.2 million dollars was spent for faculty and student research. In the same year, a total of 1,700 students and 600 faculty received support from these funds. To date, the MBS program has pro-

vided assistance to 1,676 students in obtaining their B.S.
degrees. Some 1,227 (73%) of these students have entered
advanced studies in health-related programs (See Table 2).

The Minority Access to Research Careers (MARC) program
was initiated by the National Institutes of General Medical
Sciences (NIGMS) in 1972 to strengthen faculty capabilities
at minority academic institutions. The MARC program provides
stipend and tuition support for pre- and post-doctoral training of faculty members at major institutions throughout the
country. In 1977, the MARC program initiated an undergraduate training component. The undergraduate program provides
stipend and tuition support to undergraduate students who are
interested in careers in the biomedical sciences. The goal
of the undergraduate program is to increase the number of
minority students who can successfully compete for entrance
into biomedical graduate programs. On an annual budget of
$5 million, the MARC program supports 50 faculty in pre- and
post-doctoral training and has funded 16 undergraduate programs with a combined student enrollment of 115.

A more recent and smaller effort to train minorities for
science careers has been launched by the National Heart, Lung
and Blood Institute (NHLBI). NHLBI has funded the development of 15 Hypertension Training Centers at major research
institutions throughout the country. The centers are designed to involve faculty members and predoctoral students
from minority institutions in basic and clinical research on
the epidemological aspects of hypertension and hypertensive
patient compliance. In the past two years the Hypertensive
Centers have involved 150 preceptors, 80 faculty, and 40
graduates from 46 minority institutions in a concerted effort
to research the problem of hypertension in the American population.

As a result of the development of special programs at
NIH, support for research training at minority institutions
increased from $12 million during Fiscal Years 1967-71 to
$65 million during Fiscal Years 1972-76. The NIH support to
black colleges increased from $10 million to $52 million
during the same period.

DHEW-National Institute of Mental Health (NIMH)

In 1970, the National Institute of Mental Health initiated a program entitled the Centers for Minority Group Mental Health Program. The Centers were developed to provide
leadership for application of new knowledge toward the solution of mental health problems utilizing a minority perspective. Center activities at NIMH include the processing and

Table 2

MBS Accomplishments

Career Choices of Graduates
1974-1977

	1974	1975	1976	1977	Total 1974-1977
Medical School	78	116	150	86	430
Dental School	13	22	40	14	89
Graduate School	99	120	174	101	494
Other Health Related Schools	35	39	87	53	214
Total Enrolled in Advanced Training	225	297	451	254	1,227
Total MBS Graduates	295	399	648	336	1,676

Source:

MBS Program, Division of Research Resources, National Institutes of Health, Annual Report (1978)

monitoring of grants and contracts; arranging for intramural
and extramural consultation; providing limited consultation
to agencies, groups and organizations on the mental health
of minority groups; and participating in the drafting, reviewing and editing of major policies and legislation re-
lating to mental health.

The center also provides support for faculty and students who are engaged in mental health related research projects through the funding of five national research and development centers. These centers are: the National Research
and Development Mental Health Center for American Indians
and Alaskan Natives, University of Oregon; National Research
and Development Mental Health Center for Asian Americans,
University of California, San Diego; National Research and
Development Mental Health Center for Blacks, Howard University and Drew Postgraduate Medical School–Los Angeles; and
National Research and Development Mental Health Center for
Hispanics, University of California, Los Angeles.

DHEW–Health Resource Administration – Health Centers Opportunity Program (HCOP)

In 1972 the Health Resources Administration initiated
the Special Health Careers Opportunity Grants (SHCOG) Programs. The program provides funds for universities, colleges,
health professional schools, and community organizations to
recruit and offer pre-professional training and financial
assistance to racial minorities and other disadvantaged
groups interested in careers in the health professions, including medicine, dentistry, optometry, veterinary medicine,
and public health. From the initial budget of $5 million
in Fiscal Year 1972, the budget has increased to $14.5 mil-
lion in Fiscal Year 1978. These funds supported the special
training of more than 10,000 students on 142 projects
spread across 40 states, the District of Columbia, and
Puerto Rico. Currently the program is entitled Health
Careers Opportunity Program (HCOP) and in Fiscal Year 1979
will allocate more than $18 million for student training
and assistance.

DHEW–Office of Education

In Fiscal Year 1979, the Office of Education, through
its Graduate and Professional Opportunity Program, allocated
$8 million in fellowship support for minority and disadvan-
taged students' graduate education in all fields. Also in
1979, the Office of Education received congressional author-
ization to establish a Biomedical Enrichment Program to pro-

vide funds for special educational enrichment opportunities
in the basic and biomedical sciences to disadvantaged secondary school students. This program, which was budgeted at
$4 million, is designed to increase the interest of high
school students in biomedical careers through innovative
teaching techniques. As of this writing, the detailed plans
and regulations for the program are under development by the
staff of the Assistant Secretary for Education (DHEW).

National Science Foundation (NSF)

In 1971, the National Science Foundation initiated what
is now known as the Minority Institution Science Improvement
Program (MISIP). MISIP is designed to accelerate the development of science capabilities in historically black institutions and other four- and two-year colleges that primarily
serve disadvantaged ethnic minorities. Under this program,
institutions can receive a maximum of $300,000 over a 36-
month period to support faculty release time for curriculum
design and development in the physical and life sciences.
Since 1972, 184 awards totaling approximately $35 million
have been made available by the MISIP program.

In 1978, NSF received appropriations to initiate the
development of regional Resource Centers for Science and
Engineering. Through the establishment of a series of
centers at Universities throughout the country, this program
was designed to increase the number of doctoral-trained
minority and disadvantaged persons in science and engineering.
The first Resource Center was established at Atlanta University in Fiscal Year 1978 and funded at 2.8 million for a
four-year period. A second Resource Center was established
in Fiscal Year 1979 at the University of New Mexico (Albuquer-
que), and New Mexico State University. The original plan was
to distribute the Centers geographically so that they would
serve as magnets for the development of academic and research
capabilities at nearby colleges and universities. In addition, the centers were also to assist secondary school
programs by providing information and counseling to high
school students on career opportunities available in science
and engineering. Center sponsored activities include academic year and summer workshops and programs for both college
faculty and students and high school faculty and students.

Private and Philanthropic Foundations

Several private and philanthropic foundations have also supported various aspects of higher education for blacks and other minorities (see Appendix II for specific examples. Much of the support from these foundations has been expended for training minorities in biomedicine. The Macy Foundation has provided funds to enhance the premedical curriculum at a number of black colleges. Funds have been used to provide for adequate premedical counseling, improvement of student test-taking skills, and organization of Health Professional Clubs. The Robert Wood Johnson Foundation has provided funds for financial aid for minority medical and dental students and also supports a number of summer enrichment programs in a medical environment for minority undergraduate students. These programs frequently involve cooperative arrangements with nearby undergraduate institutions. Some institutions which have received financial support from the Robert Wood Johnson Foundation include the University of Southern California Medical School, New Jersey College of Medicine and Dentistry, The University of Mississippi Medical Center, Tulane University Medical School and the University of Texas Health Science Center at Galveston.

Efforts to increase the participation of blacks and other minorities in science careers have been enhanced by federal and privately funded programs. However, the full participation of these groups in the basic sciences is yet to be realized. Several factors continue to retard the flow of blacks into scientific careers. Among them are: (1) the lack of adequate financial resources, (2) too few role models and (3) poor high school preparation and counseling.

An important ingredient for the preparation of students for science careers is the development of adequate mathematical and verbal skills at the high school level. A recent survey of a local school district in Berkeley, California indicated that only 20% of the black students were receiving college prep training in math as compared to over 72% of the white and 79% of the Asian students (Sells, 1979a). Also, a study of entering freshmen at the University of Maryland in the fall of 1977 showed that 63% of the white men had 3.5 years of pre-calculus high school math, as compared to only 31% of white women, 27% of black men and 19% of black women (Sells, 1979b). Interested federal and private agencies may therefore wish to give a higher priority to curriculum development in high school in an effort to increase the number of minority students in math and science tracks. Other

areas of intervention that should be given special consideration include: (1) pre-college and early college counseling
to inform minority students of career opportunities in
science; (2) the development of laboratory-based science
curricula to increase minority student motivation and interest in science; (3) the provision of greater financial
support for science research and training for minority students at minority and majority colleges and universities;
(4) the provision of more tutorial services for minority
students at majority institutions; and (5) the expansion of
science-related work-study and undergraduate research experiences for minority students.

The past two-and-a-half decades have produced extraordinary and profound social, economic, and technological
changes in this country. These changes have greatly affected the lives of American citizens and have gone beyond regional boundaries to put this country in the forefront of
the world in terms of power, influence, and scientific
eminence. However, true national progress can be achieved
only by the full participation of all of the diverse segments of our society. As eloquently noted by former United
Nations Ambassador Andrew Young (1977), "... science and the
scientific endeavor will be enriched by the full participation of a broader group of people. Often, questions in
science reflect the human experience of the investigator.
Thus, the participation of citizens from all segments of
society will ensure a more equitable and compassionate
distribution of the fruits of science and application of
technology."

References

Bleich, M.
    1977   "Funding of minority programs from the private
           sector: a perspective from the Josiah Macy Jr.
           Foundation." Pp. 143 in V.L. Melnick and F.D.
           Hamilton (eds.), Minorities in Science. New York:
           Plenum Press.

Brown v. Board of Education of Topeka 347 U.S. 483 (1954).

Malcolm, J.M., J. Cownie and J.W. Brown
    1976   Programs in Science for Minority Students, 1960-
           1975. Washington, D.C.: American Association
           for the Advancement of Science.

Melnick, V.L.
    1977   "Public policy for minority self actualization
           present realities and future possibilities."

References Continued

Melnick, V.L. (continued)
        Pp. 86 in V.L. Melnick and F.D. Hamilton (eds.)
        Minorities in Science. New York: Plenum Press

Mingle, J.R.
    1978 "Black enrollment in higher education: trend in
        the national and the south." Atlanta: Southern
        Regional Education Board."

National Research Council and National Academy of Sciences
    1977 "Report to committee on personnel needs for
        biomedical and behavioral research."
        Washington, DC

National Science Foundation
    1975 Characteristics of doctoral scientists and
        engineers in the United States. (NSF-77-309).

Sells, L.W.
    1979a "High school mathematics enrollment."
        Manuscript in preparation.

    1979b "Counseling the Young." Science 203:4377

Vetter, B., E. Babco and J. McIntire
    1978 "Professional women and minorities, a manpower
        data resource service." Washington, DC.:
        Scientific Manpower Commission.

Young, Andrew
    1977 "Foreword." P. XIV, V.L. Melnick and F.D.
        Hamilton (eds.) Minorities in Science.
        New York: Plenum Press

Appendix I

Federal Agencies with Programs for Minorities
in the Basic Sciences

Dr. Clay Simpson
Health Career Opportunity Program
Office of Health Resources Opportunity
HRA-DHEW Rm. 10-50
Center Building 3700 East West Highway
Hyattsville, MD   20782

Mr. Ciriaco Gonzales
Minority Biomedical Science Program
Division of Research Resources
National Institutes of Health
Bethesda, MD   20014

Dr. James Rutherford
National Science Foundation
5225 Wisconsin Avenue
Washington, DC   20550

Mr. Edward Bynum
Minority Access to Research Careers,
   National Institutes of Health
National Institute of General Medical
   Sciences
Westwood Building
Westwood Avenue Bethesda, MD   20014

Office of Education
Bureau of Higher and Continuing
   Education
400 Maryland Avenue, SW
Washington, DC   20202

Center for Minority Group Mental
   Health Programs
National Institutes of Mental Health
Rockville, MD   20013

Appendix II

Private Foundations with Programs
for Minorities in Science

The Carnegie Corporation of New York
437 Madison Avenue
New York, New York   10022

The Danforth Foundation
222 South Central Avenue
St. Louis, MO   63105

The Ford Foundation
320 East 43rd Street
New York, New York   10017

Josiah Macy Jr. Foundation
1 Rockefeller Plaza
New York, New York   10020

The Andrew W. Mellon Foundation
140 East 62nd Street
New York, New York   10021

The Rockefeller Foundation
111 West 50th Street
New York, New York   10020

Alfred P. Sloan Foundation
630 5th Avenue
New York, New York   10020

The Robert Wood Johnson Foundation
P.O. Box 2316
Princeton, New Jersey   08540

22

Impact: A Summer Enrichment Program for Minority/Disadvantaged Undergraduates at the University of Minnesota

PHILLIP CAREY, BALDAVE SINGH, and BARBARA PILLINGER _____

Introduction

Recent studies indicate that minority student access and retention rates in higher education are disturbingly low (Carey, Singh and Smith, 1979; Rouche and Snow, 1977; Armstrong and Hall, 1976). Therefore, developing effective strategies to increase the access and retention of blacks and other minorities in higher education remains a current challenge.

Several reasons why minorities have not achieved maximum success in higher education have been suggested -- for example, parent and teacher indifference as well as the poor quality of the elementary and secondary education that minorities receive. Also, the educational expectations and the perceptions that minorities have concerning their chances of success at various levels of higher education affect minority achievement in higher education (Thomas, 1979; Gurin and Epps, 1975). Other factors affecting minority access and retention include inadequate financial aid (Morris, 1979), low self-concept, and a lack of adequate individual and group-centered support systems in the college environment.

As black enrollment patterns shift from the traditional segregated settings to more integrated settings, the problem of minority access and retention on predominantly white campuses is of particular concern. Carey (1976), Griffin (1975), and Willie and McCord (1973) estimate that the current national attrition rate for black students at white colleges and universities could be as high as 70 percent. Interestingly, studies have shown that black college students' retention is much higher at the predominantly black colleges (Institute for the Study of Educational Policy, 1976).

Several programmatic strategies and points of intervention have been suggested by Grant and Engleman (1968) and
others (Davis, 1975; Cash, 1970; Green, 1969) for increasing
the likelihood of minority access and retention in predominantly white institutions. These strategies include:
(1) special admission programs which lower traditional
college entry requirements for blacks and other minority
students; (2) pre- and post-college academic and non-academic
enrichment programs designed to improve the academic and
motivational skills of "high risk" students; (3) the development of college orientation programs to familiarize minorities with the academic and social aspects of their college
environment; (4) the development of general studies degree-
granting programs specifically designed for students who have
not fared well academically during their secondary and
previous schooling, and (5) adequate financial assistance.

Many of the program strategies on predominantly white
campuses have concentrated on providing academic remedial
services and/or financial aid to minorities (Davis, 1975),
but many social scientists and educators believe that more
extensive pre-college enrichment and orientation programs
for disadvantaged minority students are needed to increase
retention.

Background and Assumptions of the Program

The University of Minnesota has a total student enrollment of over 73,000 students. Approximately 4.5 percent of
its undergraduate and graduate enrollees are racial minorities, half of whom are black. In 1978 a summer program for
incoming freshmen was established by the University's Office
for Minority and Special Student Affairs (OMSSA). The program was basically designed to sharpen the academic skills
of the disadvantaged/minority students and to familiarize
them with the subculture, norms, and expectations of the
university environment. In addition, OMSSA provided total
financial support (including necessary transportation and
child care expenses) to all students who participated in
the program. The basic philosophy underlying the program
is that black and other minority disadvantaged students
could perform more successfully in higher education given
adequate academic, social, and financial support by a highly
structured group of competent and committed faculty and
educational administrators.[1] In addition, the program stressed and encouraged the involvement and support of all seg-

ments of the University to facilitate the goals of the
program.

Program Activities

The initial aspect of the college summer program (which
began in the summer of 1978) involved recruiting students to
participate in the pilot program. The program offerings were
advertised in the local schools and communities where minority
students were largely represented. From the student responses, sixty-eight students were selected based on the severity
of their financial and/or academic needs.[2] The general requirements for admission to the program were that students be
academically and/or financially deficient, members of a recognized racial-cultural minority group, and interested in attending the University of Minnesota in the Fall. The racial-
cultural composition of the participants included thirty-
three blacks, fifteen Asian Americans, twelve Chicanos/Lati-
nos, six American Indians, and two Whites.

At the beginning of the five-week Summer Institute the
students were introduced to the university campus by an orientation tour and the provision of vital information about
the system. A series of informational and counseling seminars offering specific material and suggestions on all relevant aspects of university life were provided. These included financial aid, course offerings, major concentrations
within the colleges, and other special supportive services.
Additional discussion seminars on how to manage the complexities of a large university environment were held throughout
the summer session. Social events were developed with input
and direction from the students. These activities included a
bowling league, a weekly newsletter, a picnic, local plays,
concerts and other social-cultural events. The final event
was a recognition banquet.

After housing and financial aid arrangements were made
(50 percent of the participants lived in prearranged on-
campus housing), students were interviewed and evaluated to
determine specific class assignments and course loads. All
participants were permitted to enroll in either a Math or
English course and personal orientation class that emphasized how to study and succeed in college.[3] Also offered
was a bilingual/bicultural English composition class that
was designed specifically for Asian Americans, primarily
from Vietnam, Cambodia and Thailand.

Staff and counselors also provided students with continuous counseling and assistance. Special counseling units
were established in the dormitory which housed minority

students; thus immediate assistance was available to the
students. These activities were augmented by faculty and
staff participants who developed an informational network
among themselves and with certain students to monitor the
class attendance and academic progress of students. Students who were consistently absent from classes were con-
tacted and received immediate consultation. Faculty and
staff meetings were held on a weekly basis to assure effective and continuous functioning of the program. Another
important activity provided for the students throughout the
program was tutorial assistance on an individual basis.
Tutors were available on demand in the students' dormitories,
classrooms, and at the counseling center.

Program Results

      Because the summer program was short-term,and a first-time
pilot effort, the results of the program's progress should be
considered tentative. Results were obtained from the students' course performance, their pre- and post-test scores on
the standardized Basic Skill test, and from the student assessment of the program. These results indicated in general that
the academic enrichment and orientation program was successful in achieving its goals. For example, the thirty-five
students enrolled in the three sections of math(two courses
of Basic Math and one of Intermediate Algebra) earned a class
grade point average of 3.10 or a "B". The class grade point
average for those students who were enrolled in English Composition was a 2.8 or "C+".[4] Also, the Asian-American students, in their bilingual-bicultural compositon class,
earned a class grade point average of 2.5 or received an "S"
(Satisfactory) grade.

      The Writing and Math subtests of the McGraw-Hill Basic
Skills System Test were administered to the program participants prior to their five-week courses. Due to time limitations and logistical problems, both pre- and post-testing had
to be done outside the time and space allotted for classes.
We were also able to schedule one post-testing session only,
and this was administered after four weeks of classes. Thus
pre- and post-test results were available for only fifty-five
of the sixty-eight (81 percent) of the program participants.
The results indicated general improvement in the students'
test performance. Although we cannot be certain that the
test score gains that these students made were totally attributable to the effects of the program, we believe that their
intensive course experiences in the program contributed
substantially to their test gains.

The post-test results showed that the thirty-five students who enrolled in math courses had increased their mean percentile rank from 19.37 percent to 35.2 percent. Usage of the Difference of Means Test indicated that this gain was significant (t = 5.28, p $\leq$ .001). The twenty students with pre- and post-test data who were enrolled in the English Composition course had a pre-test mean percentile rank of 27.05 percent; upon completing the summer program their percentile rank had increased to 40.31. The greatest improvement of these students was on the Language Mechanics section of the English test, which showed significant pre- and post-test differences (t = 4.64, p $\leq$ .01). However, the post-test gains that the students made on the Sentence and Paragraph Pattern sections of the English test were not statistically significant.

The post-test results for the Bilingual/Bicultural English course for the Vietnamese and other Southeast Asian students were the most impressive. Upon enrollment in the Summer Institute, these students scored in the twenty-first percentile of the national sample of incoming freshmen. After concluding the course, they increased their national percentile. This improvement was statistically significant (p $\leq$ .005). An examination of the results on three parts of the test showed raw score improvements of 50 percent in Language Mechanics, 53 percent in Sentence Patterns, and 30.2 percent in Paragraph Patterns.

In summary, the students' grades, instructors' reports, and the pre- and post-test results indicated substantial improvement in the students' acquisition of English and mathematics. To gauge the possible indirect effects of the Summer Institute on retention, these students' registration in subsequent quarters was followed up. Eighty-four percent (57) of the participants in the Summer Institute completed the program. Sixty-five percent (44) of the original program participants registered for the Fall quarter at the Minneapolis campus. Two of the original participants had previously decided to attend another university; and eight attended another University of Minnesota campus. Information on the three students who did not enroll for the Fall was unavailable. Of the 44 original program participants who registered for the Fall quarter, 40 registered for the Spring quarter. Eighty-four percent (37) of the 44 students who entered the university in the Fall were retained throughout the academic year. Also, three additional Summer Institute participants later returned to the Minneapolis campus who had not registered in the Fall.

Although they were not required to do so, many of the
summer program faculty and staff maintained communication
with these students during their freshman year. Because no
special provisions were made for additional support services
during the academic year, students were encouraged to take
advantage of the existing support services. That approximately eighty-four percent of the program participants who
entered the University in the Fall of 1978 persisted throughout the entire year suggests that the Summer Institute was
effective to some extent. However, an even greater level of
program success and more long-term progress of the program
participants is expected to be achieved by future efforts.

Several limitations of the current programs must be
addressed to achieve this goal. For example, all participants in the program agreed that the current five-week span
of the program needs to be expanded to more adequately meet
its objectives and additional student needs. We observed,
for instance, that some of the students in our program needed
more extensive tutoring in English and Math. However,
because of time and staff limitations, students could enroll
only in one or the other course. Time and staff limitations
also restricted our efforts to maintain extensive contact
and follow-up with the summer participants. Finally, our
present program can only facilitate a general evaluation
of students at the end of the freshman year. However, it
is important that these students be followed at the end of
each year. The validity of our program results might be
enhanced by evaluations involving similar programs at other
colleges and universities and by future comparisons of
minority and majority group within the University. In addition, the random assignment of eligible minority students
to the program might enhance the evaluation design for the
program.

Conclusion and Discussion

The academic performance of minority students in the
summer program along with their post-test performance supports our belief that efforts to provide disadvantaged minority students with college enrichment experiences during the
summer can be extremely beneficial when approached from a
"holistic" perspective. The overall favorable reports from
the participants themselves further substantiate this contention. Given a concerted effort by competent and sensitive program sponsors and administrators, these types of
enrichment and orientation programs can provide disadvantaged
minorities with greater confidence in their ability to perform at the college level by pre-exposing them to the norms

and subcultural expectations operating in most large, complex
college environments.

As previously noted, one of the aims of the program was
to identify economically and/or academically deprived minority and high risk students interested in entering college
who had potential for performing college work, but whose
chances to succeed were diminished because of dysfunctional
attitudes and skills. A more important aim of the program,
however, was to assure the successful completion of their
first year of college. The achievement of this objective
was especially crucial, given the high rate of minority
student attrition in the first year of college. Presently
it is believed that the attrition rate for minority and
disadvantaged students at the University of Minnesota is as
much as 85 percent.   For the American Indian students, the
situation is even worse; Beaulieu (1978) reports that nine
out of every ten entering freshmen from the American Indian
community (reservation and/or urban) drop out before receiving a college degree.   Furthermore, the pattern of retention suggests that as many as 50 percent decide to leave
college during the first few weeks of classes.

Despite the limitations of the Minnesota program, the
data suggest that the program had a positive effect on the
academic performance and retention of the majority of the
student participants throughout the freshman year. Furthermore, we believe that the provision of effective pre-college
preparation to disadvantaged minority students greatly
enhances their chances of college access and retention.

References

Armstrong, R. and W.V. Hall
  1976   "A comparative study of the Martin Luther King pro-
         gram and randomly selected freshmen entering the
         University of Minnesota in Fall 1970: entrance data
         and subsequent performance." University of Minne-
         sota: Office for Student Affairs Research
         Bulletin 16:14.

  1978   "The relationship of course characteristics to
         differential performance of Martin Luther King
         program and other students in selected college
         of liberal arts courses." University of
         Minnesota: Office for Student Affairs Research
         Bulletin 16:15.

Beaulieu, D.
  1978   "The college retention of American Indians."
         Unpublished paper presented to the Board of
         Regents, University of Minnesota (Nov.)

Burnette, R.
  1971   The Tortured Americans. Englewood Cliffs,
         New Jersey: Prentice-Hall.

Carey, P.
  1976   White Racism and Black Higher Education.
         Washington, D.C.: Minority Fellowship Program.

Carey, P., B. Singh and S. Smith
  1979   "The higher education of minorities: the summer
         of seventy-eight, a creative response to minority
         higher education." University of Minnesota:
         Office for Minority and Special Student Affairs.

Cash, C.
  1970   "Educationally inferior students: getting in and
         out of college." Columbia, Mo.: paper presented
         for EPDA Institute, University of Missouri.

Clark, B.R.
  1960   The Open Door College: A Case Study. New York:
         McGraw Hill.

Cross, R.P.
  1976   Accent on Learning: Improving Instruction and
         Reshaping the Curriculum. San Francisco:
         Jossey-Bass, Publishers.

References Continued

Crossland, F.
  1978   "Statistics on the higher education of minorities."
         Unpublished manuscript.

Davis, J.A.
  1975   The Impact of Special Services Programs in Higher
         Education for Disadvantaged Students. Princeton,
         N.J.: Educational Testing Service.

Eagerton, J.
  1968   Higher Education for "High Risk" Students.
         Atlanta: Southern Education Foundation, Inc.

Grant, C. and S. Engleman
  1968   "A Pre-admission program for students with low
         academic promise." Journal of College Student
         Personnel 46:12-20.

Green, R.
  1969   "The black quest for higher education: an
         admissions dilemma." Personnel and Guidance
         Journal 47:26-31.

Griffin, T.A.
  1975   The Southern Education Foundation Report.
         Atlanta: Southern Education Foundation, Inc.

Gurin, P. and E. Epps
  1975   Black Consciousness, Identity, and Achievement.
         New York: John Wiley.

Hamachek, D.C.
  1971   Encounters with the Self. Chicago: Holt,
         Rinehart and Winston.

Institute for Study of Education Policy
  1976   Equal Educational Opportunity for Blacks in U.S.
         Higher Education: An Assessment.
         Washington, D.C.: Howard University Press.

Katz, I.
  1969   "A critique of personality approaches to Negro
         performance: Research Suggestions." Journal of
         Social Issues 3:12-19.

References Continued

Kvaraceus, W.
1965   "Negro youth and social adaption: the role of
        the school as an agent of change."   Pp. 34-41.
        Negro Self Concept: Implications for School and
        Citizenship.   New York: McGraw Hill.

Kardiner, A. and L. Ovesey
1962   The Mark of Oppression: Exploration in the
        Personality of the American Negro.   Cleveland:
        World Publishing Co.

Morris, L.
1979   Elusive Equality: The Status of Black Americans
        in Higher Education.   Washington, D.C.:   Howard
        University Press.

National Urban League
1979   The State of Black America.   Washington, D.C.:
        National Urban League, Inc.

Poussaint, F.A.
1972   Why Blacks Kill Blacks.   New York: Emerson Hall
        Publishers.

Rouche, J.E. and J.J. Snow
1977   Overcoming Learning Problems.   San Francisco:
        Jossey-Bass Publishers.

Sample, D. and W. Seymour
1971   "The academic success of black students: a
        dilemma."   Journal of College Student Personnel
        12:18-23.

Thomas, G.E.
1979   The influence of ascription, achievement and
        educational expectations on black-white post-
        secondary enrollment."   The Sociological
        Quarterly 20 (Spring):   209-222.

U.S. Department of Labor
1971   Black Americans: A Chart Book.   Washington, D.C.:
        Bulletin #1699

Willie, C.V. and A.S. McCord
1973   Black Students at White Colleges.   New York:
        Praeger Press.

Footnotes

1. The administrative staff positions in the Summer Institute were as follows: a Director, an Assistant Director, a Secretary, and Administrative Assistant/Financial Aid Counselor, and one Administrative Assistant for Administration. Faculty positions included two math professors, an instructor for the personal orientation class, and four instructors in English composition, writing, and bi-lingual education. In addition, there were six counselors and three tutors. A one-day seminar was conducted which focused on cultural/racial differences in areas of learning, communicating, perception of the world, goal setting, career choice, and other related factors.

2. As many as one hundred eligible students requested permission to participate, but due to funding limitations the program could accomodate only sixty-eight of these students. The participants were selected on the basis of academic and financial need, and the order of registration completion. Also, eight students were advanced freshmen from one of the four coordinate campuses of the University of Minnesota system. These students were permitted to participate by special request in an attempt to help their academic standing and performance.

3. In the selection of course offerings, emphasis was naturally geared toward Math and English for purposes of skill building. Because both General College and College of Liberal Arts students were participating, there was an attempt to offer courses taught by instructors from both Colleges. Courses offered were GC 1445 Intermediate Algebra, GC 1431-33 Math, Comp 1001 English Composition, GC 1421 Writing Lab, PO 1001 Personal Orientation. Of significance was the fact that the students' individual test scores and college acceptance were the two main criteria used in class assignments. The students were directed toward the areas where test scores indicated the most help was needed.

4. It should be noted that in evaluating and assigning grades to the participants, faculty members made no exceptions in assigning grades because of the program's status. They employed the same methods of evaluating and grading that they apply to all students during the regular academic year.

Footnotes   (Cont'd)

5.   Historically, attrition has been a rather difficult
socio-educational phenomenon to measure. Nevertheless,
Armstrong and Hall (1976, 1978) suggest that this is the
situation at the University of Minnesota. This finding is
consistent with national date (See Fred Crossland (1978):
Ford Foundation, Statistical Profile of Minorities in Higher
Education, unpublished data).

6.   Recent findings by a number of sociologists and educators
support these conclusions by David Beaulieu, Chair
Indian Studies Department, University of Minnesota,
unpublished paper, presented to the Board of Regents,
University of Minnesota, November 1978. See also Robert
Burnette, "The Long and Losing Fight of the American
Indian," in the Tortured Americans, Prentice-Hall, Inc.,
Englewood Cliffs, N.J., 1971, pp. 11-25.

23

A Successful Model for Articulation and the Development of a Two-Plus-Two Program at a Predominantly Black and a Predominantly White Institution

PAUL B. MOHR, SR. and JAMES C. SEARS

In the 1978 Virginia Plan for Equal Opportunity in State Supported Institutions of Higher Education, hereafter referred to as the Virginia Plan, Commonwealth of Virginia officials made a commitment to eliminate educationally un- necessary duplication between its traditionally black and traditionally white institutions in the same service area. As a means of accomplishing this objective, a study of alleged program duplication in Tidewater was conducted during the summer of 1978. The Tidewater Duplication Study, hereafter referred to as the Study, proposed elimination of duplication, and utilization of specialization and co- operative programs as methods of resolution to the problem of alleged program duplication in the Tidewater Virginia area. These methods were acceptable by both the Virginia Plan and the amended criteria established in the second supplemental order of April 22, 1977 in the case of Adams vs. Califano.

Three institutions, Norfolk State University (a pre- dominantly black institution), Old Dominion University, and Tidewater Community College (both predominantly white institutions), located in Tidewater Virginia, were respon- sible for meeting and implementing requirements found in the Study. Norfolk State University (NSU) and Tidewater Community College (TCC) were charged in the Study with developing two-plus-two transfer programs in the areas of office administration/secretarial science, accounting and business education. As defined on page 15 of the Study, "... a 2+2 program is one in which students interested in a particular four-year degree program can take two years at a community college and then automatically transfer to a senior college for two more years of study upon successful comple- tion of the two years at a community college." Furthermore, the two-plus-two articulation arrangement was characterized in the Study as program specialization, which was one of the three recommended ways to resolve the problem of program duplication.

The Tidewater Study Advisory Committee stated on page 17 of the Study that ".. such articulation agreements .. will prove advantageous to the objectives of the Virginia Plan in that other race students will be encouraged to attend Norfolk State College." Furthermore, it was believed by local college officials that the two-plus-two agreements would expand mobility between the two-year and four-year institutions, assist in student recruitment and admissions, reduce attrition, promote faculty and staff exchanges, and eliminate unnecessary program duplication. It is especially noteworthy that discussions leading to resolution of the program duplication issue were held at the college level as well as the state level. Institutional boards, presidents, vice presidents, deans, faculty and students were provided opportunities for participation in the development of articulation agreements. Resolution of alleged duplication was greatly enhanced by the direct involvement of institutional parties. Enhancement occurred because extending negotiations and discussions to the college level placed college personnel in a vested-interest position, thereby resulting in increased college interest in meeting stipulated requirements.

The development of an articulation agreement between a predominantly black university (NSU) and a predominantly white community college (TCC) was seen by many as a natural vehicle by which the two-fold purpose of desegregation could be accomplished. The purpose of the agreement was the successful recruitment of non-black students to a predominantly black university. The mandate in Adams v. Califano placed a priority on achieving a greater racial mix of students at the traditionally black and white institutions.

Two studies (Brown, 1973; Standley, 1978) indicated that non-black students are amenable to attending traditionally black institutions. Both studies were conducted by the Southern Regional Education Board of Atlanta, Georgia. The results can be summarized as follows:

1. White students indicate a high level of positive feelings regarding their overall educational experiences at the respective traditionally black colleges and universities.

2. Over 73 percent of the students feel that administrators do not exert leadership in recruiting non-black students.

3. Most white students perceive teachers as
    being committed to good teaching.

4. Most white students feel that they have a
    keener appreciation of different ways of
    life as a result of being at the black
    institution.

5. Most white students feel that race does
    not affect a student's ability to learn.

6. The decision of the students to enroll
    in a black institution received the
    support of more than 70 percent of the
    parents involved.

Another desegregation goal can be accomplished by providing black college students with realistic higher education goals. Far too often, community colleges have been
characterized as "revolving door" institutions for minorities, meaning that students enter such institutions but are
tracked into terminal programs that restrict their educational and job mobility. Therefore, students leave these
institutions with little aspiration for greater achievement.
A full treatise on the revolving door syndrome is given by
Reginald Stuart (1975).

This chapter presents a successful cooperative and
collaborative articulation model that was voluntarily con-
ceptualized by a predominantly black university (NSU) and
a predominantly white community college (TCC). Secondly,
it provides an example of institutional responses to the
amended criteria that Judge John Pratt approved as guidelines in developing state desegregation plans.[1] Thirdly,
this chapter describes a model for achieving greater access
of blacks to higher education and achieving greater desegregation in the two aforementioned institutions.

Description of the Affected Institutions

Tidewater Community College, founded in 1968, is one of
several multi-campus institutions in the twenty-three college
state-supported Virginia Community College System. Serving
a district of over one thousand square miles, the college
was established to meet the educational needs of the cities

of Chesapeake, Norfolk, Portsmouth, Virginia Beach, a part
of Suffolk and a part of Isle of Wright County. It presently operates on three permanent campuses, two centers, and at
several off-campus locations in various military installa-
tions and in the community.

The college annually serves over 25,000 credit commuter
students, many attending on a part-time basis. Curricula
are offered in fifty-two different areas, culminating with
either a certificate, a diploma, or associate degree. TCC
also serves a student population comprised of 77.6 percent
majority, 19.1 percent black, and 3.3 percent other minority. The college has increased its minority population from
12 percent in 1972 to 22 percent in 1978. Currently, individual campuses tend to reflect the racial mix of the community served, while the College reflects the racial mix of the
Tidewater area. College student growth at TCC is projected
at an average rate of 5 percent over the next several years,
with enrollments leveling in the mid-1980s.

Norfolk State University was founded as the Norfolk Unit
of Virginia Union University in 1935 to provide training on
the junior-college level for high school graduates of the
Norfolk-Portsmouth area. During the depression of the thir-
ties, educators and civic leaders felt more keenly than
ever their commitment to unemployed youth who were unable to
continue their education outside of their community, and
were therefore deprived of the opportunity to obtain training for certain jobs that might be available in the community.

The Norfolk Polytechnic College was chartered in March,
1942, to take over the functions and assets of the Norfolk
Unit of Virginia Union University. The Norfolk Division of
Virginia State College was created by an act of the 1944
General Assembly of Virginia, which directed Virginia State
College to establish and operate a Division in the City of
Norfolk. The act further provided for the transfer of the
facilities of the Virginia Polytechnic College to Virginia
State College. On February 1, 1969, the Norfolk Division of
Virginia State College became Norfolk State College; an
independent, four-year, degree-granting institution with its
own Board of Advisors, its own President, and its own tradition of rendering quality service to its students and its
community, and its Commonwealth. In 1972, the College was
authorized by the General Assembly of Virginia to grant the
master's degree. An Act of the General Assembly of 1979
changed the name of the institution to Norfolk State University, effective July 1, 1979.

Norfolk State University is a co-educational (40 percent male and 60 percent female) urban institution offering curricula in liberal arts and sciences, technology, and professional programs at the associate, baacalaureate and master's levels. Head count enrollment at the institution is currently 7,303. In-state students constitute nearly 90 percent of the total enrollment, 64 percent reside in the Tidewater area, and 35 percent are from non-commuting distances. Out-of-state enrollment has increased over the last five years, and it is expected that this trend will continue.

Since Norfolk State was founded by black citizens of the Tidewater region, it has traditionally served that community. Minority enrollment (white) has increased significantly during the past five years, partially due to the addition of graduate programs. This increase in minority population is expected to continue as a result of articulation agreements with the Virginia Community College System and the addition of high demand programs not offered by other institutions in the area.

The Specific Charge--Two-Plus-Two Agreements

The Study, which became a part of the Virginia Plan, charged Norfolk State University and Tidewater Community College with the responsibility of addressing the duplication of associate degree-level programs through the development of two-plus-two agreements. In response, the administrations at both institutions moved quickly to meet the June 1, 1979 deadline imposed by the Study. Careful analysis of both traditional articulation barriers and specific/unique problems associated with HEW/OCR's mandate to desegregate had the effect of preparing the presidents, academic dean, and academic vice president to effectively respond to problems, issues, and concerns raised by institutional constituencies.

The first meeting of institutional representatives was held on February 5, 1979 at Tidewater Community College at the invitation of the Tidewater Community College president. Teaching faculty from the three discipline areas of accounting, office procedures/secretarial science and business education, and upper-level management participated in the meeting. From the first meeting, an articulation model emerged which served to guide institutional represenatives through not only the three required two-plus-two agreements, but eight such agreements. Other programs which follow the articulation model are currently under development.

Traditional Issues of Articulation

Transfer of academic credits from one institution to
another often has been inhibited and characterized by
policies based on excessive bureaucratization, antiquated
premises, and general lack of interest. Historically, fac-
ulties have protected their turf by raising questions about
equality of credits, institutional image, student aptitudes,
exactness of course content, grading practices, sex, instructional methodologies, race, course prerequisites, residency
requirements, faculty preparation, grade point averages,
academic calendars, and validity of non-traditional credits.

Administrators, like faculty, have not had a very solid
record in support of articulation and transfer of credits.
They have often failed to fund offices for articulation,
neglected to staff special counseling positions, resisted
developing and publishing transfer information understandable
to students, ignored opportunities to encourage personal
interaction between professionals from sending institutions,
placed little emphasis on establishing clearly-defined
standards for recognizing non-traditional studies, and failed
to support or establish articulation conferences. College
administrators should have responded more positively by
(1) developing communication networks to aid transferring
students, (2) establishing hearing boards to ensure students
an opportunity to appeal transfer of credits, (3) providing
better consumer information and research opportunities to
access transfer problems, (4) performing validation studies
of non-traditional credits, and (5) clearly defining institutional goals to be communicated to students.[2]

Not all the blame for the lack of effective articulation policies can be placed on the faculty and administrators
of colleges and universities. At the institutional level,
the president and board also should be in full support of and
committed to the concept of articulation for it to be a
viable practice. If the president and board had been more
committed to the concept of articulation, the faculty and
administrative problems cited above would have become nonexistent over a period of time. In other words, articulation would become an institutional goal toward which all
parties would strive.

In some states, the transfer of credits from one state

supported institution to another is a legislative requirement. In Virginia, however, the transfer of credits is an
institutional matter and the value or worth of credits varies
from one institution to another. Therefore, the presidents
of Norfolk State University and Tidewater Community College
had to display unusual leadership to overcome many of the
transfer barriers cited in this section of the paper. However, a legitimate question is: "What accounted for the
presidents' involvement?" It is probably fair to conclude
that the external stimulus of the HEW/OCR negotiations
motivated the presidents to act. Regardless of the "why,"
the facts are clear that both presidents were forceful and
directive in leadership efforts to overcome existing traditional barriers to articulation.

Social, Political, and Educational Issues

Articulation between competing institutions located in
a relatively small geographic area with a limited and slowly
growing population presents its own set of problems, with
competition serving to further heighten many traditional
barriers to the transfer of credits. To add to this situation an imposed HEW/OCR settlement between a predominantly
four-year black institution and a predominantly white two-
year institution would seem to result in an environment so
tense and politicized that little if any substantive discussion could be held.

Prior to the two-plus-two discussions, the history of
the two institutions had not shown a single articulated
program, even though both state-supported institutions had
practically existed side by side since the inception of
Tidewater Community College in 1968. At one time, history
kept these institutions apart. However, the political
realities of current historical decisions have now forced
them together. The working environment within and between
these institutions was characterized by a combination of
traditional barriers associated with articulation between
four-year and two-year colleges and the tensions, emotions,
suspicions, fears, and generally, the intense political
atmosphere present during negotiations between HEW, state
and college officials.

In addition to social and political concerns, substantive educational issues were present in the working environment. The crucial question of academic standards was the
most serious of the educational issues. Once the question
of academic standards was resolved, the other educational
questions seemed to dissipate. The articulation model

employed to handle the development of the two-plus-two
agreements treated the academic standards question and other
educational questions through an educational equality theory
which incorporated the idea that two-plus-two efforts should
not lead to lowering academic standards or modifying curr-
culum goals for either institution, but that new and different ways for treating credits, degrees, students, records,
and an assortment of other concerns needed to be considered
and adopted as the way of thinking. The educational equality
theory assumed that the academic and professional motiva-
tions, preparation, and quality of the faculty and students
at the two institutions in similar course levels was sufficiently equal to permit transfer and acceptance of credits,
courses, degrees, and students, without extensive analysis
of every course contained in a curriculum of study. It was
decided that the chief concern would be that students receive college level preparation in their particular field
of study and be able to compete successfully if transfer
occurred between the two institutions.

Having addressed educational questions through the
educational equality theory and having presidential commitments which served to defuse political and social issues,
institutional representatives were able to develop two-plus-
two agreements in an environment absent of elitist ideas,
turf protection, excessive bureaucratic rules, arguments
about equality of credits, and other barriers to articulation.

The Articulation Model

Articulation between two institutions serving different
clientele, having different goals, emerging from different
histories and, basically, having more differences than similarities must be addressed through sober exchanges by institutional representatives committed to the concept of articulation, possessing knowledge of articulation pitfalls, and
following a prescribed systematic process. Institutional
representatives involved in the negotiations between Norfolk
State University and Tidewater Community College developed a
model for articulation which included the following basic
assumptions:

1. Presidential commitment, involvement,
    and leadership would facilitate the
    process.

2. Faculty involvement in curriculum an-
    alysis and modification would be crucial
    to any lasting agreement.

3. Deadlocks in negotiations would be a reality.

4. Varying forms of resistance to change would emerge periodically.

5. All participants would have an equal voice in negotiations.

6. Some mechanism would have to be developed to handle conflicts and deadlocks during and after negotiations.

7. In the final analysis the student-customer would stand to gain or lose.

8. An educational equality theory would serve to benefit both institutions.

9. NSU and TCC would continue to be viable institutions for many years to come.

A steering committee with equal faculty and administrative memberships from each institution, co-chaired by the college presidents, was responsible for: (a) analyzing the Virginia Plan, the Study, and the state and national political climate; (b) establishing an educational equity theory; (c) developing guidelines for two-plus-two agreements; (d) defining curricula for consideration; (e) charging the Resolutions Committee with the responsibility of developing task groups of faculty and division administrators to formulate the two-plus-two agreement; (f) deciding all deadlocks which were not resolved by the Resolutions Committee; (g) preparing all formal reports and reporting all findings to higher authority; (h) gaining governing board approval through the co-chairmen; and (i) acting in the capacity of a hearing board for one year after agreements were instituted to resolve faculty, administrative, and/or student conflicts.

A Resolutions Committee consisting of the Norfolk State University academic vice president and the Tidewater Community College academic dean was similarly responsible for: (a) establishing task groups of faculty and division administrators to develop two-plus-two agreements; (b) defining tasks and timetables to task groups; (c) monitoring task group activities; (d) breaking deadlocks and resolving conflicts; (e) maintaining a professional environment for negotiation; (f) insuring consistency of agreements and compli-

ance with Steering Committee guidelines; (g) preparing the
agenda and documents for Steering Committee meetings; and
(h) serving as day-to-day institutional contact points.

Eleven task groups were formed to develop two-plus-two
agreements while two task groups handled administrative de-
tails. Administrative task groups dealt with admission procedures, registration procedures, miscellaneous forms, de-
tails of transcript requirements, costs, publicity requirements, and related paper flow. The main objective of the
administrative task groups was to streamline the transfer
process so students would be treated as if they had initially
enrolled in the four-year institution. In other words, students would perceive the two institutions as one single institution.

Conclusion

The articulation agreement between NSU and TCC began
with a plan that the two institutions would have transfer
programs in two areas. This modest beginning was accepted
by the U.S. Office of Civil Rights in January, 1979. Voluntary efforts on the part of institutional representatives
resulted in the approval of eight program agreements with
program options in five areas. Thus, community college
students have thirteen choices that would result in their
pursuing bachelor's degrees at NSU.

NSU offered ten two-year degree programs at the time
articulation agreements were approved. Since that time,
the University has begun to emphasize four-year and masters
degree programs. A total of four two-year degree programs
were voluntarily terminated by the NSU Board of Visitors.
Presently, NSU will seek "replacement" programs that would
provide an expanded vehicle for articulation agreements with
TCC and other community colleges. Presently, institutional
representatives are working on articulation agreements in
other areas such as Nursing and Early Childhood Education.
Norfolk State University has as its future goal, additional
articulation agreements with Tidewater Community College and
all other community colleges in the Commonwealth of Virginia.

The model presented in this chapter is easily adaptable
to other state systems of higher education. Both institutions have administrators with community college experience.
As a result, the model is well within the mainstream of coordinated systems of higher education that rely upon community colleges as good feeder systems to four-year colleges and
universities. The model also provides other states with a

vehicle by which black students can increase their access to post-community college experiences. This is especially critical in light of minority under-representation in higher education.

In brief, one can say that two institutions of higher learning without a history of cooperation or communication developed, within a six-month period, mutual respect which resulted in curriculum agreements and activities which exceeded recommendations by the <u>Virginia Plan</u>. The methods employed in development of the articulation agreements created an atmosphere characterized by friendly and respectful deliberations leading to eight articulation agreements rather than the three recommended. Curricula modifications and policy changes evolved relatively easy and were guided by the goal of better meeting the needs of students in the Virginia community. Absent from negotiations were elitist ideas, extensive turf protection and serious disagreements about equality of credits and grade point averages and systems. Present in negotiations were cooperation, acceptance of the basic goals of the program and a desire by all parties involved in the negotiation process to comply with state and institutional policies on admission and financial procedures. It is believed that increased cooperation and communication, which was an outcome of successfully implementing the articulation model, will result in increased enrollment of students of other races, greater student retention, faculty and staff exchanges, and an elimination of duplicated programs.

References

Airlie House
   1973   College Transfer Working Papers and Recommendations. Airlie House Conference (Dec. 2-4).

Brown, C.
   1973   The white student on the black campus.
           Atlanta, Georgia: Southern Regional Education
           Board.

Mohr, P.
   1975   Black Colleges and Equal Opportunity in Higher
           Education. Lincoln, Nebraska: University
           of Nebraska.

Standley, N.
   1978   White students enrolled in black colleges and
           university: their perceptions and attitudes.

Atlanta, Georgia: Southern Regional Education
Board.

Stuart, R.
    1975   Black perspectives on state controlled higher
            education: the Florida report.   New York:
            John Hay Whitney Foundation.

Footnotes

1. The institutions mentioned in this report established a precedent in personally developing an acceptable desegregation plan.

2. An extensive analysis of college transfer issues may be found in College Transfer, Working Papers and Recommendations from the Airlie House Conference, 2-4, December 1973.

24

Legislative Remedies
for Increasing the Educational Access
and Retention of Minorities

FRANK BROWN

Introduction

Within the past two decades, federal and state governments have implemented a number of educational programs and
policies aimed at increasing the academic skills and success
of blacks and minority students at all levels of education.
Programs and strategies have ranged from community school
control and busing at the lower school levels to desegregation efforts in elementary, secondary and postsecondary
schools. But, despite these various efforts, minority students have not made impressive gains in educational achievement (Austin, Rodgers and Walbeser, 1974; Morris, 1979;
Institute for the Study of Educational Policy, 1976).

This chapter argues that: (1) increased federal and
state legislative involvement in the education of minorities
must take place to facilitate greater educational achievement of blacks and other racial minorities; (2) the nature
of legislative involvement necessitates major changes in some
already existing programs; and (3) increased legislative
involvement should be in the form of a series of formal
incentives aimed at motivating teachers and administrators
to better educate and facilitate the academic needs of minority students. It is also maintained that recent controversy
regarding school desegregation has seriously diverted attention from what should be the major goal of achieving a better
quality education for minorities as well as for all American
students. W.E.B. DuBois (1935) succinctly summarized the
matter as follows:

> . . .theoretically, the Negro needs neither segregated
> schools nor mixed schools. What he needs is education.
> What he must remember is that there is no magic, either
> in mixed schools or in segregated schools. A mixed

school with poor and unsympathetic teachers, with
hostile opinion, and no teaching concerning black
folk, is bad. A segregated school with ignorant
placeholders, inadequate equipment, poor salaries,
and wretched housing, is equally bad . . .(DuBois,
1935).

One attempt to increase the quality of education for
disadvantaged minorities and improve their basic educational
skills has been through compensatory education (CE) programs.
These programs were established in the mid-sixties during
the Johnson Administration under the Elementary and Secondary Education Act (ESEA). Their intent was to increase the
reading skills and language development of disadvantaged
pre-school, elementary, secondary school children. Although
evaluations of the effects of these programs are limited,
the few that have been conducted generally indicate that
these programs have had a minimal effect on increasing the
academic achievement gains of disadvantaged students (Miller
and Woock, 1973; Liddle, 1967; Austin, et.al., 1974; Krider
and Petsche, 1977). Two major criticisms of compensatory
educational programs are that they affected only a small
percentage of disadvantaged students and initial achievement
gains made by program participants do not persist over time
(Krider, 1967; Holmes, 1966; Chorost, 1967). In addition,
no systematic evidence exists to support the programs'
claims of providing disadvantaged students with more instructional time and/or superior instruction. (Brown, 1976;
Miller, et.al,. 1973).

Given the limitations or at best ambiguities regarding
the effectiveness of compensatory education, several alternatives to these programs have been suggested. For example,
Havighurst and Stiles (1961) have suggested that a more
intensive and long-term focus on a smaller number of disadvantaged students be employed. Jencks (1968), adopting
a more extreme view, proposed that public schools and compensatory programs be replaced by a system which would allocate
educational expenditures directly to parents who would then
have the freedom to select a school for their children.
Jencks' (1968) basic assumption is that in a free market
situation, parents can spend money on their children in a
manner that would maximize the achievement of their own
self-interests, as well as upgrade the quality of education
as a result of increased competition among schools.

This chapter proposes a legislative strategy somewhat different from Jencks' (1968) proposal. Instead of
providing parents with direct economic incentives, it is

suggested that economic incentives be directly provided to teachers, individual schools, and school districts. More specifically, it is recommended that beyond the basic educational expenditures, cash bonuses and similar economic incentives be distributed to public schools based on their success in increasing the academic achievement and persistence of disadvantaged students. In addition, various rewards should be distributed to high schools based on their success in transferring minorities from high school to college. Replacing current compensatory educational programs with a broad range of incentives directly accessible to teachers and administrators might be a more effective strategy at the lower schooling level. This approach should enable a greater number of disadvantaged students to receive more long-term and quality academic assistance than past and present compensatory efforts.

In addition to legislative intervention at the elementary and secondary schooling levels, various legislative policies need to be considered at the higher educational levels to better promote the access, retention, and educational achievement of minorities. For example, special legislation needs to be designed to better identify and assist some two-year institutions in establishing, as a priority, the transfer of minorities from two-year to four-year colleges. The National Committee on Black Higher Education (1978) had noted that the future access of blacks to higher education is largely dependent on the extent to which some of the current overrepresentation of blacks in two-year colleges can be subsumed by the four-year colleges. Therefore, economic and other governmental incentives might be provided to encourage two-year institutions to increase the transition of minority students to four-year colleges. It has been noted, however, that some minority two-year students do not aspire to a college education or are not adequately prepared for advanced higher education (Tschechtelin, 1981; Friedlander, 1972). Therefore, some of the two-year colleges might be encourged to provide better vocational training for minorities to increase their access to the world of work.

Regarding four-year colleges, one important change may be needed in federal guidelines concerning student admissions to Equal Opportunity Programs (EOP). Under existing guidelines, EOP candidates must be both economically and educationally disadvantaged to qualify for program participation. However, it is recommended that the requirement that minority students be academically disadvantaged be deleted so that economically disadvantaged students who are in good academic standing will also qualify for EOP. This approach would extend the opportunity for a larger number of disadvantaged students to pursue higher education. In addition, it would increase the quality of minority students in higher education.

Special governmental aid and incentives are also needed to help four-year colleges and universities increase the representation of blacks and minorities in the technical and natural sciences and other academic fields in which they are currently underrepresented (Brown and Stent, 1977; Thomas, 1980). An increase in scholarship awards and other financial aid opportunities in areas where blacks and minorities are underrepresented may also be needed. However, these student awards would only be useful if there is a substantial increase in the proportion of minorities who have the interest and academic background to pursue careers in the technical and hard sciences. Therefore special academic programs and effective counseling opportunities must be developed at the elementary level of schooling and maintained throughout the secondary and postsecondary levels to achieve a greater interest and participation rate of minorities in the sciences and in other fields where they are poorly represented (Young, 1981; Melnick and Hamilton, 1981).

There is also a need to increase the proportion of research, internship and teaching assistantship opportunities for minorities in graduate and professional schools. Burbach and Thompson (1971) observed that alienation and lack of academic involvement are pressing problems that confront black and other minority students in large higher educational institutions. Reed (1978) noted that this problem is even greater at the graduate and professional levels in majority white institutions where there is little opportunity for minorities to develop student support systems, given their small numbers as a group. He also observed that the social and professional interaction of minority students with faculty outside of classroom was infrequent and, as a result, the opportunity for black students and other minorities to develop and practice their academic skills beyond the classroom was greatly limited (Reed, 1978).

It is therefore proposed that a greater variety of research and teaching opportunities be provided to help facilitate greater intergration and interaction of minority students with majority faculty and students. Some federal governmental agencies have recently sponsored a number of pre- and post-doctoral opportunities for minorities, in an attempt to increase the career development and marketability of minority students (Melnick, et.al., 1981; Malcolm, Cownie and Brown, 1976). It is also important that these programs be established at predominantly black institutions, given that a substantial number of black graduate and professional students continue to obtain their training from these institutions.

A final recommendation is that the federal and state government assume a greater role in helping higher educational institutions develop more effective recruitment, admissions and retention programs for minorities. For example, the development of small scale, exploratory efforts such as the University of Minnesota's undergraduate program (Carey, Singh and Pillinger, 1981) and the University of Rochester's tutorial program for minority medical students (Geertsma, 1981) should be encouraged and expanded.

Formal and systematic evaluations of the success of higher educational institutions in recruiting and retaining minorities also should be immediately developed and administered by the federal and state governments. Subsequent governmental incentives ranging from public recognition to additional technical and financial incentives should be given to those institutions that most successfully achieve these outcomes. These kinds of governmental incentives in conjunction with previously suggested legislative interventions are necessary for blacks and other minorities to achieve equality of educational access and retention in the near future.

References

Austin, G.R., B.G. Rodgers and H.H. Walbeser, Jr.
  1974   "The effectiveness of summer compensatory
         education: a review of the research." Pp. 470-493
         In M.D. Gall and B.A. Ward (eds.) Critical Issues
         in Educational Psychology. Boston, Toronto:
         Little, Brown and Company.

Brown, F.
  1976   "Title I: is it compensatory or just a partial
         equalizer." Emergent Leadership 1:13-18.

Brown, F. and M.D. Stent
  1977   Minorities in U. S. Institutions of Higher Educa-
         tion. New York: Praeger Press.

Burbach, J.J. and M.A. Thompson
  1971   "Alienation among college freshmen: a comparison

of Puerto Rican, black and white students."
Journal of College Student Personnel 10:248-252.

Carey, P., B. Singh and B. Pillinger
1981 "A pre-college orientation program for minority undergraduates at the University of Minnesota."
Pp. 294-305 in G. Thomas (ed.), Black Students in
Higher Education: Conditions and Experiences in
the 70s. Westport, Connecticut: Greenwood Press.

Chorost, S.B.
1967 An Evaluation of the Effects of a Summer Head Start
Program. Sten Bland, N.Y.: Walcoff Research
Center.

DuBois, W.E.B.
1935 "Does the Negro need separate schools."
Journal of Negro Education. 4 (July) 328-335.

Friedlander, S.L.
1972 Unemployment in the Urban Core: An Analysis of
Thirty Cities with Policy Recommendations. New
York: Praeger Press.

Geertsma, R.H.
1981 "A special tutorial for minority students: An
account of a year's experience." Pp. 272-281 in
G. Thomas (ed.), Black Students in Higher Education: Conditions and Experiences in the 70s.
Westport, Connecticut: Greenwood Press.

Havighurst, R.J. and L.J. Stiles
1961 "A national policy for alienated youth."
Phi Delta Kappa 42:283-291.

Holmes, D.
1966 An Evaluation of Differences Among Different
Classes of Head Start Participants. New York:
Associated YM-YWHA's of Greater New York.

Institute for the Study of Educational Policy
1976 Equal Education Opportunity for Blacks in U.S.
Higher Education. Washington, D.C.: Institute for
the Study of Educational Policy, Howard University.

Jencks, C.
1968 "Is the public school obsolete?"
The Public Interest Winter: 18-27.

Krider, M.A. and Petsche, M.
    1967   An Evaluation of Head Start Pre-School Enrichment.
            Programs as They Affect the Intellectual Ability
            and Social Adjustment and the Achievement Level
            of Five Year Old Children Enrolled in Lincoln,
            Nebraska. Lincoln: Nebraska University.

Liddle, G.P.
    1967   Educational Improvement for the Disadvantaged in an
            Elementary Setting. Springfield, Ill.: Charles
            C. Thomas.

Malcolm, M.M., J. Cownie, and J.W. Brown
    1976   Programs in Science for Minority Students, 1960-
            1975. Washington, D.C.: American Association for
            the Advancement of Science.

Melnick, V.L. and F.D. Hamilton
    1981   "Participation of blacks in basic sciences: assess-
            ment and strategies." Pp. 282-293 in G. Thomas
            (ed.), Black Students in Higher Education: Con-
            ditions and Experiences in the 70s. Westport,
            Connecticut: Greenwood Press.

Miller, H.L. and R. R. Woock
    1973   Social Foundations of Urban Education.
            Hinsdale, Ill.: The Dryden Press Inc.

Morris, L.
    1979   Elusive Equality: The Status of Black Americans in
            Higher Education. Washington, D. C.: Howard
            University Press.

National Advisory Committee on Black Higher Education
and Black Colleges and Universities
    1979   Access of Black Americans to Higher Education:
            How open is the door? Washington, D.C.:
            Government Printing Office.

Reed, J.
    1978   "Increasing the opportunities for black students in
            higher education. Journal of Negro Education
            48:18-24.

Thomas, G.E.
    1980   "Equality of representation of race and sex groups
            in higher education: institutional and program en-
            rollment statuses." American Educational Review
            Journal. 17 (June).

Tschechtelin, J.D.
    1981   "Black and white students in community colleges."
            Pp. 152-166 in G. Thomas (ed.), Black Students in
            Higher Education: Conditions and Experiences in
            the 1970s. Westport, Connecticut: Greenwood
            Press.

Young, H.A.
    1981   "Retaining blacks in science: an affective model."
            Pp. 261-271 in G. Thomas (ed.), Black Students
            in Higher Education: Conditions and Experiences
            in the 1970s. Westport, Connecticut: Greenwood
            Press.

Section VI
Broad Level Structural Policies Affecting the Future of Blacks in Higher Education: Overview _____

The previous chapters in this book described the status of black enrollment, retention, internal conditions, and experiences within higher education. In addition, methods for increasing black access and retention were discussed. As pointed out in the introductory chapter, issues concerning minority higher education do not exist within a vacuum. Instead they are defined and operationalized within the context of the broader society. As a result, there are a variety of external conditions and broader social policies that impinge upon the current and future status of blacks in higher education.

The final section in this volume evaluates broad educational, governmental and economic policies affecting the future of blacks in higher education. The first chapter by Leonard Haynes examines the Adams decision, institutional, state and federal responses to the decision and the current and future impact of the Adams mandate on blacks in higher education. The second chapter by Thomas, McPartland, and Gottfredson takes a more extensive look at the current status of segregation in higher education and its effect on black participation in higher education and black colleges. The final chapter by Gloria Scott addresses the broad question of the economic future of blacks in higher education.

25

The *Adams* Mandate:
A Format for Achieving Equal
Educational Opportunity and Attainment

LEONARD L. HAYNES III

Introduction

The most important legal action to affect the educational aspirations and achievements of blacks and other
minorities since the 1954 Brown decision has been the
recent court decision in Adams v. Richardson (1973). Having
become a mandate, the Adams decision is especially important
to the welfare of black Americans because it seeks to:
(1) increase black and minority access to higher education
in those states that formerly operated dual systems of higher
education; (2) formulate policies to insure that the participation and completion rates for blacks increase at all levels
of higher education; and (3) strengthen and enhance historically black colleges so that they can become full partners
in the delivery of educational services to their states,
regions, and the nation.

The Adams case was filed by the NAACP Legal Defense
Fund (LDF) in 1970. LDF felt that HEW was not enforcing
Title VI of the 1964 Civil Rights Act against those states
which operated dual segregated systems of higher education.
Title VI of the Civil Rights Act prohibits the allocation of
federal funds to segregated public educational institutions.

Although the federal courts assisted in developing
equitable solutions to the problem of implementing public
school desegregation, they had not been involved, before
Adams, in fashioning equitable solutions for desegregating
public higher education. Because of its previous success in
pursuing legal action to desegregate public schools, LDF felt
that legal action would result in a remedy that would force
HEW to enforce the provisions of Title VI in higher education.

During the Adams litigation, both the court and legal

representatives found it difficult to establish an equitable
method to desegregate higher education. Part of the reason
was the court's reluctance to intervene in an area that was
generally constitutionally reserved for state governments;
but apart from this, there were many difficulties due to the
complexities inherent in determining higher education
policies and practices. For example, the rules and regulations in higher education are determined and controlled by a
variety of authorities (e.g., coordinating boards, institutional boards, legislatures) who often do not share common
views about the function and purpose of higher education.
Moreover, unlike public schools, participation in American
higher education is neither required nor compulsory. As a
result, principles established in <u>Brown</u> (1954), which led to
the use of racial percentages to desegregate public schools,
are difficult to apply to higher education. Thus the <u>Adams</u>
case, which has produced a court-ordered mandate, marks the
first comprehensive legal attempt to extend the principles
established in <u>Brown</u> to public higher education.

The mandate in the <u>Adams</u> case calls for Southern and
Border states to eliminate the vestiges of racial segregation
by desegregating their systems of public higher education.
The ten states that were identified as maintaining dual
segregated systems in the <u>Adams</u> litigation were Arkansas,
Florida, Georgia, Louisiana, Maryland, Mississippi, North
Carolina, Oklahoma, Pennsylvania and Virginia. The adjudica-
tion of the <u>Adams</u> case revealed that predominantly white
colleges and universities have not been responsive nor
committed to providing sufficient access to blacks who wish
to enter various types of higher educational institutions.
However, historically black public colleges (without the
benefit of full support and equitable treatment by white
controlled state governments and coordinating boards) have
responded positively to the educational aspirations of
blacks and other minorities (Jencks and Riesman, 1968). For
example, these institutions have graduated a disproportionately high number of all blacks earning baccalaureate
degrees. Mingle (1979) and others have indicated that the
historically black colleges still award about 69 percent of
all bachelor's degrees earned by blacks, despite the fact
that these institutions only enroll about 43 percent of the
nation's black college population.

HEW's Desegregation Criteria

On July 5, 1977, after a long process of legal maneuver-
ing, the <u>Adams</u> court released guidelines under which default-
ing states could prepare their systemwide desegregation plans

to comply with the requirements of Title VI and meet the
objectives of the litigation. The guidelines were prepared
by HEW and the Legal Defense Fund, and represent the most
comprehensive attempt by the federal government to provide
the Adams states with specific criteria for desegregating
their systems of higher education.   The criteria are divided
into four major parts (The Federal Register, 1978), which
include (1) disestablishment of the structure that had
perpetuated the dual system of higher education; (2) desegregation of student enrollment on a statewide basis to maximize
access and completion for black students at all levels of
higher education; (3) desegregation of faculty, administrative staffs, non-academic personnel and governing boards and
(4) commitments of the states to a monitoring and evaluation
process designed to see that progress is made toward stated
goals and objectives.

One of the most significant aspects of HEW's criteria
is the requirement that states include, in their desegregation plans, methods to strengthen and enhance their traditionally black colleges. No other federal regulations or
laws have ever acknowledged that these institutions should
receive special treatment to improve and expand their capacity to continue to educate blacks and other minorities.
Specifically, the criteria require the Adams states to
commit themselves to and demonstrate methods that would make
their state black colleges full partners in the higher
educational system. The criteria state that acceptable
plans must include methods that will be employed to aid
historically black institutions in fulfilling their missions,
and a commitment to give these institutions comparable
resources to other institutions having similar missions.

The Adams plan also requires states to "eliminate
program duplication" between black and white institutions in
the same area. The criteria emphasize, however, that this
goal cannot be achieved at the expense of the black colleges.
Additionally, they require states to give public black
colleges prime consideration in establishing new graduate
and professional programs.

The desegregation planning process for the Adams states
is scheduled to conclude in 1982-83. At the end of this
period, the plans to desegregate state systems of higher
education are supposed to be well into the stage of implementation. Should any of the Adams states default in meeting
the specified guidelines and requirements to desegregate,
HEW's Office for Civil Rights (OCR) can at this point begin
administrative proceedings against such states. OCR's action

could include terminating outstanding federal grants and funds awarded to institutions in non-complying states.

HEW's criteria represent the broadest attempt to achieve equity and parity for blacks and other minorities in higher education. Furthermore, the criteria constitute an important policy and program guideline by which the federal and state governments can evaluate the efforts and progress that higher educational institutions have achieved in retaining and educating minorities. No other educational policy resulting from legal action has come close to developing such a comprehensive plan for correcting the vestiges of segregation in higher education.

The Current Status and Reaction to the Adams Plan

After a series of extensive negotiations, six of the Adams state plans have been accepted by OCR (Arkansas, Florida, Georgia, North Carolina, Oklahoma and Virginia). Florida and North Carolina's plans received provisional acceptance. However, it is anticipated that both plans will be fully accepted prior to 1980. Pennsylvania is currently negotiating an out-of-court settlement with HEW in an attempt to produce an acceptable desegregation plan. Maryland's suit against HEW is presently pending in the court of appeals; and the Justice Department has taken action against the states of Mississippi and Louisiana for their failure to comply with HEW's guidelines.[1]

The reactions to the Adams plan and current progress by the Adams states have been mixed. With some exceptions, black educators contend that the Adams criteria, if fully complied with, would represent a great step toward achieving equality for blacks in higher education. At the same time, some educational administrators have expressed displeasure regarding the federal government's heavy involvement in an area that has constitutionally been preserved for state direction and administration. Other state officials have indicated reluctance to commit themselves to plans that require them to allocate greater finances (Chronicle of Higher Education, 1979). Proponents of the Adams plan fear that the displeasure and uncertainty expressed by state

---

[1]HEW has recently visited sites in Alabama, Tennessee, Texas, Ohio, Kentucky and South Carolina. It ordered (1977) the merger of the University of Tennessee at Nashville and Tennesse State which took place July 1, 1979. Any of these states found to have dual, segregated systems of higher education will also be required to produce acceptable plans.

officials, coupled with the tentative nature of their commitment, may lead to a new series of Adams litigations.

Some concern also exists regarding the continued role
of HEW in consistently and vigorously executing the Adams
mandate. Part of the concern is that OCR officials who
currently support the goal of desegregation and the Adams
plan may not remain in office for the duration of the implementation period. Gerry (1976) has stated that the likelihood that uncommitted federal officials will replace some
of the presently committed officials remains a reality.
Federal officials who are now in charge of monitoring and
evaluating the states' planning processes are themselves
concerned that some states may purposely delay activities
until such replacement occurs. Finally, some black college
presidents are concerned that the Adams plan will place
black colleges in competition with white colleges
and universities for students, faculty and facilities before
black colleges can be adequately strengthened to compete
effectively (NAFEO, 1979).

Specific Limitations of the Adams Proposal

Although HEW's criteria constitute a promising plan
which, if followed, will achieve greater educational opportunities for blacks and other minorities, the plan does have
some specific limitations. For example, a major weakness
concerns plans for strengthening the traditionally black
colleges. Despite the court's requirement that the special
needs of black colleges be addressed so they become equal
partners in the desegregation process, the present criteria
suggest that states do not have to develop the type of
"Marshall Plan" that is needed to fulfill this requirement.
For instance, the criteria require states to provide black
colleges with programs, course offerings, facilities and
resources at least comparable to programs at white institutions within states. However, black colleges are primarily
being compared to white institutions that occupy low positions (e.g., baccalaureate offerings only). This may be
viewed as a biased application of the comparability test
when one considers the fact that black colleges were established by states as special purpose institutions for blacks
under the "separate but equal" doctrine.

A second weakness of the Adams plan is that it does not
adequately challenge white institutions to increase their
current level of minority undergraduate, graduate and professional enrollments. No state, for example, is required to
increase black admissions by more than 150 percent above the

admissions rate for the academic year preceding the year in
which the plan is requested by HEW. This limited requirement
may be inadequate because the number of blacks presently
enrolled in predominantly white colleges in the Adams states
is on the average less than six percent.

Also, the plan is not aggressive enough in requiring state institutions to increase their black faculty
enrollment and their representation of blacks on higher
educational boards. What is needed is a stronger demonstrated effort by the Adams states (and other predominantly
white state systems of higher education) to increase the
representation of blacks and other minorities at all levels
of higher education.

A third limitation of the Adams plan is its failure to
regard the desegregation process as part of a comprehensive
long-range state master plan that provides constructive
approaches in the delivery of educational services. Desegregation planning under the new guidelines cannot be effective
unless it reflects a long-term higher education state
planning process. A fourth and final limitation of the plan
is its unrealistic prediction that the desegregation process
will be completed by 1982-83. Currently, no provisions
exist to ensure that states keep and promptly meet their
present plans for implementation. If one considers the time
problems in implementing Brown, and the complexities of the
governing structure that exists in higher education, it can
realistically be forseen that the Adams planning and implementation process will have to extend beyond 1982-83.

Conclusion

The Adams plan has limitations that must be addressed
before it may effectively achieve its maximum potential.
However, despite these limitations, the plan provides, for
the first time in history, a federal format for eliminating
dual segregated systems of higher education and providing
greater equality of higher educational opportunity for blacks
and other minorities. But for the Adams plan, the initial
efforts by the NAACP which motivated the plan, and the current enforcement efforts by the Office of Civil Rights,
racial disparities and inequalities in higher education would
be even greater today. Furthermore, the Adams plan, if implemented, will represent a landmark achievement towards
eliminating what DuBois (1899) described as the twentieth
century problem of the "color line".

References

Adams v. Richardson   488 F.2d 1159 (D.C. Cir 1973).

Brown v. Board of Education 347 U.S. 483 (1954).

Chronicle of Higher Education
    1979   "State Colleges Confronting the Politics of
          Frugality." 17:1,10

DuBois, W.E.B.
    1899   The Philadelphia Negro: A Social Study.
          Philadelphia: University of Pennsylvania.

The Federal Register
    1978   43(32): 6658-6664

Gerry, M.
    1976   Proceedings of Southern Education Foundation
          Conference on Status of the Adams Case.
          Atlanta, Georgia: Southern Education Foundation.

Jencks, C. and D. Riesman
    1968   The Academic Revolution. New York: Doubleday
          and Co.

Mingle, J.R.
    1979   Black Enrollment in Higher Education. Trends in
          the Nation and the South. Atlanta, Georgia:
          Southern Regional Education Board.

National Association for Equal Opportunity in Higher
          Education (NAFEO)
    1979   Blacks in higher education.   Fourth Annual
          Conference of National Association for Equal
          Opportunity in Higher Education. Washington, D.C.

26

Desegregation and Black Student Higher Educational Access*

GAIL E. THOMAS, JAMES M. McPARTLAND, and DENISE C. GOTTFREDSON _____

Introduction

Desegregation in American higher education has been of major concern within the last decade only. The 1973 Supreme Court ruling in Adams--which held that it was unconstitutional for states to maintain segregated colleges and universities-- became the stimulus for higher education desegregation. As stated in the previous chapter by Haynes (1981), some states have still not produced satisfactory desegregation plans, and all states have experienced some degree of difficulty in desegregating their colleges and universities. One reason is that there are unique and complex features of higher education that distinguish it from the elementary and secondary school- ing levels. For example, the organizational hierarchy of colleges and universities is much more complex than the structure of lower level schooling, which is primarily differ- entiated by grade levels. Astin (1977) noted that the stratification system within higher education ranges from the least competitive two-year and junior colleges to the most competitive graduate and professional schools, with four year colleges in the middle of the hierarchy.

The fact that higher education is noncompulsory in atten- dance and requires admissions standards and financial invest- ment from its clientele further distinguishes it from public elementary and secondary schooling. Most four-year and higher level institutions employ some measure of standardized test performance in the admissions process (Bailey, 1978; Morris, 1979). The issue raised in Bakke concerning how these tests should be used in admitting minority students to higher educa- tion continues to be heavily debated. The data in this study do not permit an examination of institutional admissions

---
*This research was supported by the United States National Institute of Education, Department of Education.

criteria and their impact on black-white enrollments and higher education desegregation. This limitation should be kept in mind throughout the analyses.

The existence of the traditionally black colleges and other institutions with special missions also constitute a distinct feature of higher education. The role of the traditional black colleges in the desegregation process was a major issue addressed in Adams and remains a point of controversy. In specifying guidelines for the Adams states to desegregate, HEW stated that: (1) The burden to desegregate should not be assumed by the black colleges, given the historical necessity of their existence, and (2) Black colleges should be strengthened and further enhanced so that they can compete more effectively in the desegregation process (see the Appendix in Haynes, 1978, for detailed statements of the HEW guidelines).

Black college presidents have expressed that prior to being enhanced, the colleges need to be assured of their continued existence (National Association for Equal Opportunity in Higher Education, 1977). These administrators point to traditionally black colleges that have become predominantly white (Bluefield State, West Virginia State, Lincoln University at Missouri) and to the currently increasing white student and faculty enrollment at Chaney State and other traditionally black colleges. Black college administrators and other advocates for the black colleges contend that despite HEW's guidelines, many black colleges are being required to desegregate beyond the level required by white colleges (Raspberry, 1980). However, a contrary opinion held by others is that higher education desegregation can be achieved more effectively by further desegregating the black colleges.

The varied opinions and vested interests regarding higher education desegregation may be partly related to a lack of clarity concerning the goals of higher education desegregation and its relevancy for achieving greater equality of educational opportunity for minorities. In its guidelines for the Adams states, HEW did attempt to clarify the major goal of desegregation and its relevancy for increasing higher educational opportunity for black students. The guidelines stated that states should desegregate in a manner that would maximize the access and completion of black students throughout higher education (Haynes, 1978). This description suggests that higher education desegregation is not an isolated phenomenon and should be treated as a process within a broad context designed to increase minority access and success throughout higher education. Much of the controversy about desegregation in higher education has not considered these factors.

This chapter assesses higher education desegregation progress in a broader manner that; (a) extends beyond the achievement of various student racial mixes and (b) relates more specifically to the achievement of positive educational outcomes for minorities (i.e., access, retention, job attainment, etc.). Racial and ethnic enrollment data collected by the U.S. Office of Civil Rights are used to show black-white proportional enrollments and the extent to which black and white students are racially isolated throughout higher education for the nation, for the four major geographic regions, and for the 50 states and the District of Columbia. These data are also used to examine the relationship between desegregation and black enrollment when the traditionally black institutions in the South are considered.

Measures of Black-White Enrollment and Segregation

Table 1 presents measures which show; (a) differences in the higher education enrollment of blacks and whites and (b) the degree to which blacks and whites are racially isolated at various levels of higher education in major regions of the country and in the nation as a whole. The statistics are calculated from the 1976 survey of racial and ethnic enrollment data collected by the U.S. Department of Education from all 3,068 institutions of higher education in this country. Tabluations are presented for full-time students at four levels: two-year, four-year, graduate, and professional. The four regions represent the geographic divisions defined by the U.S. Census.

Student enrollments are indicated in Table 1 by the percent black and percent white of the full-time students for each region and level, and by the ratio of the number of white-to-black students enrolled full-time. For example, columns 1, 3 and 5 show that among two-year undergraduates in the nation, 13.3 percent are black, 76.4 percent are white, and the white-black enrollment ratio is 5.7 to 1.

Racial isolation between blacks and whites is indicated by several measures. Means and distributions of school racial compositions are measured from the perspective of white and black students. Values in Table 1 of "the percent black in the school attended by the average white student" are calculated by assigning to each white student the percent black in his or her school, and averaging for all white students in a particular region and level of higher education. For example, column 2 of Table 1 shows that the average white two-year undergraduate in the nation attends a school that is 8.9 percent black. In this case, about 9 of every 100

Table 1

Black-White Enrollment Ratios and Segregation Indices for
Full-Time Students in Higher Education, By Region and Higher Educational Level, 1976

Region and Level [a]	Percent Black	Percent Black in the school attended by the average White student	Percent White	Percent White in the school attended by the average Black Student	Ratio White-Black Enrollment	Segregation Index
Nation						
Two-Year	13.3	8.9	76.4	51.2	5.7:1	33.0
Four-Year	9.1	5.5	84.4	50.7	9.2:1	40.4
Graduate	5.1	4.3	79.5	66.2	15.5:1	17.2
Professional	4.5	3.7	90.0	73.0	19.7:1	19.4
Northeast						
Two-Year	11.4	6.9	82.0	49.6	7.2:1	39.9
Four-Year	6.4	5.3	87.9	72.4	13.6:1	17.4
Graduate	4.0	3.8	80.8	77.4	20.1:1	4.6
Professional	4.3	4.2	91.5	88.0	21.0:1	4.2
Midwest						
Two-Year	13.4	6.8	83.1	41.6	6.2:1	50.0
Four-Year	6.6	5.6	89.9	75.6	13.5:1	15.5
Graduate	5.0	4.7	80.4	75.7	16.0:1	5.9
Professional	3.7	3.6	91.4	87.8	24.1:1	3.4

Table 1 Continued

Region and Level	Percent Black	Percent Black in the school attended by the average White Student	Percent White	Percent White in the school attended by the average Black Student	Ratio White-Black Enrollment	Segregation Index
South						
Two-Year	19.5	15.5	71.4	56.6	3.6:1	20.8
Four-Year	16.5	6.7	78.4	31.9	4.8:1	59.4
Graduate	7.9	5.3	79.1	52.8	9.9:1	33.1
Professional	6.4	3.9	90.1	54.1	14.0:1	40.2
West						
Two-Year	8.5	6.0	72.7	51.2	8.6:1	30.1
Four-Year	3.7	3.3	81.2	72.8	21.8:1	10.6
Graduate	2.9	2.8	77.5	74.5	26.6:1	5.4
Professional	2.9	2.8	84.9	78.4	28.4:1	7.2

a
Northeast (NE) = CT, ME, MA, NH, NJ, NY, PA, RI, VT
Midwest (MW) = IL, IN, LA, KS, MI, MN, MO, NE, ND, OH, SD, WI
South (S) = AL, AR, DC, DE, FL, GA, KY, LA, MD, MS, NC, OK, SC, TN, TX, VA, WV
West (W) = AK, AZ, CA, CO, HI, ID, MT, NM, OR, UT, WA, WY

340

fellow-students encountered by the average white two-year
undergraduate will be black. An analogous measure, shown
in Table 1, from the perspective of black students is the
"percent white in the school attended by the average black
student."

A Segregation Index is also provided in Table 1 which
measures the racial separation of enrollments standardized
for the number of available blacks and whites enrolled in a
particular region and level of higher education. The Segregation Index is based on a comparison of the actual school
racial composition of the average student and the expected
racial composition if the available black and white students
were randomly distributed across the schools. For this
index, the actual school racial composition is indicated by
the measure of (1) "the percent black in the school attended
by the average white student" or (2) "the percent white in
the school attended by the average black student." It can
be shown that the expected values for these measures if the
available blacks and whites were randomly distributed among
the schools is equal to (1) the overall percent black enrollment, or (2) the overall percent white enrollment for the
particular region and level (Becker, McPartland and Thomas,
1978). For example, column 2 of Table 1 shows that the
average two-year undergraduate white student in the nation
attends a school that is 8.9 percent black, while column 1
shows that under a random distribution of students we would
expect the average white to attend a school that is 13.3
percent black. The combination of these two values yields
a Segregation Index of 33.0 in column 6.[1] The analogous
measures from the perspective of the black student are shown
in columns 4 and 3, the "percent white in the school attended
by the average black student," and the "percent white" at
each region and level, which yield a similar Segregation
Index in column 6. The Segregation Index can assume values
between 0 and 100; it will have the value 100 whenever black
and white students attend entirely separate schools and zero
whenever the actual racial separation of enrollment is the
same as a random allocation of the students in the region
and level, with larger values between 0 and 100 indicating
greater racial separation. The Segregation Index has several
important properties that include its independence of group
size and aggregate racial proportions that permit direct
comparisons between educational groups, and its equivalence
to the between-group proportion of variance in race that
permits decomposition of the index into analytically interesting components (Becker, et. al., 1978).

Comparisons of Levels of Higher Education

Opposite trends across levels of higher education are
shown in Table 1 for the enrollment access of black students
and the degree of racial isolation between blacks and whites.
Blacks have gained much greater proportional enrollment in
undergraduate schools (especially in two-year programs) than
in graduate or professional schools. However, undergraduate
schools are much more racially segregated than graduate or
professional schools. That is, the levels of higher education where blacks have gained the highest enrollment relative
to whites are the levels where the races are most likely to
attend separate schools. Conversely, blacks and whites are
most likely to be randomly distributed among the schools at
those levels of higher education where there are relatively
few blacks enrolled.

The trend of increasing white-black enrollment ratios
as one moves from two-year undergraduate to four-year undergraduate, and from four-year undergraduate to graduate or
professional schools, is clearly shown in Table 1 within each
of the four regions of the country. For example, in the
Northeast, there are 7.2 whites for every black two-year
undergraduate student, 13.6 whites for every black four-year
undergraduate student, 20.1 whites for every black graduate
student, and 21.0 whites for every black professional student.
For this region and level, the percent black of student
enrollment declines from 11.4 in the two-year undergraduate
programs, to 6.4 in four-year undergraduate programs, to 4.0
and 4.3 in graduate and professional programs.

At the national level, Table 1 also shows that the
white-black enrollment ratio increases as one compares two-
year to four-year undergraduate students and undergraduate to
graduate or professional students. Whereas there are 5.7
white students for every black in two-year undergraduate
programs, the white-to-black enrollment ratio is 9.2 to 1 in
four-year undergraduate programs. Whereas the white-black
enrollment ratio among two-year students is less than the
population ratio of 18- to 24-year-olds in each region,
the white-black enrollment ratio is significantly greater than
the population ratio for the other levels of higher education,
and dramatically so for graduate or professional enrollments[2].
The relative enrollment of whites to blacks is three to four
times greater among professional students than among two-year
undergraduate students, in each of the separate regions and
in the nation at large.

On the other hand, the racial separation of available
black and white enrollments within regions tends to be least

among graduate or professional students, followed by four-
year undergraduates, with most racial segregation among two-
year undergraduates. For example, the Segregation Indices
in the Northeast have values of 4.6 and 4.2 for graduate,
and 39.9 for two-year undergraduates. In each region, the
same pattern of greater segregation for two-year than four
four-year undergraduates, and for four-year undergraduates
than for graduate or professional students, is evident, with
the major exception of Southern two-year undergraduates.

Comparisons of Public and Private Institutions

Table 2 compares public and private institutions of
higher education in terms of segregation and enrollment
access for the separate regions and levels.

The general importance of private institutions is one
major way that higher education differs from elementary-
secondary schools in America. But this difference depends
upon the level of higher education under consideration. Less
than 10 percent of elementary-secondary students in this
country attend private schools. The last column of Table 2
shows that only two-year undergraduates are similar to these
rates. Across the nation, only 6.4 percent of two-year
undergraduates are in private institutions, while the
regional percentages range from a low of 1.7 percent in the
West to a high of 13.1 percent in the Northeast. In contrast,
in the nation, almost 30 percent of four-year undergraduates,
about one third of graduate students, and over one half of
professional students attend private schools. Each region
shows the same trend of greater use of private schooling in
graduate and professional than four-year undergraduate
programs, with the Northeast as the region with greatest percentage enrollments in private institutions at each of these
levels. Thus, two-year colleges are like elementary-
secondary schools in the predominance of public institutions,
but the rest of higher education in this country has a significant proportion of its enrollment in private institutions.
Segregation of enrollments was found to be most severe outside
of the South in two-year undergraduate programs, and this is
primarily an issue for the public institutions which enroll
most of the students at this level. At other levels where
there is a much higher percentage of private institutions
there are consistent differences between public and private
institutions in segregation and white-black enrollment
ratios.

Comparing public and private institutions at the
three highest levels in each of the four regions, we again
see the same pattern of opposite trends for white-black

Table 2

Segregation Indices and White-Black Enrollment Ratios
for Public and Private Institutions of Higher Education,
by Region and Level, 1976

	Public Institutions			Private Institutions		
	Seg. Index	Wh.-Bl. Enroll. Ratio	% of Total in Pub. Inst.	Seg. Index	Wh.-Bl. Enroll. Ratio	% of Total in Pri. Inst.
Nation						
Two-Year	32.0	5.8:1	93.6	45.4	4.7:1	6.4
Four-Year	38.2	9.2:1	69.5	45.4	9.2:1	30.5
Graduate	15.2	17.3:1	66.1	18.5	12.8:1	33.9
Professional	19.4	19.6:1	44.0	8.8	19.9:1	56.0
Northeast						
Two-Year	41.2	7.1:1	86.9	27.3	7.5:1	13.1
Four-Year	24.8	11.3:1	50.8	6.3	16.9:1	49.2
Graduate	3.0	21.1:1	35.5	4.8	19.5:1	64.5
Professional	3.4	14.6:1	24.6	3.2	24.3:1	75.4
Midwest						
Two-Year	49.3	6.4:1	94.0	53.4	3.7:1	6.0
Four-Year	12.9	14.2:1	71.8	21.8	12.0:1	28.2
Graduate	4.8	18.1:1	78.0	6.8	11.1:1	22.0
Professional	4.2	21.3:1	47.8	3.6	28.0:1	52.2

Continued

Table 2 Continued

	Public Institutions			Private Institutions		
	Seg. Index	Wh.-Bl. Enroll. Ratio	% of Total in Pub. Inst.	Seg. Index	Wh.-Bl. Enroll. Ratio	% of Total in Pri. Inst.
South						
Two-Yr. Undergrad.	18.2	3.7:1	93.0	50.0	2.9:1	7.0
Four-Yr. Undergrad.	53.7	5.1:1	76.0	79.4	3.8:1	24.0
Graduate Students	28.3	11.7:1	74.6	40.6	6.6:1	25.4
Professional Students	17.0	20.0:1	55.4	55.8	10.0:1	44.6
West						
Two-Yr. Undergrad.	29.4	8.7:1	98.3	60.0	24.6:1	1.7
Four-Yr. Undergrad.	10.8	22.2:1	80.2	8.4	20.2:1	19.8
Graduate Students	4.0	31.4:1	74.3	2.4	18.1:1	25.7
Professional Students	7.2	21.0:1	43.1	7.7	37.5:1	56.9

enrollment ratios and segregation of enrollment. With only
one exception within regions, where the white-black enrollment ratio is high, the segregation index is low. That is,
where blacks have gained greater proportional enrollment,
the schools are more racially segregated. This is true for
public and private institutions at the same levels within
regions. The trend is evident in eleven of the twelve
comparisons between public and private institutions for particular regions and levels beyond two-year institutions, with
the exception of professional students in the West, where
private institutions have a larger segregation index and
white-black enrollment ratio than public institutions.

Table 2 also shows some discrepancies between public
and private institutions for various regions. For example,
in the Mid-West and particularly the South, private institutions are more segregated than public institutions. However,
in the Northeast and West, differences in segregation between
public and private schools are not as distinct, with public
schools as segregated or more segregated at several institutional levels.

Comparison by Attendance Areas

Higher education also differs from elementary-secondary
schools in attendance areas for school enrollments, which
also affects analyses of desegregation. Public elementary-
secondary schools are organized into separate school
districts within states. Therefore, students are usually
eligible to enroll in schools in their own local district
only , and often are assigned to the school within the
district that is closest to their residential neighborhood.
The situation is different in higher education, especially for
four-year undergraduate and graduate or professional programs.
The more selective the admissions policies of an institution
of higher education, the wider the area for student recruitment is likely to be. Two-year colleges, which often will
admit a large fraction of candidates who graduate from high
school, tend to service mostly a local computer population
that is drawn from throughout a single city or from a large
section of a city (Willingham, 1970). Four-year colleges
will draw from throughout a state or from other states,
especially if they are more selective in their criteria for
student admissions. And graduate or professional institutions,
which are usually much fewer in number and more selective
than undergraduate programs, will often draw from throughout
a state and across states, again depending somewhat on their
prestige and selectivity.

The Segregation Indices presented earlier in Tables 1 and 2 measured the racial separation of enrollments of the black and white students available throughout an entire region (in the case of regional Segregation Indices) or available throughout the entire nation (in the case of national Segregation Indices). That is, these Segregation Indices are based on comparisons of actual racial enrollments and expected enrollments if all the black and white students in the region (or nation) were randomly distributed among all the institutions of the region (or nation). Table 3 is presented to show the degree of segregation in terms of the availability of black and white students within different state boundaries.

Table 3 gives Segregation Indices for each of the 50 states and the District of Columbia for the four separate levels of higher education we have been studying. The same trends of racial separation found for regional comparisons in Table 1 are evident for states within the regions. Southern states have the highest enrollment segregation at the four-year undergraduate, graduate and professional levels; the fifteen states with the highest segregation indices for four-year undergraduate enrollments are Southern, and all the states with Segregation Indices above 10 at the graduate or professional level are Southern (11 states at the graduate level and 7 states at the professional level). Among four-year undergraduate programs outside the South, only five states show Segregation Indices greater than 10 (New York, Pennsylvania, Illinois, Missouri, Ohio), while 16 of the 17 Southern states have Segregation Indices greater than 10, and most are greater than 40.

Also similar to earlier regional comparisons, non-Southern states show greater segregation for two-year undergraduates than four-year undergraduates, while the opposite is the case in the South. In every one of the 14 non-Southern states where the Segregation Index for two-year or four-year undergraduates is greater than 10, the Segregation Index is higher for two-year than four-year undergraduate enrollments. In the South, all 18 states have greater segregation of four-year than two-year undergraduates. Of the twelve states with most segregation at the two-year under-graduate levels (Segregation Indices higher than 25), 8 are in the non-South and 4 are in the South.

State analyses also confirm the relationship found earlier between school segregation and white-black enrollment ratios across different sets of institutions. Calculations were made of the rank-order correlation between the State Segregation Indices (shown in Table 3) and the state white-

Table 3

Segregation Indices for State Higher Education
Enrollments, by Level, 1976

	Northeast					Midwest			
State	2-Yr	4-Yr	Grad	Prof	State	2-Yr	4-Yr	Grad	Prof
CT	19.6	0.8	0.3	2.6	IL	65.2	17.0	9.6	4.1
ME	0.4	1.2	0.0	0.0	IN	7.4	4.2	0.3	5.2
MA	26.3	4.6	0.4	3.7	IA	0.6	2.8	2.2	4.8
NH	0.0	8.7	1.2	0.0	KS	11.8	2.6	0.8	2.0
NJ	38.8	4.2	0.6	5.2	MI	53.1	18.6	3.8	3.0
NY	41.2	21.4	6.0	3.2	MN	0.2	0.8	0.1	4.1
PA	38.4	21.4	0.2	2.4	MO	32.8	15.3	0.2	2.6
RI	0.0	3.1	1.0	0.0	NE	9.7	3.2	1.4	1.0
VT	1.9	5.0	4.0	0.0	ND	0.6	0.4	0.2	0.2
					OH	36.6	15.8	5.2	5.7
					SD	0.2	3.9	0.6	0.0
					WI	16.2	1.2	0.0	0.6

Continued

Table 3 Continued

Segregation Indices for State Higher Education
Enrollments, by Level, 1976

	South					West			
State	2-Yr	4-Yr	Grad	Prof	State	2-Yr	4-Yr	Grad	Prof
AL	33.0	65.6	26.9	40.9	AK	0.0	5.9	1.5	--
AR	28.8	39.4	7.3	1.6	AZ	4.1	0.1	0.5	0.6
DC	0.0	77.4	60.8	51.1	CA	30.1	9.6	2.0	5.4
DE	9.6	44.8	0.0	--	CO	21.3	5.8	0.8	5.3
FL	7.2	47.2	9.3	2.6	HI	1.2	0.0	0.2	0.0
GA	22.7	63.4	43.4	59.2	ID	0.2	1.0	1.0	0.0
KY	0.4	21.0	2.5	0.0	MT	0.8	5.6	0.2	0.0
LA	31.4	56.6	40.6	40.6	NV	6.6	3.0	0.1	--
MD	46.2	51.7	27.8	1.4	NM	6.6	3.0	9.4	0.0
MS	37.6	69.6	63.4	0.3	OR	0.7	4.9	0.4	0.1
NC	14.2	74.0	32.3	17.2	VT	0.1	1.3	0.8	0.9
OK	6.2	24.5	0.8	0.0	WA	13.7	3.5	0.4	5.8
SC	14.9	62.5	45.4	1.2	WY	0.8	0.0	0.0	0.0
TN	39.0	49.4	26.9	70.4					
TX	9.1	51.3	32.7	34.6					
VA	20.8	74.4	34.2	1.6					
WV	4.9	7.8	0.2	0.0					

black enrollment ratios (not shown) for the states in each
region. Using only states with at least 1,000 black students
to obtain stable measures, the relationship between segregation and black access is found in both the South and non-
South, at both the two-year and four-year undergraduate
levels. States with the lowest level of black enrollment
relative to whites tend to be the least segregated, and states
with the highest relative enrollment access for blacks tend to
be most segregated. The rank order correlation between state
white-black enrollment ratios and state segregation indices
is .80 for Southern four-year undergraduate institutions
(among the 17 states enrolling at least 1000 blacks), .71 for
Southern two-year undergraduate schools (15 states), .75 for
non-Southern four-year undergraduate institutions (19 states),
and .85 for non-Southern two-year colleges (16 states). (At
the graduate and professional levels there were not enough
states enrolling at least 1000 blacks to permit similar calculations: 1 state at the professional level, and 2 Southern
and 5 non-Southern states at the graduate level.)

The Special Case of Traditionally Black
Institutions in the South

Throughout these analyses, it was found that the South
differed from many of the patterns shown in other regions;
it was the region where black-white student isolation was
most severe at all higher educational levels except for
two-year colleges. To further explore the differences found
for the South and to more closely examine the relationship
between black enrollment and segregation in the South, we
will examine the role of the traditionally black Southern
institutions.

There are 103 institutions in this country that have
been identified as Traditionally Black Institutions (TBI)
which are still predominantly black (Turner and Michael, 1978;
National Advisory Committee on Black Higher Education and
Black Colleges and Universities, 1978). These are institutions "serving or identified with service to Black Americans
for at least two decades, with most being fifty to one
hundred years old" (Blake, Lambert and Martin, 1974). All
but five are in the South, and only 16 are two-year institutions. About sixty percent of these institutions are privately controlled, but the public institutions have a much
larger average enrollment size and serve nearly 70 percent
of all students in the traditionally black institutions.
Until the 1960's, the majority of black college students in
the country attended one of the Traditionally Black
Institutions. These institutions continue to play a major

role for blacks in higher education, containing more than 18 percent of the total black college and university enrollees in the United States in 1976. It is estimated that one-half of the bachelor degrees received by black students in 1974 were awarded by the Traditionally Black Institutions (Institute for the Study of Educational Policy, 1976).

Table 4 has been constructed to highlight the critical role that the traditional black colleges play in facilitating black access at all levels of higher education. In addition, it demonstrates that segregation (as measured by our index) could be substantially reduced in the South by eliminating black colleges. However, this policy would prove impractical and counterproductive to the major goal of desegregation, which is to maximize black students' access and retention throughout higher education. The table presents Segregation Indices and black enrollment figures for all remaining Southern institutions if private TBI's were removed, if public TBI's were removed, and if all TBI's were removed. Because there are far fewer TBI's among two-year colleges in the South than among four-year undergraduate and graduate or professional programs, the results in Table 4 are much more dramatic at the upper levels of higher education.

Table 4 shows that by removing private TBI's, the segregation index among four-year undergraduates would be reduced from 59.4 to 50.2 at the expense of eliminating 22.1 percent of the black enrollment; by removing public TBI's, from 59.4 to 39.6 with the elimination of 39.8 percent of the black enrollment, and by removing both private and public TBI's, from 59.4 to 9.6 with the elimination of 61.9 percent of black enrollment. The changes at the graduate and professional levels are also striking. By removing all public and private TBI's, the segregation index in the South among graduate students would change from 33.1 to 5.1 at the cost of 36 percent of the black enrollment, and among professional students the segregation index would change from 40.2 to 2.2 with the loss of about half of the black enrollment.

It is interesting to note from Table 4 that the pattern of differences in segregation and enrollment access are the same in the South as noted in other regions when the traditionally black institutions and their student population are removed. The last column of Table 4 shows the decreasing trend of segregation indices as one moves from two-year (15.2) to four-year (9.6) to graduate and professional institutions (5.1 and 2.2) with an increase in the white-black enrollment gap.

Table 4

Segregation Indices and Black Enrollment for
Southern Institutions of Higher Education, With and Without Public and
Private TBIS By Higher Educational Level, 1976

Level		All Southern Institutions	Without Private TBI	Without Public TBI	Without Private and Public TBI
Two-Year	Seg. Index	20.8	15.2	19.2	15.2
	Black Enroll.	89,343	87,092	84,011	81,760
	% Black Loss		2.5	6.0	8.4
Four-Year	Seg. Index	59.4	50.2	39.6	9.6
	Black Enroll.	220,388	171,694	132,687	83,993
	% Black Loss		22.1	39.8	61.9
Graduate	Seg. Index	33.1	23.6	20.4	5.1
	Black Enroll.	9,322	7,894	7,389	5,961
	% Black Loss		15.3	20.7	36.0
Professional	Seg. Index	40.2	12.3	37.1	2.2
	Black Enroll.	4,108	2,437	3,747	2,076
	% Black Loss		40.7	8.8	49.5

The comparisons in Table 4 may be somewhat artificial since some black students in TBI's could enroll in other institutions if TBI's were actually eliminated. However, these results clearly show the danger of employing restricted measures of desegregation which do not take into considera- tion black access, retention, and achievement in higher education. In addition, they highlight the necessity to enhance and strengthen black colleges to assure their continued existence and their continued role in contributing to black attainment.

Summary and Conclusions

We have noted that higher education is organized differently in several major ways from elementary-secondary education. These differences have important implications for higher education desegregation policy and research. Our data showed that the various structural arrangements and complex features of American colleges and universities operate to produce either a lower enrollment of blacks where segregation is low or a high degree of racial isolation where blacks are more proportionately enrolled relative to whites. This finding was consistent across all levels of higher education, in non-Southern regions, in public and private institutions, and within states. The consistency of this result highlights the need to examine both enrollment access and desegregation in higher education.

Secondly, our findings illustrated the danger of viewing desegregation as an isolated phenomenon which does not consider black enrollment and retention and the role of black institutions in facilitating black educational attainment. Fortunately, recent federal policy has begun to recognize the importance of simultaneously evaluating desegregation and minority access and attainment. However, researchers and the educational community do not have a clear understanding of the underlying processes that create the relationship between desegregation and equity outcomes for minorities in higher education.

Further research is therefore needed to more adequately explain why black-white racial isolation is less severe at levels and localities where black enrollment access is lower relative to whites. To what extent are the negative relation-ships between desegregation and enrollment equity explained by structural features of higher education organization (such as admissions policies and financial requirements of public and private institutions at each level), by demographic features (such as the racial composition of particular community college attendance areas), or by social-psychological features (such as white reluctance to be in a racial minority, black preferences for programs with an ethnic perspective, and community stereotypes of minority and white institutions)? Do restrictive admissions policies that have historically contributed to the creation of black colleges and universities still constitute the major segregating force in four-year colleges? Better information on these questions will require alternative measures of segregation and richer data for research than are now available. Upon obtaining better data and segregation measures, we can more effectively analyze and assess the progress of desegregation and black achievement in higher education.

References

Astin, A. W.
    1977   "Equal access to postsecondary education: Myth or reality?" The UCLA Educator 19 (Spring): 8-17.

Bailey, R. L.
    1978   Minority Admissions. Lexington, Massachusetts: Lexington Books (D.C. Heath and Co.).

Becker, H. J., J. M. McPartland, and G. E. Thomas
    1978   "The measurement of segregation: The Dissimilarity Index and Coleman's Segregation Index Compared." Social Statistics Section, Annual meetings of the American Statistical Association.

Blake, E., Jr., J. Lambert, and L. Martin
    1974   Degrees Granted and Enrollment Trends in Historically Black Colleges: An Eight-Year Study. Washington, D. C.: Institute for Services to Education.

Coleman, J. S., S. D. Kelly, and J. A. Moore
    1975   Trends in School Segregation, 1968-73. Washington, D.C.: Urban Institute.

Cortese, C. F, R. F. Falk, and J. Cohen
    1976   "Further considerations on the methodological analysis of segregation indices." American Sociological Review 41: 630-37.

Haynes, L., III
    1978   The Adams Cases: A Critical Sourcebook. Washington D.C: Institute for Services to Education.

1981   "The Adams Mandate: A format for achieving equal
        educational opportunity and attainment." Pp. 329–335
        in G. Thomas (ed.) Black Students in Higher
        Education: Conditions and Experiences in the
        1970's. Westport, Connecticut: Greenwood Press.

Institute for the Study of Educational Policy
  1976   Equal Educational Opportunity for Blacks in U.S.
          Higher Education: An Assessment. Washington, D.C.:
          Howard University Press.

Morris, L.
  1979   Elusive Equality: The Status of Black Americans
          in Higher Education. Washington, D.C.: Howard
          University Press.

National Advisory Committee on Black Higher Education and
Black Colleges and Universities
  1978   Higher Education Equity: The Crisis of Appearance
          Versus Reality. Washington, D.C.: National
          Advisory Committee on Black Higher Education and
          Black Colleges and Universities.

Rasberry, W.
  1980   "The State and Morgan State." The Washington Post
          (Feb. 14): 12–13.

Turner, W. H. and J. A. Michael
  1978   A Definitive List of Traditionally Black Institu-
          tions. Washington, D.C.: NCES.

U.S. Bureau of the Census
  1977   Statistical Abstract of the United States: 1977.
          (98th edition) Washington, D.C.: U.S. Government
          Printing Office.

Willingham, W. W.
  1970   Free-Access Higher Education. New York: College
          Entrance Examination Board.

Zoloth, B. S.
  1976   "Alternative measures of school segregation."
          Land Economics 52:278–398.

Footnotes

1. The calculation formula for the Segregation Index has two equivalent forms:

$$S = \frac{(\text{Percent White}) - \left(\begin{array}{l}\text{Percent white in the school at-}\\ \text{tended by average black student}\end{array}\right)}{(\text{Percent White})}$$

OR:

$$S = \frac{(\text{Percent Black}) - \left(\begin{array}{l}\text{Percent black in the school at-}\\ \text{tended by average white student}\end{array}\right)}{(\text{Percent Black})}$$

The two calculation formulas will give the same value if blacks and whites are the only two groups in the population, and slightly different values if there are other not very large ethnic groups besides blacks and whites in the population. For this paper, an average is presented of the two values calculated by the above formulae. This index was selected because it does not have the problems of bias that other familiar segregation indices have which can produce misleading comparisons (Cortese, Falk, and Cohen, 1976). It is critical to the major findings in this paper that values of the selected Segregation Index are not mathematically dependent on the racial proportions of students in a particular locality or level. For proof of this property and other properties of the selected index, see Becker et.al., 1978; Coleman et. al., 1975; and Zoloth, 1974.

2. The white-black population ratio in 1975 was 9.3:1 in the Northeast, 10.6:1 in the Midwest, 4.3:1 in the South, and 17.3:1 in the West, and 7.6:1 in the nation as a whole (U.S. Bureau of Census, 1977, p. 31).

27

The Economic Future:
Institutional and Student Financial Aid
for Blacks in Higher Education

GLORIA RANDLE SCOTT

Introduction

As black colleges and universities move into the last two decades of the twentieth century, and as black Americans continue to pursue the economic and social benefits to be gained by higher education, the economic future of blacks in higher education looks rather bleak. The major reason is that the economic future of the country, itself, looks bleak. The economic future of blacks will be decided in the political/social arena rather than in the halls of higher educational institutions. People who are in positions to influence the decision should scrutinize all of the current legislation, and the proposed new legislation on higher education. Through its many agencies, the federal government directly and indirectly controls the shape and direction of American higher education. This chapter will focus primarily on the impact of the federal government, private businesses and philanthropic organizations, and current economic conditions on the economic future of blacks in higher education.

Factors Affecting the Economic
Future of Higher Education for Blacks

There are many factors affecting the economic future of higher education for blacks. These major factors are: the socioeconomic status of students and institutions; the nature of higher education as a service industry; inflation; economic and social recession; a lack of public policy on the importance of higher education; and a continued commitment to provide higher education for black Americans at a level of equity. Among these factors, the service industry role of higher education and inflation pose the most serious threats.

The service industry role of higher education affects the financial health of colleges and universities in several ways. First, unlike many other industries, productivity improvements in higher education are difficult to achieve. Increases in productivity enable other sectors of the economy to absorb higher costs, especially high labor costs, without suffering serious financial distress or raising the prices of their products drastically. However, in higher education, over 80 percent of expenditures are for personnel-faculty, administrators, clerical and maintenance support. Colleges and universities are under constant pressure to increase salaries and wages to match increases in other sectors of the economy. Without "products" to sell, the increased wages in higher education lead to higher tuition which often price out of the market those individuals who need to be attracted to higher education.

Another basic problem is inflation. Productivity increases in other sectors reduce some of the impact of inflation on costs and prices. Higher education, on the other hand, must adjust in other ways, such as by limiting salary increases and persuading its clientele that higher education is a bargain even at present tuition and fee levels. In fact, the cost of a higher education has not changed much recently (Noell, 1978).

Black students and black institutions receive their finances from the same basic sources as do white students and white institutions. The major difference is that the majority of white students come from families with adequate socioeconomic status while the majority of black students come from families with inadequate socioeconomic resources. Also, the support of the majority of white institutions is clearly tied to alumni fortunes and the influence that these organizations have on state and federal policies in the interest of their institutions. Obviously, the same economic conditions will affect all students and institutions, but the impact of inflation and other economic strains will be much more devastating for blacks and black institutions than for most white institutions.

Socioeconomic Environment

The socioeconomic status of students and institutions of higher education among states is also a factor that will affect access to higher education to black students in the 80s and 90s. State environments and state needs vary within the

United States so that an assessment of the socioeconomic
condition of each state gives valuable nationwide information that extends to the impact of higher education availability for blacks within those states.

In 1972, between 300,000 and 500,000 academically able
(meaning students with very good high school grade averages)
high school graduates did not enter college (National Advisory Committee on Black Higher Education, 1979). The estimate is that at least one of every ten of these students
did not start college because they could not afford the financial cost involved. The most recent estimate is that as
many as 500,000 high school graduates who have college ability are currently not attending college because of financial
reasons. Among these students is a disproportionately high
number of low income and minority youth who are not attending college although they have college ability.

Looking ahead to the 80s and beyond, support models
which must emerge should go beyond the debate of tuition
cost (i.e. that low cost or no tuition in public higher education is the answer). The absence of tuition charges or
having low tuition rates does reduce some of the financial
burden but does not eliminate the problem for the students
involved. Most of the black students who cannot afford college find the "support dollars for room-board, books and
personal incidentals" as well as the "separation dollars"
from the family that is dependent on the earnings of a family member are as or more important than the tuition costs,
in preventing college attendance.

In 1944, the Veteran's Bill (i.e. the G.I. Bill) was
enacted to allow for men and women who had been honorably
discharged from the armed forces to attend the college or
university of their choice. This bill provided students
with subsistence and the cost of books and tuition. This
was the first major federal effort to provide expenditures
for students to attend higher education. These programs
were administered through higher education institutions and
funded by the federal government. Thus, the inclusion of
subsistence as a direct aid to students is not a new model.
A similar program should be given strong consideration for
full student funding during the 1980s. Also, basic principles for establishing state student aid programs should be
expanded to consider the socioeconomic conditions of students
and institutions within states.

Institutional Support for
Higher Education

Private institutional support (all sources other than
federal and local tax dollars)coupled with the basic support
from governmental agencies, is rendered in five ways through:
direct institutional support, student support (i.e., student
financial aid), investment income or endowment., indirect
support of specific programs, and by direct purchase of specific goods and services through grants and contracts. The
fifth approach is more closely related to direct purchase;
it is included, however, because it has an impact on the institution's economic condition through its direct support of
overhead costs.

The provision of student support is largely dependent
on the federal government. The Higher Education Act of 1965,
as amended, the National Defense Education Act of 1958, and
the Public Health Act provide the statutory authority for
seven student assistance programs. They include:

1. Grants - Basic Educational Opportunity Grant Program (BEOG), State Student Incentive Grant Program (SSIG)
Supplemental Education Opportunity Grant Program (SEOG);

2. Loans - National Direct Student Loan Program (NDSL)
Guaranteed Student Loan Program (GSL), Public Health Act Loan
(HEAL) Program, and;

3. Work Programs - College work-study.

In September 1978, at an open hearing of the National
Advisory Committee on Black Higher Education and Black Colleges and Universities (NACBHEABCU), several presenters
from predominantly black schools identified the internal
impact that the administration of the BEOG Program caused.
The implications of this unique phenomenon is not present
in the predominantly white institutions because of the lower
percentage of students attending those institutions with
Basic Education Opportunity Grants. In the absence of full
funding of the Institutional Support provisions and the
Higher Education Foundation section of the Education Amendments of 1972, black institutions will heavily invest support dollars that should be utilized for other general expenditures. This will affect the future of economic resources.

Direct Institutional Support

There is presently very little activity in the private
sector among foundations and donors, for pure institutional
support or development funds awarded to black institutions.
The Ford Foundation grants to several selected private
black colleges in the late 60s and early 70s have been
discontinued. Groups such as the United Negro College Fund,
which produces a major fund-raising effort on the behalf of
the private black colleges, provides annual support based on
a formula of funds raised, and several other variables.
Where there are supporting denominational organizations
which support private black colleges, they provide support
in ways agreed upon with the institutions.

Federal involvement in higher educational support has
been primarily through the implementation of Title III of
the 1965 Higher Education Act (HEA), as amended, since 1965.
This support has taken several forms in response to the new
iterations of the regulations developed with each set of
amendments, and with the advent of each new administration
(which brings a new head of the Department of Health, Education and Welfare, with their own policy views of what Title
III should do). The original language of the Title III in
the HEA of 1965 provides that:

> "The Commissioner shall carry out a program of
> special assistance to strengthen the academic
> quality of developing institutions which have
> the desire and potential to make a substantial
> contribution to the higher education resources
> of the Nation, but which are struggling for
> survival and are isolated from the main currents
> of academic life." (Higher Education Act of
> 1965 - Preamble)

Many different uses and purposes of Title III have been
proposed. Many institutions which were not considered under
the original description have increasingly qualified under
later amendment waivers, and congressional intent. Title
III continues to be the only federally based program which
provides some institutional support for development of institutions in accordance with the language of the Title.
Historically black colleges find themselves in the 1970s
heavily dependent on this institutional aid. It is expected
that their needs may escalate during the 80s as they try to
provide higher education for the increased populations of
young blacks and as they attempt to cope with inflation
and the impact of recession.

The NACBHEABCU has repeatedly expressed concern about the movement of Title III funds away from the historically black colleges. In its latest response (June, 1979) to the Secretary of H.E.W., (whom it is authorized to advise) it recommended targeting Title III for the historically black colleges.[1] This is within the spirit of the intention of the agreed legislation. The future direction of this legislation, and the regulations and interpretations implementing it, will have a significant impact on the economic status of the black institutions in the 80s. Some of the institutions will not be able to survive without revisions in this legislation.

Additional Sources of Support for Black Institutions

Endowments: When interest rates drop, income from invested endowment funds drop. At the same time, inflation is running rampant with goods and services increasing in price. The income from investment dollars still buys fewer services and goods needed in the operation of the institution. For 97 black colleges and universities there are no significant levels of endowment. This represents one of the major sources of vulnerability for most black institutions. Among those which do have significant investment, the inflationary impact hits twice as hard as it does white institutions.

Many efforts are underway by black colleges to build endowments. A recent effort included a consortium of six black colleges which raised $2.4 million that was matched by loans from nine insurance companies. The $2.4 million will be the basis of an endowment fund, which, when invested, will help to maintain school operations and repay the initial loan. Such endeavors and endowment activities are increasing because of the great need.

Private Foundations and Business Corporations

Private foundations have been a rather stable source of support (especially Ford, Rockefeller and Moton) for black

colleges in the past (Southern Education Foundation, 1972).
But, in recent years, their support has been reduced by a
decrease in their returns on investments. There has been,
however, an increase in the direct contributions of business
corporations to higher education. In the past, businesses
have more often purchased goods and services from some colleges and universities rather than award direct gifts. Recently a more popular approach of providing dollars to match
contributions by alumni has emerged among business corporations.

Alumni gifts represent an increasing percentage of private gifts to the institutions. However, the institutions
provide services to the alumni, (i.e., alumni magazines,
newsletters, mail services). The college also solicits
alumni contributions for its support.

From an economic point of view, black alumni represent
a group to be "mined" to produce more dollars. The inflationary style of the 80s and recent introduction of tax
legislation in the United States Congress to remove some
types of contributions from the status of tax deduction,
may end up restricting the amount of dollars that will be
given by the alumni who have recently recognized their responsibilities to black institutions.

Boards of Trustees are also potential sources of the
support in higher education, but in general, they have not
been effective in obtaining funds for black institutions.

Student Fees

In the 1960s the average private institution was receiving about 55% of its total operating income from student
tuition and fees. The average public insitution was deri-
ving approximately 18% of its total operating income from
student tuition and fees.

In the 1970s H.E.W. Comptroller General's Office reported student tuition and fees covered 65% of income at private
institutions and 22% at public institutions. Public institutions have traditionally had lower tuition and fees than
private institutions. This is due to direct subsidy of public, state and local institutions. Private black institutions depend more heavily on student tuition than any other
institutions (Ford Foundation Report, 1976).

Since black students come from families which have a disproportionately high representation in the under $7,500 a year income category, they are more dependent on external sources of funds for tuitions and fees. They are highly dependent on student financial aid programs. When black institutions receive financial contributions to assist with student support, they are able to compete and attract students who have the academic ability but who without total financial support, could not and would not attend college.

Institutional Contracts and Grants

The Federal Inter-Agency Committee Report showed that for fiscal year 1975, (the latest data available) very few contracts went to black colleges. For example, the National Institute of Education funded thirteen-million dollars to all colleges for educational research and development of which only forty-one thousand went to black colleges (Federal Inter-Agency Committee on Education, 1975). The National Institute of Education since its chartering in 1972 had reported no funds to black colleges and universities prior to 1975.

Table 1 reports the federal funds awarded to black colleges and universities from 1970 to 1975. Although it shows a small increase between 1970-75, it still shows a very small percentage of dollars allocated to black institutions when compared to predominantly white institutions. If one operates under the assumption that grants and research contracts are a form of institutional aid, then the impact of the absence of negotiations with and use of black colleges further adds to the economic plight of these institutions. This further affects the level of services that black institutions can provide to the students they serve. The overhead expenses and purchase of human and program resources that contracts bring into an institution, on a continuous annual basis does in fact represent a form of institutional support, because those dollars are available for use in the institution in some regular way for duration of the project.

White colleges and universities which have received federal grants and contracts should also be encouraged to involve black students enrolled in these institutions in research assistantships and jobs provided by such contracts and grants. While there are no statistics on this phenomenon, informal reviews at several levels suggest that black students both graduate and undergraduate are excluded from

Table 1

Federal Funds for Black Colleges, By Agency, FY 1970-1975
(In Thousands of Dollars)

	1970	1971	1972
ACTION	923.7	1,118.9	1,043.5
Agency for International Development	102.0		1,500.0
Atomic Energy Commission/Energy	202.0	308.0	210.4
Research and Development Agency 4/			
Department of Agriculture	1,127.0	1,049.1	14,091.9
Department of Commerce	295.0	430.0	961.5
Department of Defense	199.2	262.2	575.3
Department of Health, Education			
and Welfare	(100,410.6)	(145,917.7)	(209,068.0)
National Institute of Education			
Office of Education	85,213.6	118,307.9	166,058.9
Office of Human Development/			11,199.8
Other HEW 4/			
Public Health Service	14,384.0	26,050.6	29,592.1
Social and Rehabilitation Service	813.0	1,559.2	2,217.2
Department of Housing and Urban	10,009.6	5,928.0	5,171.0
Development			
Department of Interior	107.8	20.0	152.6
Department of Justice	489.1	660.1	1,610.6
Department of Labor	1,790.5	2,014.9	3,957.1
Department of Transportation	455.0	242.0	240.0
Environmental Protection Agency		146.7	178.3
National Aeronautics and Space Administration	640.0	831.0	897.0
National Endowment for the Arts	33.0	42.9	137.0
National Endowment for the Humanities	291.6	481.6	1,257.1

Continued

365

Table 1 Continued

Federal Funds for Black Colleges, By Agency, FY 1970-1975
(In Thousands of Dollars)

	1973	1974	1975
ACTION	1,544.5	678.0[1]	611.3[1]
Agency for International Development	25.0	1,219.0	0
Atomic Energy Commission/Energy Research and Development Agency[4]	392.5	172.0	220.0
Department of Agriculture	17,744.9	17,439.0	16,425.0
Department of Commerce	745.3	41.0[2]	0
Department of Defense	1,152.6	844.0[2]	307.0
Department of Health, Education and Welfare	(202,004.7)	(234,209.0)[3]	(205,305.0)
National Institute of Education			41.0
Office of Education	154,926.0	177,876.03	160,658.0[3]
Office of Human Development/ Other HEW[4]	12,430.8	640.0	14,968.0
Public Health Service	33,192.7	54,994.0	29,632.0
Social and Rehabilitation Service	1,455.2	699.0	0
Department of Housing and Urban Development	3,287.9	3,000.0[1]	671.0
Department of the Interior	41.4	0	0
Department of Justice	1,154.2	1,154.0	953.0
Department of Labor	5,478.3	150.0	163.0
Department of Transportation	331.0	155.0	208.0
Environmental Protection Agency	496.3	720.0	566.0
National Aeronautics and Space Administration	1,319.0	2,277.0[1]	2,512.0[1]
National Endowment for the Arts	109.5	180.0[1]	58.0[1]
National Endowment for the Humanities	309.5	919.0[1]	341.0[1]

Table 1 Continued

	1970	1971	1972
National Science Foundation	3,185.0	3,073.6	9,391.7
Office of Economic Opportunity/ Community Services Administration 4/	5,189.0	6,981.0	6,513.0
Veterans Administration	29.0	48.9	61.9
TOTAL	125,479.1	170,556.6	257,081.0

	1973	1974	1975
National Science Foundation	6,977.4	8,166.0	5,284.0
Office of Economic Opportunity/ Community Services Administration 4/	6,912.2	4,576.0	6,000.0 [1]
Veterans Administration	68.2	80.0 [1]	
TOTAL	250,979.0	275,979.0	239,664.3

[1] Estimate

[2] Includes Estimate for ROTC AND NESEP (Navy Enlisted Scientific Education Program)

[3] Includes Estimate for National Direct Student Loans

[4] The names listed before the slash are those which were valid for the years 1970-74. In 1975, legislation expanded the AEC and named the new agency ERDA. Legislation also changed the name of OEO to CSA, but the agency is the same. Also, OHD money was not separated out in FY 1975 so it is now a part of the "Other HEW" category.

Source: Federal Inter-Agency Committee Report, 1975.

access to full participation in federal contracts and grants
awarded to predominantly white institutions. This exclusion
further impedes the educational development of black students. The financial support from assistantships can help
black students achieve their college education in black and
white institutions.

The Graduate and Professional Education
of Blacks

A brief look at graduate and professional education further emphasizes the need for better economic support for
blacks in the 1980s. Table 2 shows the degree data for
blacks in law and medicine in 1976, the last year for which
information is available. Blacks represented 4.7% of the
law degrees, 5.2% of the medical degrees and 3.6% of the
other graduate degrees at the doctoral level.

Financial support for professional education for black
students is primarily centered around the predominantly
white institutions. However, 19 percent of the blacks
pursuing first professional degrees were enrolled in the
historically black institutions.

At the graduate level, black students are much more likely than the average white student or other minority student
to be enrolled on a part-time basis, thereby assuming the
burden of combining study and work more often than other
students.

At the doctoral level in 1976, more than three times as
many degrees were conferred to non-resident aliens (4,068)
than were conferred to black Americans (1,213). For the
Master's Degree conferred by institutions other than historically black colleges, non-resident aliens received the
same proportion as did black Americans. However, institutions in twenty-nine states conferred more Master's Degrees
to non-resident aliens than to black Americans.

In Alabama, all of the veterinary medicine degrees that
were awarded to blacks in 1976 came from Tuskegee Institute.
Meharry Medical College and Howard University Medical College awarded 75% of all degrees awarded to blacks in medicine in 1976. Texas Southern and North Carolina Central
awarded 60% of all law degrees to blacks awarded in the United States in 1976 (National Advisory Committee on Black
Higher Education, 1979). These data emphasize the need for
some specific direction in the 80s aimed at improving the social and economic conditions related to black access and re-

TABLE 2

Higher Education Degrees Earned by Racial/Ethnic
Group and Sex Aggregate United States
1975-1976

Level of Degree		Total		White		Black		Hispanic		American Indian/ Alaskan Native	
		No.	%	No.	%	No.	%	No.	%	No.	%
Masters	Total	310,493	100.0	262,851	84.7	20,351	6.6	6,379	2.1	795	0.3
	Male	165,971	100.0	139,539	84.1	7,809	4.7	3,316	2.0	432	0.3
	Female	144,522	100.0	123,312	85.3	12,542	8.7	3,063	2.1	363	0.3
Medicine	Total	13,487	100.0	11,993	88.9	708	5.2	304	2.3	47	0.3
	Male	11,294	100.0	10,163	90.0	504	4.5	245	2.2	36	0.3
	Female	2,193	100.0	1,830	83.4	204	9.3	59	2.7	11	0.5
Law	Total	32,483	100.0	29,520	90.9	1,519	4.7	858	2.6	75	0.2
	Male	26,237	100.0	23,999	91.5	1,102	4.2	697	2.7	59	0.2
	Female	6,246	100.0	5,521	88.4	417	6.7	161	2.6	16	0.3
Ph.D. or Ed. D.	Total	33,799	100.0	27,435	81.2	1,213	3.6	407	1.2	93	0.3
	Male	26,016	100.0	20,853	80.2	771	3.0	294	1.1	77	0.3
	Female	7,783	100.0	6,582	84.6	442	5.7	113	1.5	16	0.2

SOURCE: U.S. Department of Health, Education and Welfare, Office of Civil Rights and National Center for Education Statistics, unpublished tabulations, 1976.

Continued

		Asian Pacific Islander		Nonresident Alien	
		No.	%	No.	%
Masters	Total	4,037	1.3	16,080	5.2
	Male	2,499	1.5	12,376	2.6
	Female	1,538	1.1	3,704	2.6
Medicine	Total	227	1.7	208	1.5
	Male	177	1.6	169	1.5
	Female	50	2.3	39	1.8
Law	Total	312	1.0	199	0.6
	Male	230	0.9	150	0.6
	Female	82	1.3	49	0.6
Ph.D or Ed. D	Total	583	1.7	4,068	12.0
	Male	480	1.8	3,541	13.6
	Female	103	1.3	527	6.8

SOURCE: U.S. Department of Health, Education and Welfare, Office of Civil Rights and National Center for Education Statistics, unpublished tabulations, 1976.

370

tention in graduate and professional schools.

From the 70s to the 80s
Economic Trends

Projections of estimated average charges in constant
1976-77 dollars for 1980-1987 show a geometric increase in
higher education tuition, room and board (See Table 3).
Institutions will be forced to pass on the inflationary
increased to its students. The Comptroller General's office
stated that one-fourth to one-third of all private institutions are experiencing financial difficulty due to interre-
lated problems created by declining enrollments, increasing
tuition gaps between public and private colleges, competition for students brought on by the growth of the community colleges, rising costs and inflation, and lack of effective adminstrative controls.

The institutions listed in the Carnegie Commision's
classification of schools as Liberal Arts II Colleges, (includes 38 private HBCs and 2 NPBCs) are the most affected.
Forty-nine of the 74 colleges and universities listed as
delinquent on HUD Reserve Bank listings and HEW facility
construction loans in 1975 belonged to the Liberal Arts II
group. Twenty-nine of the 38 private institutions which
closed between 1970 and 1975 were Liberal Arts II Schools
(Carnegie Council on Policy Studies in Higher Education,
1979).

The Annual Statistical Report (United Negro College Fund,
1976) for 41 private historically black colleges presents
a bleaker picture of the precarious nature of finances at
the private institutions. Although, revenues and expenditures were roughly equal in 1974-75, expenditures increased
37.3 percent in the period from 1971-72 to 1974-75 while
revenues increased only 32 percent over the same period.
Table 4 reports similar differences for revenues and expenditures per student. These findings are based on aggregate
data and do not indicate deficits or surpluses at individual
institutions. The United Negro College Fund report shows
that in 1974-75, half of its member institutional experienced budget deficits.

Many of the present and future problems affecting the
historically black colleges are directly related to their
service to large numbers of low-income students. The higher
dependence of black private institutions on federal funds
for current funding revenue (38% in 1975, compared to 14%
for other private institutions) make them exceedingly vul-

Table 3

Estimated average charges (1976-77 dollars) per full-time equivalent student in institutions of higher education with alternative projections, by type and control of institution: United States, 1980-81 to 1986-87. (Charges are for the academic year and in constant 1976-77 dollars)[a]

Year and control (1)	Total tuition, board and room				Tuition and required fees			
	All (2)	University (3)	Other 4-year (4)	2-year (5)	All (6)	University (7)	Other 4-year (8)	2-year (9)
1980-81:								
Public.........	1,900	2,110	1,903	1,666	576	729	619	445
Nonpublic......	4,188	5,012	3,904	3,025	2,694	3,302	2,510	1,641
1981-82:								
Public.........	1,906	2,119	1,916	1,681	582	738	632	460
Nonpublic	4,220	5,052	3,936	3,030	2,726	3,342	2,542	1,646
1982-83:								
Public.........	1,912	2,128	1,928	1,697	588	747	644	476
Nonpublic......	4,253	5,093	3,968	3,036	2,759	3,383	2,574	1,652
1983-84:								
Public	1,919	2,137	1,940	1,712	595	756	656	491
Nonpublic......	4,285	5,133	4,000	3,041	2,791	3,423	2,606	1,657
1984-85:								
Public.........	1,925	2,147	1,953	1,728	601	766	699	507
Nonpublic......	4,318	5,174	4,032	3,046	2,824	3,464	2,638	1,662

Table 3 Continued

Estimated average charges (1976-77 dollars) per full-time equivalent student in institutions of higher education with alternative projections, by type and control of institution: United States, 1980-81 to 1986-87. (Charges are for the academic year and in constant 1976-77 dollars)[a]

Year and control (1)	Board (7-day basis)				Dormitory rooms			
	All (10)	University (11)	Other 4-year (12)	2-year (13)	All (14)	University (15)	Other 4-year (16)	2-year (17)
1980-81:								
Public.........	736	765	704	748	588	616	580	473
Nonpublic......	813	888	777	770	681	822	617	614
1981-82:								
Public.........	736	765	704	748	588	616	580	473
Nonpublic......	813	888	777	770	681	822	617	614
1982-83:								
Public.........	736	765	704	748	588	616	580	473
Nonpublic......	813	888	777	770	681	822	617	614
1983-84:								
Public.........	736	765	704	748	588	616	580	473
Nonpublic......	813	888	777	770	681	822	617	614
1984-85:								
Public.........	736	765	704	748	588	616	580	473
Nonpublic......	813	888	777	770	681	822	617	614

Continued

373

Table 3 Continued

Year and control (1)	Total tuition, board and room				Tuition and required fees			
	All (2)	University (3)	Other 4-year (4)	2-year (5)	All (6)	University (7)	Other 4-year (8)	2-year (9)
1985-86:								
Public	1,931	2,156	1,965	1,744	607	775	681	523
Nonpublic......	4,350	5,215	4,065	3,051	2,856	3,505	2,671	1,667
1986-87:								
Public.........	1,938	2,165	1,977	1,977	1,759	614	784	693
Nonpublic......	4,383	5,255	4,097	3,057	2,889	3,545	2,703	1,673

374

Table 3 Continued

Year and control (1)	Board (7-day basis)				Dormitory rooms			
	All (10)	University (11)	Other 4-year (12)	2-year (13)	All (14)	University (15)	Other 4-year (16)	2-year (17)
1985-86:								
Public...........	736	765	704	748	588	616	580	473
Nonpublic........	813	888	777	770	681	822	617	614
1986-87:								
Public...........	538	736	765	704	748	616	580	473
Nonpublic........	813	888	777	770	681	822	617	614

[a] Constant 1976-77 dollar amounts calculated by applying the Consumer Price Index (See constant-dollar index, Table B-4) to charges for the years in current unadjusted dollars as shown in Table 36.

SOURCE: NCES, Projection of Education Statistics, to 1986-87, 1978

TABLE 4

TOTAL AND PER STUDENT REVENUE AND EXPENDITURES
FOR UNCF INSTITUTIONS

1971-72 and 1974-75

	1971-72	1974-75	% Change
Revenues	$125,167,367	$165,242,006	+32.0
Expenditures	120,266,739	165,174,808	+37.3
Revenues Per Student	3,675	4,710	+28.2
Expenditures Per Student	3,531	4,708	+33.3

(Based on 34 of the 41 member Institutions)

SOURCE: United Negro College Fund, Annual Statistical
Report, 1976, pp. 30 and 31.

nerable to fluctuations in federal policy even though much
of this funding is directly tied to the services provided
for low-income and disadvantaged students (Brimmer, 1971;
Trent, 1978). Table 5 illustrates the rates of dependency
on revenue from public funds for private and public black
institutions as compared to all other colleges and universities. The financial gap between actual student needs and
the needs met by federal financial aid programs, is met by
the institutions themselves. Black colleges tend to rein-
vest assets in student aid efforts rather than placing these
funds into long-term investments such as endowments. This
restricts their potential for building the capital necessary
for future viability. This is true at both undergraduate
and graduate levels.

There are still other factors on the horizon which affect
the future financial health of black colleges both public
and private. The major factors include: (1) The Adams
case for desegregating public higher education; (2) The
re-authorization of the Higher Education Act of
1965, especially the parameters of Title III - Developing
Institutions and Title IV - Student Financial Aid purview;

TABLE 5

PERCENTAGE OF CURRENT FUNDS REVENUES FROM PUBLIC
SOURCES FOR 102 HISTORICALLY BLACK COLLEGES
AND ALL COLLEGES AND UNIVERSITIES
1974-1975

PUBLIC SOURCE	CONTROL	HBC'S	ALL COLLEGES AND UNIVERSITIES
FEDERAL	Public	21 percent	14 percent
	Private	38 percent	14 percent
	Total	29 percent	14 percent
STATE	Public	45 percent	44 percent
	Private	1 percent	2 percent
	Total	24 percent	31 percent
LOCAL	Public	1 percent	6 percent
	Private	1 percent	1 percent
	Total	1 percent	4 percent

Data derived from HEGIS and may not necessarily be comparable to other data gathered from Federal agencies because
institutions are not able to identify original source of all
current funds revenues.

SOURCE: Library of Congress Congressional Research Service,
"The Historically Black Colleges Prospects and
Options for Federal Support" Education and Public
Welfare Division, January 17, 1977, p. 27.

(3) The type of federal policy and commitment that is
developed concerning the future of America's higher education; (4) The economic conditions of the Nation which will
have a detrimental impact on the families and students as
consumers, and educational institutions as consumers;
(5) Private donation patterns, and (6) Policy direction
which will shape access to higher education for America's
blacks. These topics, and others discussed in this chapter,
suggest many questions for in-depth research that will provide direction for policies which will affect the economic
future of blacks in higher education in the decade of the
eighties.

References

Brimmer, A.
  1971   "The economic outlook and the future of the
          Negro college," Daedalus 100:539-572.

Carnegie Council on Policy Studies in Higher Education
  1979   Next Steps for the 1980s in Student Financial
          Aid. Berkeley, California: The Carnegie
          Foundation for the Advancement of Teaching.

Federal Interagency Committee on Education
  1975   Federal Agencies and Black Colleges: Fiscal
          1972. Washington, DC.: U.S. Government
          Printing Office.

Ford Foundation Report
  1976   Paying for Schools and Colleges. New York:
          Ford Foundation

Library of Congress Congressional Research Service
  1977   The Historically Black Colleges: Prospects
          and Options for Federal Support. Washington,
          DC.: Education and Public Welfare Division.

National Advisory Committee on Black Higher Education and
Black Colleges and Universities
  1979   Access of Black Americans to Higher Education:
          How Open is the Door? Washington, DC.: U.S.
          Government Printing Office.

National Center for Education Statistics
  1978   Projections of Education Statistics, 1986-1987.
          Washington, DC: U.S. Government Printing Office.

Noell, J.
  1978   The Condition of Education: Statistical Report,
          Washington, DC: U.S. Government Printing Office

References

Scott, G.D.
  1976   Research Issues Relevant to the Monitoring and
          Support of Present and Future Directions for
          Blacks in Higher Education. (Unpublished).

Southern Education Foundation
  1972   Small Change, A Report on Federal Support for
          Black Colleges. Atlanta. Southern Education
          Foundation.

Trent, W.J., Jr.
  1971   "The future role of the Negro college and its
          financing." Daedalus 100:647-659.

United Negro College Fund
  1976   Annual Statistical Report. Atlanta: United
          Negro College Fund

U.S. Department of Health, Education and Welfare, Office
of Civil Rights and National Center for Education Statistics
  1976   Higher Education Degrees Earned by Racial/Ethnic
          Group and Sex Aggregate United States 1975-76.
          (Unpublished tabulations).

Footnotes

1. The National Advisory Committee on Black Higher Education
    and Black Colleges and Universities, was chartered by
    Secretary of Health, Education and Welfare, Arid Matthews
    in December, 1976. Its purpose is to advise the Secretary
    of HEW and the Assistant Secretary of HEW for Education
    directly on matters affecting higher education for blacks
    in the United States. It has an official charter for
    activity in 13 areas. This committee started its work in
    September, 1977 and has published two annual reports and a
    major research paper. Several research studies are under
    commission for publication during 1979 and 1980.

28

The Future of Blacks in Higher Education: Recommendations and Conclusions

GAIL E. THOMAS

When examining the current status of blacks in higher education in light of their past historical struggles, one has to conclude that blacks have made extensive progress in higher education. The more than one million black Americans now participating in higher education as compared to less than one thousand just five decades ago clearly supports this point. However, despite the enrollment gains that blacks have achieved in absolute numbers, the data in this volume indicate that greater progress is needed for blacks to achieve full equality of higher educational opportunity.

The concept of full equality in higher education has been expanded to include (1) the relative enrollment and achievement gains of blacks in higher education as compared to their representation in the population and their progress in comparison to other groups; (2) the increased access of blacks to graduate and professional schools; (3) the retention and prompt promotion of blacks at all levels of higher education; and (4) the achievement of quality and diverse educational skills which assure blacks realistic and competitive job opportunities.

An application of the present definition of full equality to the status and conditions of blacks in higher education in the 70s reveals that the major progress of blacks has been in access to undergraduate schools--primarily in two-year colleges. Blacks have only begun to approximate parity of representation in higher education at the undergraduate level in proportion to their distribution in the college age population. They fare less successfully than whites in graduate and professional school enrollment, diversity of major field choices, obtaining a quality higher education, and prompt promotion and retention throughout higher education. Given these facts, and the belief that an investment in higher education is the major means of black mobility in U.S. society, many of the authors in this volume have outlined alternatives for achieving greater minority progress in higher education. This chapter summarizes and expands these alternatives and discusses broader policy and research issues and recommendations, concerning the current and future status of blacks in higher education.

Increasing Black Access to Four-Year Colleges

A future increase in the access of blacks to four-year colleges will greatly depend on the ability of high schools and two-year colleges to provide the nation's four-year colleges with a larger and more competent pool of blacks. This will require earlier identification and more appropriate channeling of a greater number of college-bound blacks. This places greater responsibility on elementary and secondary schools to improve the basic skills of minority students and greater responsibility on parents to support the schools and better prepare their youngsters for schooling.

The constructive and earlier use of competency-based testing (before the late high school years) might also play a critical role in producing a more competent pool of black college candidates. Constructive use is emphasized here to mean the early application of testing to identify the strengths and weaknesses of minority students in order to subsequently administer appropriate interventions to get these students out of high school and into four-year colleges.

Secondary schools must increase their retention rates of blacks and the proportion of these students enrolled in college preparatory programs. In 1977, 24 percent of all blacks aged 18-24 were not enrolled in school and were not high school graduates as compared to 15 percent of the whites in the same age cohort (U.S. Bureau of the Census, 1978). Also, on the average, a greater proportion of whites were enrolled in college preparatory programs in 1972 (National Advisory Committee on Black Higher Education, 1979). Furthermore Jencks et. al. (1972) and Rosenbaum (1976) have indicated that the academic tracking and selection procedures within high schools have a significant effect on student access to college, and that most colleges and universities automatically accept high school selection procedures without further examination.

Two-year and junior colleges have an equal if not greater role to assume in promoting the access of minorities to four-year colleges. These institutions have been largely neglect-

ed; they must be seriously evaluated and better organized
to meet the existing challenge. Careful consideration should
be given to separating these institutions into: (1) vocational institutions that provide non-four-year college bound students with marketable job skills and, (2) pre-college preparation and feeder institutions to four-year colleges. The
latter goal of community colleges as feeder institutions is
already in effect at some institutions, as the chapter by
Mohr and Sears has demonstrated. These programs can serve
a critical function. More of these institutions are needed,
particularly to serve students who have the potential for a
four-year college education but who need additional time for
preparation beyond high school. In addition, the transfer
function between institutions should involve black two-year
colleges feeding into four-year white institutions as well as
white two-year colleges transferring students to black four-
year colleges. The ability of predominantly black and white
two-year colleges to better promote the "two-plus-two" articulation function should not only increase the quality of
college-bound minorities, but should also help reduce the
need for remediation at higher levels of education, and help
increase minority retention in four-year colleges and throughout higher education.

Increasing Black Graduate and Professional School Access

As previously noted, one of the most important missions
confronting blacks in the coming decade is greater representation and attainment in graduate and professional schools.
Blacks cannot expect to have an impact on higher education,
in their own community or in society in general without
achieving advanced educational credentials. Therefore, a
well-defined set of channeling activities needs to be employed to expand the present black professional pool.

Identification and sponsorship of potential graduate
and professional school students need to take place as early
as the college freshman year (certainly no later than the
sophomore year). More specifically, follow-through transfer
programs which assure black undergraduates immediate transfer
to graduate and professional school might be considered by
some institutions. Students who are selected for such programs should have a clear and early understanding that the
purpose of their undergraduate training is to prepare them
for graduate or professional school. A series of summer programs and ongoing activities that offer students pre-graduate
and professional school specialization, career counseling,
and academic and social exposure to graduate and professional
schools also may be useful. The purpose of these activities

(as were those suggested to increase black four-year college access) is to prepare blacks as early as possible for higher education through more uniform and long-term programming and channeling.

In addition to formal sponsorship and channeling, the establishment of mentor relations between minority students and faculty at the undergraduate level is critical to encourage blacks to pursue advanced schooling. As noted, this is especially important for first generation blacks, most of whom lack relevant role models and support. More objective support to potential black graduate and professional students in the form of grants and fellowships (as opposed to loans) is also important to increase access and retention. Increased commitment in similar forms from public and private industry should also be encouraged.

Increasing Black Access in the Hard and Natural Sciences

Merely publicizing opportunities available to minorities in the sciences does not adequately stimulate participation. Early intervention at the elementary and secondary school levels is also important to achieve this goal. As suggested in past chapters, reconstructing the science curriculum and developing new and more appealing methods of teaching science to disadvantaged students is also necessary. The "affective approach" described by Young should be investigated as an alternative strategy. Finally, the value of experiential learning through field trips, and other out of classroom activities that put students directly in contact with science and scientists should be further explored.

At the postsecondary level, evaluations and expansions of such programs as Minority Introduction to Engineering (MITE) might enhance the participation of minorities in science. However, unlike MITE, which focuses on students who demonstrate scientific capabilities, more programs should be oriented toward encouraging and developing the hidden potential of disadvantaged students. Also, private and federally sponsored science programs for minorities should focus more on the traditionally black colleges as a source for recruiting black students. In addition, the science curricula at these institutions should be expanded and strengthened, because these institutions remain primarily teaching and social science oriented.

Increasing Minority Retention Throughout Higher Education

We can hypothesize, in summary, that the better the quality of elementary and secondary education for minorities **and** the earlier their pre-exposure and sponsorship to higher education, the greater their chances of higher educational promotion and retention. The strategies previously suggested (constructive and early testing, the establishment of pre-college bound and pre-career awareness programs at the two-year college level and so on) should improve the motivation and competencies of minority youth. However, structural changes and improvements are also necessary to promote greater minority retention, throughout higher education.

National and statewide training of faculty and staff—including sensitivity workshops on race relations, minority culture, teacher attitudes and prejudices, and the educational needs of disadvantaged students—is greatly needed. It is unrealistic to think that disadvantaged students can be adequately motivated, socialized, and academically prepared to succeed in nonsupportive and prejudice environments that are insensitive to change and to the needs of these students.

Further investigations of race relations and minority academic and social adjustments on predominantly white campuses are also needed. A recent report indicated that white colleges currently enroll 70 percent of the black college students, but about 7 out of 10 blacks fail to graduate from these institutions (Friedlein, 1979). In contrast, black colleges graduate over 50 percent of their black enrollees (Fiedlein, 1979). Staff and faculty at the predominantly white institutions should leave their "tours d'ivoire" and visit black colleges to learn more about how to retain minority students. Another practical approach involves conducting a series of workshops among college faculty and administrators from predominantly black and white institutions to promote information and communication networks and to formulate better methods to address the problem of minority retention (Goodrich, 1979). Finally, as past chapters have pointed out, an increase in grant as opposed to loan aid to disadvantaged minorities may have a positive effect on retention at all levels of higher education.

Future Policy and Empirical Issues to be Addressed

Several policy and research issues must be given top priority on the higher education agenda for the 1980s. One issue concerns the effects of the increased use of standardized testing on minority high school completion and college access. Special committees with adequate black representation need to be appointed within each state to determine

(1) how secondary and postsecondary institutions use tests,
(2) what benefits are derived from increased test usage, and
(3) what purposes these tests serve for various institutions
and for black and white students. More research is needed on
the ability of traditional standardized tests to predict the
educational performance of blacks. It is also important to
learn more about the educational and status outcomes of minorities who **score** low on traditional standardized tests but
who are admitted under special admissions programs at various
levels of higher education.

A second issue for the 80s entails examining the impact
of higher educational desegregation and affirmative action
on minority attainment. Such evaluations are presently nonexistent, and are needed to inform policy of how effective
current equality of educational opportunity (EEO) efforts are
and what the needs and direction of future efforts should be.
Such research should put many controversial policies in a
better perspective and should suggest how these policies can
be improved and possibly achieve greater acceptance.

Closely related to the evaluation of EEO programs **is**
the need to determine the impact of higher education on the
job and status attainment of blacks and other minorities.
The relationship between higher education and job attainment
is largely a neglected research and policy topic. A recent
report indicated that being a high school graduate as opposed
to a high school drop-out reduced the probability of white
youth unemployment but had no additional effect on black
youth employment (Thomas and Scott, 1979). Past research on
adult job attainment also indicated that blacks with similar
ability and educational credentials as whites obtained lower
occupations and income returns than whites (Coleman et. al.
1972; Gottfredson, 1978). More updated studies on the labor
market returns of race and sex groups who have achieved various levels of higher education are needed to further evaluate EEO efforts.

Research and policy addressing the future role of black
colleges must also receive immediate attention and a higher
priority than in the past. Major attention should focus on
assuring the identity of these institutions and increasing
their quality. Data presented in this volume and elsewhere
show that the traditionally black institutions remain the
major educational alternative for many blacks, including those
students whose low SAT scores and high school achievement
would deny them entry to many of the predominantly white institutions. A recent report showed that 75 percent of blacks

with advanced degrees from white institutions obtained their
undergraduate training from a black institution (Brown, 1979).

Despite the past and present necessity for these institutions, much of the discussion since Adams still centers on
whether these institutions should survive. Many blacks fear
that these institutions will not survive due to a lack of
aggressive federal support and due to the burden that is being placed on black institutions to desegregate beyond that
required of most white institutions. Describing the severity of the situation, Brown (1979) noted that the predominantly black institutions are "slowly fading to white." For
example, Bluefield State, which was once predominantly black,
is now predominantly white. Brown (1979) also cited the 45
percent white faculty at Langston University and Morgan State
University's 30 percent white graduates among its recent
graduating class as examples of the substantial white influx
on black campuses.

Another side effect that desegregation has produced for
the black colleges is competition with white institutions for
quality black students and black faculty. These institutions
will remain largely unable to compete for a greater number
of the top black students unless an adequate number are
relieved of their compensatory role and are helped to become
top quality research and teaching institutions. The emphasis
here on producing an adequate number of quality black institutions is in sharp contrast to Kenneth Clark's (1979) recent proposal that all black institutions become training
academies to better prepare black students for entry into
major colleges and universities. After identifying the black
colleges that should become top quality institutions, those
remaining and better suited to continue their compensatory
role should be strengthened and further developed to better
serve this function.

Ideally, the achievement of greater racial equality
among institutions of higher education should entail the
existence of predominantly black-and white-controlled institutions that offer quality education, diverse cultural
perspectives, and an equal chance of access and retention
for promising students of all races. More importantly, the
goal of achieving a greater number of high quality educational institutions should be a prerequisite to the goal
of desegregation. It is believed that merely obtaining a
specific racial mix among students and faculty will not

guarantee an increase in higher educational quality and
student acheivement. After the predominantly black institutions are offered a real opportunity to become quality
institutions and thus to compete more effectively in the
higher educational process, then it may be more appropriate
to attempt to achieve a more equitable racial distribution
of students and faculty across all higher education instit-
tutions.

A final issue that must be addressed regarding the
future of minorities in higher education concerns the racial
attitudes and values operating among all actors throughout
higher education. As previously noted, the "mind set,"
values, and attitudes of members of minorities and the majority group are as crucial in affecting higher educational
change as are structural interventions. Therefore, more
detailed information is needed on the attitudes and values
of policy makers, educational researchers, and administrators regarding desegregation and affirmative action. These
data should be useful in formulating better methods designed
to increase group support for higher educational change.
They may also be valuable in better identifying persons
who are more committed to conducting the types of research
and administering the kinds of policies that will enhance
equality of outcomes for minorities in higher education.

Conclusion

The general theme throughout this volume is that although blacks have made some gains in higher education,
their struggle for more significant access and retention
gains at all levels of higher education must be more aggressively pursued in the 80s. Many, if not all, of the strategies and recommendations offered to achieve this goal are
workable, but not without total commitment and costs which
must be sustained by all Americans. The history of conflict
which has preceded major social change in U.S. institutions
suggests that the additional "dues to be paid" and progress
to be achieved in higher education will not occur voluntarily and may quite likely entail greater racial conflict.
This may, however, be an asset rather than a detriment to
society in the long run if some of the constructive changes
necessary for further educational and societal development
do occur.

The federal government must assume the primary leadership role in promoting constructive educational change. The
establishment of past and present federal programs aimed at
increasing educational opportunity for all Americans shows

some initiative by the federal government. However, this initiative must be accelerated, expanded and better coordinated to promote more effective change, especially for minority students.   Any initiative by the government must be encouraged and supported by the active engagement of its citizens. William Graham Sumner (1959) noted in his classic, Folkways, that the masses are generally conservative and apathetic to social change and thus unquestionably accepting of the folkways (e.g. norms and regulations) prescribed to them by the ruling class. Sumner's observations of the early 1900s seems quite applicable to the present status of American sentiment: Whites appear to be becoming more conservative while blacks and minorities in general appear to be increasingly apathetic and individualistic. Unless minorities regain some momentum and a collective consciousness, and unless all Americans become more actively engaged, future educational growth and development will not take place within this decade.

The question of whether America is to become more progressive in educational as well as societal growth is becoming less of a matter of choice. This is particularly true given our fading image as a "great society" in the wake of inflation, strained domestic and foreign relations, and declining test scores and college enrollment. These events suggest that many dimensions of American society may be on the brink of social change. Thus, this volume sets the stage for the real question of: Will we reassess our national priorities and better prepare ourselves for constructive social change, or will we risk a greater deficit in our schools and in American society in general?

References

Brown, T.
    1979   "Black colleges fight to make it." News World
            Forum (Wed: Sept. 19). New York.

Clark, K.
    1979   "The continuing struggle to desegregate U.S.
            education." The Chronicle of Higher Education.
            19(1): 1

Coleman, J.S., A.D. Blum, A.B. Sorenson and P.H. Rossi
    1972   "White and black careers during the first decade of labor force experience, Part. I: occupational status." Social Science Research
            1:243-270.

Friedlein, K.
    1979   "Slow fade to white integration's price:
            black colleges?" The Charlotte Observer
            (Sun. Sept. 9) Charlotte, N.C.

Goodrich, A.
    1979   A Data Driven Model for Minorities in Predomin-
            antly White Institutions. Paper presented at
            the Desegregation Conference (June). Raleigh,
            N.C.

Jencks, C., M. Smith, H. Acland, M.J. Bane, D. Cohen,
H. Gintis, B. Heyns and S. Michelson
    1972   Inequality. New York: Harper and Row.

National Advisory Committee on Black Higher Education
    1979   Access of Black Americans to Higher Education
            How Open is the Door? Washington: U.S. Govern-
            ment Printing.

Rosenbaum, J.E.
    1976   Making Inequality. New York: John Wiley.

Sumner, W.G.
    1959   Folkways. New York: Dover Publishers

Thomas, G.E. and W.B. Scott
    1979   "Black youth and the labor market: the unem-
            ployment dilemma." Youth and Society: (Decem-
            ber).

U.S. Bureau of Census
    1978   Current Population Reports Series, P-20.
            No. 361.

Index

About the Contributors

Walter R. Allen is Assistant Professor of Sociology and the Center for Afroamerican-African Studies, University of Michigan and was formerly a member of the faculty at the University of North Carolina. His research has been focussed on explicating the relationships of culture, socio-economic context, family setting and interpersonal interactions to individual socialization outcomes. Among Journals where his work is published are the *Sociological Quarterly, Journal of Negro Education, Journal of Marriage and the Family, Signs* and *Journal of Comparative Family studies*.

Helen S. Astin is Professor of Education at the University of California at Los Angeles. Her areas of specialization are counseling and social psychology. She is author of a variety of books and articles on higher education, and disadvantaged minority students. Among them are: *Higher Education and the Disadvantaged Student; Open Admissions at CUNY: An Analysis of the First Year;* and *Non-White College Graduates: Career Plans in 1965 and 1970.*

James E. Blackwell is Professor of Sociology at the University of Massachussetts in Boston. He has published extensively on minorities in higher education with a special focus on graduate and professional education. Among his works noted are: *Access of Black Students to Graduate and Professional Schools, Black Colleges as a National Resource: Beyond 1975,* and the *Black Community.*

William M. Boyd, II is President of A Better Chance, Inc. (ABC), a national academic talent search program offering quality college preparatory education to minority students. Prior to assuming the presidency of ABC, he was Executive Director of the Educational Policy Center, Inc (EPC) in

New York City. EPC has since merged with ABC as a research division. Boyd's professional activities have included service on the boards of Deerfield Academy, Wellesley and Williams Colleges, the National Association of Independent Schools, and the Higher Education Research Institute's Board of Scholars. His published writings include articles in *Change, The College Board Review, Educational Records,* and Praeger publishers.

Jomills Henry Braddock II is a Research Scientist and Co-Director of the Desegregation Studies Program at the Center for Social Organization of Schools, The Johns Hopkins University and was previously a member of the faculty at the University of Maryland. His principal research efforts have been directed to investigating the long-term effects of school desegregation on minority status attainment outcomes and social integration.

Randolph W. Bromery is Professor of Geophysics at the University of Massachusetts at Amherst and was formerly Chancellor of the Amherst campus of the University of Massachusetts and Senior Vice President for Labor Relations for the University of Massachusetts system office. He served as an exploration geophysicist with the U.S. Geological Survey for twenty years prior to joining the University of Massachusetts and has traveled throughout the United States and its territories, Africa, and other parts of the world supervising and conducting geophysical surveys for minerals and petroleum. He serves as a consultant for several U.S. companies and several African governments. He has more than 150 scientific articles published with the U.S. Geological Survey and several professional journals. He has lectured extensively on scientific, social, and educational issues and has been active in developing programs for increasing minority participation in science and engineering. He serves on the boards of directors of several major U.S. petroleum and manufacturing corporations.

Frank Brown is professor of Educational Administration at the State Univeristy of New York at Buffalo. He has conducted extensive research in policy studies and school law, urban education, local and higher education administration. He is senior author of *Minority Enrollment in U.S. Institutions of Higher Education* and numerous articles in professional journals.

E. Virginia Calkins, now Assistant Dean for Student Affairs at the University of Missouri-Kansas City School of Medicine, was previously Coordinator for Admission there. Her research interests have dealt principally with selection-prediction studies and she has published a number of articles in this field in recent years. She has also spearheaded several symposia concerning the combined baccalaureate-doctor of medicine degree programs and is the Editor of the Proceedings of the Symposium on this subject held in 1977 in Kansas City.

Philip Carey is Associate Professor of Sociology and Research and Director of the Institute for Urban Research at Morgan State University. Before accepting this position, he served as coordinator and founding director of the Office for Minority and Special Student Affairs at the University of Minnesota. His areas of academic concentration include the Sociology of Higher Education, Social Psychology, and Race Relations/Ethnic Studies. He has numerous publications in the area of higher education and minorities. Among them are: *The Sociology of Racism; New Directions in the Graduate Education of Minorities;* and *White Racism and Black Higher Education.*

Patricia H. Cross is a research analyst at the Higher Education Research Institute at the University of California at Los Angeles. Her area of specialization is higher education with particular emphasis on student development and institutional environments. She is co-author of *Characteristics of Entering Black Freshmen in Predominantly Black and Pre-White Institutions*: A narrative report. She has co-published a number of other articles with Helen S. Astin.

Ada M. Fisher, M.D. a Diplomate of the American Academy of Family Practice. She graduated from the University of Wisconsin Medical School at Madison where she was instrumental in developing programs and books for the recruitment, admission, retention, and graduation of minority students. She has served in the United States Public Health Service's National Health Service Corps in a physician manpower shortage area and held the position of Clinical Instructor in the University of North Carolina at Chapel Hill Department of Family Medicine.

John E. Fleming was previously a Senior Fellow with The Institute for the Study of Educational Policy. Dr. Fleming, a historian by training, has published *The Lengthening Shadow of Slavery, A Historical Justification for Affirmative Action for Blacks in Higher Education.* He has served as a consultant for the National Urban League, NAACP and numerous colleges and universities. Dr. Fleming has recently been appointed by the Ohio Historical Society as the Project Administrator for the Development of a National Afro-American Museum and Culture Center. He has conducted a series of profiles of colleges and universities successful in recruiting, retaining and graduating black students.

Dr. Fleming is a former employee of the U.S. Civil Rights Commission and the Kentucky Commission on Human Rights.

Robert H. Geertsma is Professor and Chairman of the Division of Medical Education and Communication at the University of Rochester's School of Medicine and Dentistry. His areas of specialization are psychology and medical education. He served previously as chairman of the Department of Medical Communication at the University of Kansas Medical School.

Denise C. Gottfredson is an Associate Research Scientist at the Center for Social Organization of Schools at The Johns Hopkins University and is completing her graduate work in the Department of Social Relations at Hopkins. She has published research on career development and the sociology of education and is currently working in the areas of personality and race differences in educational attainment.

Franklin D. Hamilton is Associate Professor of Chemistry at Atlanta University. His area of specialization is biochemistry. He is co-author with Vijaya Melnick of: *Minorities in Science: The Challenge for Change in Biomedicine.*

Leonard L. Haynes III is Director, Office for the Advancement of Public Negro Colleges in Washington, D.C. This office represents the 35 historically black public colleges and universities. He was formerly Director of the Ford Foundation sponsored Desegregation Policy Studies Unit of the Institute for Services to Education, where he initiated his research on the desegregation of higher education. He has compiled an important reference on desegregation entitled *A Critical Examination of the Adams Case: A Source Book* and is also the editor of *An Analysis of the Arkansas-Georgia Statewide Desegregation Plans.*

John L. Holland is Professor of Social Relations and Psychology at Johns Hopkins University. His research interests focus on vocational hiring and vocational interventions. He is the author of *Making Vocational Choices: A Theory of Careers,* and a popular self-help device, *The Self Directed Search.*

James M. McPartland is Co-Director of the Center for Social Organization of Schools and Associate Professor of Social Relations at Johns Hopkins University. His research interests include sociology of education, race and ethnic relations and research methodology. His earlier experience included contributions to the national studies, *Equality of Educational Opportunity* (1966) and *Racial Isolation in the Public Schools* (1967). His recent works are *Violence in the Schools* and "Desegregation and Equity in Higher Education and Employment," *Law and Contemporary Problems* (1978).

Vijaya Melnick is Professor of Biology at the University of the District of Columbia and Visiting Scientist at the International Center for Inter-Disciplinary Studies on Immunology at Georgetown University Medical School in Washington, D.C. She is Co-editor of *Biomedical Scientists and Public Policy* (with Fudenberg), 1978; *Minorities in Science: A Challenge for Change in Biomedicine* (with Franklin D. Hamilton) 1977; and *Symposium on Public Concerns of Immunization*, vol. 13 part 2, May 1979 (with Bellanti, J.A.). She holds membership in numerous professional organizations and committees relevant to science, biomedicine, minority education, biomedical policy, bioethics, and the representation of minorities and the disadvantaged in the professions.

James R. Mingle is Research Associate at the Southern Regional Education Board. In addition to his work on black enrollment he has authored several publications in the area of state planning and academic program review. He is currently project director of a Ford Foundation-sponsored study examining state and institutional responses to enrollment decline. He earned the Ph.D. degree from the Center for the Study of Higher Education at the University of Michigan in 1976.

Paul B. Mohr, Sr., is Professor of Mathematics and Vice President for Academic Affairs at Norfolk State University and was previously Professor and Dean of the College of Education at Florida A&M Univeristy in Tallahassee, Florida. His latest research and writing activities focus on equal opportunity in higher education for minorities. He is co-editor of *The Law and the Unitary system of Higher Education*. He is also editor of *Black Colleges and Equal Opportunity in Higher Education*, and *Equal Opportunity in Higher Education: Myth or Reality?*

Lorenzo Morris is a Political Scientist and a Senior Fellow at the Institute for the Study of Educational Policy at Howard University. His areas of specialization are higher education of minorities and educational and social policy research. His major publications include: *Elusive Equality: The Status of Black Americans in Higher Education* (1979); *The Chit'lin Controversy: Race and Public Policy in America* (1978); and "The Politics of Education and Language in Quebec: A Comparative Perspective", *Canadian and International Education*, 5, 2 (1976).

Barbara Baxter Pillinger is Assistant Vice President for Student Affairs and

Associate Professor of Educational Administration at the University of Minnesota, where she is a member of both the Black Learning Resource Center Advisory Board and the American Indian Learning Resource Center Advisory Board. She is the author of several articles on educational management, women in higher education administration, and the sociology of sport. Dr. Pillinger, a *summa cum laude* graduate of the University of Illinois, received her doctorate in psychology from Harvard University.

James M. Richards, Jr. is Professor of Psychology (part-time) and Social Relations (part-time) and Project Director at the Center for Social Organization of Schools at Johns Hopkins University. He has published extensively in the major journal of psychology and social psychology. His research interests include the measurement and analysis of educational environments, the diversity of human talents, and the character and impact of higher education.

Gloria R. Scott is Vice President of Clark College and Vice-Chairperson of the National Advisory Committee on Black Higher Education and Black Colleges and Universities. Her areas of specialization are higher education administration and policy evaluation. She serves as a consultant and advisor for numerous federal, national, and state educational and policy organizations.

Will B. Scott is Professor of Social Work at Clark College and Atlanta University. He is actively involved in minority undergraduate and graduate education, and minority recruitment and retention activities. He also serves as a consultant and advisor for various federal and state agencies and for educational and professional organizations in social work and sociology.

James C. Sears is Professor and Dean — Instructional and Student Services at Tidewater Community College and was previously engaged in administrative and instructional activities at several other colleges. He has interest in management-by-objectives, articulation issues, student characteristics and systems for improving management.

Baldave Singh is Director of Research and Program Evaluation at the University of Minnesota. His areas of specialization are Comparative Ethnic and Race Relations, Third World Economic Development and International Relations. He has published articles in these areas.

Ralph R. Smith is Assistant Professor of Law at the University of Pennsylvania. He was previously chairperson of the Task Force legal education and Bar Admission NCBL. He has written a number of articles on the law school experiences of black students.

James D. Tschechtelin is Director of Instructional Programs at the Maryland State Board for Community Colleges in Annapolis. He has held positions at the college and university level, and has done institutional as well as statewide research in higher education. His research has focused on the practical application of statewide student follow-up data from both entering students and graduates.

Gerald D. Williams is a Senior Associate at CSR Incorporated, Washington, D.C. His areas of specialization are Program Evaluation and Survey Research. He is author of *Evaluation of the High School Health Careers Program, School of Health Services, Johns Hopkins University* and "Student Perceptions of Occupational Congruency."

T. Lee Willoughby is Coordinator of the Evaluation Resource Center at the University of Missouri-Kansas City. His work has focused on the evaluation of medical students' knowledge and clinical performance, particularly the development of an extensive computer-assisted program for testing and instruction. He has also conducted research on the selection of minority students and the differential predictors of performance for male and female medical students.

Herman A. Young is Director of Higher Education Achievement Systems, West Louisville Education Program, and Associate Professor of Natural Sciences at the University of Louisville. His areas of specialization are higher education, science education, and chemistry. He is co-author of *Scientists in the Black Perspective*. He has also published numerous articles on black doctorates, role models for blacks in engineering and employment of black scientists.

About the Editor

Gail E. Thomas is a Sociologist and Research Scientist in Higher Education at the Johns Hopkins University's Center for Social Organization of Schools. She is also a part-time faculty member in the Department of Social Relations at Johns Hopkins. She obtained her undergraduate degree in 1970 in sociology from A & T State University at Greensboro, North Carolina. She received her masters and doctoral degrees from the University of North Carolina at Chapel Hill in 1973 and 1975. Her research interests and areas of specialization include blacks and women educational and status attainment, social and ethnic stratification, race relations theory and research, and educational research methodology. She has published in various educational and sociological journals, including the *Sociological Quarterly*, the *American Educational Review Journal, The American Journal of Education*, and *Youth and Society*. She has also been the recipient of grants and awards from the U.S. Department of Labor, the Russell Sage Foundation, the Southern Education Foundation, and Outstanding Young Women of America. She currently serves as a consultant in higher education for the federal government and other public and private organizations.